# DRIVING ME WILD
## NITRO-POWERED OUTLAW CULTURE
### Leah M. Kerr

Juno Books
NEW YORK CITY

# Driving Me Wild
## Nitro-Powered Outlaw Culture

© 2000 by **Leah Kerr**
**Published in the USA by Juno Books, LLC A. Juno:** Editor-in-Chief

ISBN 0-9651042-9-X

Library of Congress Cataloging-in-Publication Data
Kerr, Leah.
  Driving me wild : nitro-powered outlaw culture / by Leah Kerr.
    p. cm.
  Includes bibliographical references.
  ISBN 0-9651042-9-X
  1. Drag racing--Social aspects. 2. Hot rods--Social aspects. I. Title.
  GV1029.3 . K47 1999
  306.4'83--dc21                                    99-057880

**Editorial address for Juno Books and RE/Search Publications:**
A. Juno, 111 Third Avenue, #11G, New York, NY 10003
tel: 212-388-9924, fax: 212-388-1151, e-mail: ajuno@junobooks.com

**For a catalog send 6 stamps to:**
Juno Books/powerHouse Books
180 Varick Street, Suite 1302, New York, NY 10014-4606
www.JunoBooks.com/www.powerHouseBooks.com

**US Bookstore and non-bookstore Distribution:**
powerHouse Cultural Entertainment, Inc.
180 Varick Street, Suite 1302, New York, NY 10014-4606
tel: 212 604 9074, fax: 212 366 5247,
e-mail: orders@powerhousebooks.com

**U.K. Distribution:**
Turnaround
Unit 3, Olympia Trading Estate, Coburg Road
London N22 6TZ, United Kingdom
tel: 0181 829 3000, fax: 0181 881 5088,
e-mail: sales@turnaround-uk.com

**Italy Distribution:**
Logos Art srl
Via Curtatona 5/f
41100 Modena Loc. Fossalta, Italy
tel: 059 41 87 11, fax: 059 28 16 87,
e-mail: logos@books.it

**Benelux Distribution:**
Nilsson & Lamm
Pampuslaan 212, Postbus 195
1380 AD Weesp, The Netherlands
tel: 02 94 494949, fax: 02 94 494455,
e-mail: g.boor@nilsson-lamm.nl

10 9 8 7 6 5 4 3 2 1

(Andy Takakjian photo)

# *Race Crew*
## Acknowledgements

The most striking thing I learned about racing is that it's never done alone. To be successful takes the cooperation, knowledge and enthusiasm of many folks. Without love from my family, encouragement from my dear friends and experience of those deep in the field, this book would never have gotten to the top end. Thank you all very much.

### HEARTFELT THANKS TO:

*AAOW*, Armen Baghdassarian, Frances Borchardt, Mike Bumbeck, Amy Capen & Jennifer McKittrick, Steve Collison & *Drag Racing Monthly*, Cole Coonce, Walter Cotton & Steven DePinto, Ericka & Rich Dana, Roxanne Davis & Lee Howell, John Drummond & the Goodguys, Karen Erbach, John Gaby, Liz Garo, Dierdra Girardeau, Roy Lee Gittens, Jr., Amy Hobby, Shirley & William B. Kerr and family, William B. Kerr, Jr., Frank Kozik & Man's Ruin Records, Pete LaBarera, Mike LaVella, Darcy Lubbers, Ron Main, Dennis McPhail, Paige Penland, Matt Polito, Robert Post, Quartermasters, Rhino Records, Bob & Heather Sanders, Greg Sharp, Elliot Smith, Nancy Soshinsky, Andy Takakjian, Bryan Thomas & DelFi Records, Randy Thomas, Hearst Collection/University of Southern California Libraries, United Black Drag Racing Association, Sandy Viall, Dave Wallace, Jr., Todd & Caz Westover, Robert Williams, and the Woods family.

### THANK YOU TO ALL THE PHOTOGRAPHERS WHO SHARED THEIR VISION:

Jere Alhadeff, Melanie Bruck, Kevin R. Cooke, Amy Darsa, Dave DeAngelis, Carol Hakola, April Hazen, Dale Laubham, Ron Lewis, Nick Licata, John McCartney, Dave Milcarek, Sam Painter, Dave Perry, Matt Polito, Elena Liddell Ray, Steve Reyes, Paul Rosner, Mike Salisbury, Bob Snayko, Marshall Spiegel, Jack C. Stewart, Sky Wallace, Zuika, and the other photographers without whom *Driving Me Wild* would be stone-blind.

*(Rescue Photo)*

An Ace of Hearts to Jorge Vélasquez for having the patience and skill to perform under an impossible deadline.

Endless thanks to Andrea Juno, who encouraged me to go full throttle to see what this baby could do.

I would like to extend special appreciation to all those who shared their time and memories; their achievements are the reason this book exists.

*Editor-In-Chief:*
  Andrea Juno
*Art Director/Designer:*
  Jorge Vélasquez, JIV Design, Inc.
*Proofreader:*
  Caz Westover
*Front Cover:*
  Coop
*Title Page photo:*
  Steve Reyes
*Back Cover photos:*
  Above: Steve Reyes
  Below: Elena Ray

# Table of Contents

STAGING LANE

(Andy Takakjian photo)

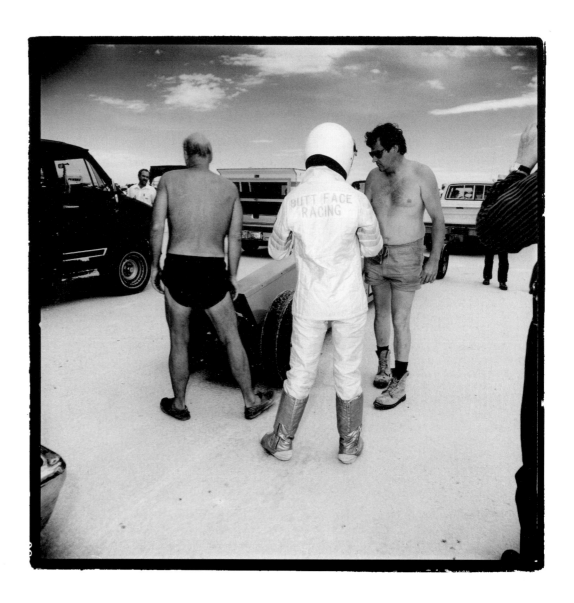

(Rescue Photo)

# The Endless Search for Purity of Tone

By 1953 hot rodders raced safely and legally at Pomona and other drag strips. (Greg Sharp collection)

**L**et's get this straight from the get go—I'm in it for the thrill. For the noise and the rumble and the shake. Sure, there's lots of other interesting stuff—stats, science, competition—but that's not what keeps me coming back for more. It's the nitro. Okay? Just so we understand each other. You should try it. Just once. Open your ears and your nose and your eyes and your mind and you'll be amazed and entertained. Once the shiver starts, you'll be sucked in. It's big, it's fun, it's drag racing. Hell, it's the whole car culture thrill. I know it's true because I've examined the sport from the innards to the stitches and, while it's not a perfect world, it's offered up events and ideas I'd never dreamed up. I've met wild-on-the-edge-folks who make me think and I want to introduce you to them. They want to take you on a journey—hell, they want to take you for a ride.

My first experience was up against a chain link fence at a race in Bakersfield—yards away from two top fuelers running over-rich with nitro, making me high and bringing tears to my eyes. Every push of the throttle shook me, and at the launch they rocked my world! I thought, "HOT DAMN! Why didn't anybody tell me about this before?" It was like laying on the monitors at a Sonic Youth show. It has a beat and you can dance to it—I give it an 11.

Me wondering how fast the dad-mobile will go. (Kerr collection)

After that first pass, I craved the rush again. I found myself slammed against that fence—nose wide open, ear drums pounding, being at one with the BRAPP, BRAPP while inhaling nitro. If you've never been to the races, the closest illustration I can offer up is Monty Hellman's existential movie *Two Lane Blacktop* (1971). Hellman nailed the purity of tone of racing—the sound, the rush of air, the smell of smoked tires, the g-force of slammed gears, the rumble of fierce motors, the barely controlled speed—the fucking thrill of drag racing. And attached to the physical stimulation are all the connotations: bad boys, good looking cars, tough women.

My compatriots in nitro addiction, the Silver Lake Racing Association. (SLRA collection)

This stuff works for me at every level. My mind is engaged, it's sexy as hell, and it's outlaw. I grew up just a little too smart and definitely requiring way too much stimulus. From early on I devoured books, movies and music in equal proportion. With time the tune running through my head changed from "Tighten Up" by Archie Bell and the Dells to "I Am the Walrus" by the Beatles to "Sheena Is A Punk Rocker" by the Ramones. Thanks to my dad's dalliance with sports cars and my family's frequent road trips, I learned that getting out there meant finding your own way. I was raised a black Army officer's child and that awarded me a full outsider status. I spent more time with white kids and sideways glances than in a "traditional" neighborhood setting. My mom blazed the trail throwing exquisite officer's wives teas and modeling fur coats the likes of which her Ohio-farm family had only seen in magazines. My father had a grace and charm, backed by his football player build, that swept him up the ranks with ease. They both assured me I could straddle the stereotypes, but, as their oldest child and only daughter, I had a tough time. I fought to express my individuality. Anything that was a little out of bounds looked just great to me.

Above, Right and Facing page: Silver Lake Racing Association at the races—Peter Deming, Leah Kerr, Caz Westover, Lee Howell, Todd Westover, April Hazen, Roxanne Davis, Nancy Soshinsky, Bill Buckingham, Cole Coonce, Roy Lee Gittens, Jr., and Elena Lidell Ray. (SLRA collection)

Writing this book introduced me to a league of outsiders. It has taken me to the drag strips and dry lakes and sat me down at the knees of guys who've been severely bitten by the speed bug. I grew up in the '60s and I can spot a Jones an arm's length away. People mention it in many ways; sometimes they call it what it is, the "sickness". I heard one racer explain his hanging onto an old dragster saying that "once the needle's in your arm, loaded and ready to go, how can you pull it out?" Folks have confessed to me that they've had to run away. They know that even one return to the track would get it back under their skin. Drag racing's similarity to drugs is that it takes "big time," as rail driver "Nitro" Neil Bisciglia would say. Takes your money—all of it, and any you plan on earning in the future. One big misconception is that racing pays. Uh-uh. It's a hobby, Jack, and not an inexpensive one. These days, running a top fuel car averages about $6,000 a pass in professional events. To win a meet takes 8 to 12 wallet-burning trips down the track. The average winning purse is $4,000. A first grader can tell you—it doesn't add up.

The fixation also takes your time. For every heart warming tale of camaraderie and opportunity for closeness with family, there's a sobering rumor of divorce. If you're not prepared to be consumed by the racing world, an attraction to a drag racer can be a futile one. There's no such thing as free time. It's eaten by working on the car, racing the car and buying parts for the car. Relationships that last seem to be bonded around racing. It's not unusual to see a racing team comprised of family members. Dad wrenches, as does Mom. Brother is on the crew and Sis drives. Or any other combination imaginable. And intermarriage? It's a disaster for the non-racing spouse. If the only people you associate with are racing fools, then that's who you're should date and perhaps spend the rest of your life with.

(SLRA collection)

Scare anyone off yet? No? Good, because here's the payoff. For the endless devotion of money and time, you get to spend hours in the face of power. If you have the sickness, then creating speed is the ultimate reward. Every mechanic and driver I spoke to would go off on a rhapsody of the pleasure of having their baby do well. I suspect it's Skinner's notion of intermittent reinforcement in action. All the hours of frustration spent working banging knuckles and furrowing brows trying to solve a "fuel management" problem are forgotten as the car successfully streaks down that track in another triumph of ingenuity over luck.

And the addiction doesn't affect only the actual participants. It spills over into the real world. Folks like me that don't know a magneto from a manifold must attend any race within a reasonable distance. Fans in the stands are all a-titter about John Force's new car or whether leaning out an engine was the cause of the last part-mangling engine fire. As in other sports you identify with someone and follow their actions like they're a close friend. You win when they win and when they lose, you go home no poorer, but perhaps a little quieter—or maybe you transfer your affections to the winner of the day. He's not such a bad guy, after all, he just had a better day.

These connections are how we define ourselves. For some it's all about Mopar versus Ford and is displayed by the car that they drive. Other enthusiasts wear their identity as a metal garb expressed by the custom world. As dragsters and hot rods yearn for power, custom cars are the sleek other side of the Detroit Sucks! dichotomy—another display of outlaw sensibilities in action. For some, purity is about form for form's sake. A chopped and lowered 1949 Merc is not likely to be your everyday car. Rather, it's your candy for working hard all week long and putting up with bullshit so you can come home and say this is who I am, and I'm damn proud of it.

(SLRA collection)

Like other novices, I envisioned racers as half wits and grease monkeys, but my trusted friends said it was more. What I found was a place where outsiders are the norm, brains are revered and it's a thrill a minute. People of color are still few, but just as hooked as anyone else. I agree with racer and activist Randy Thomas' perspective that kids need the chance to excel and racing offers that avenue. Problem solving skills mixed with the boost to the esteem are rarely instilled in today's public schools, but are commonplace in the racing environment. Encouraging kids to understand the mechanics of a motor results in future scientists, physicists, and engineers.

Teenagers trying to break away from their boring parents, defined the outlaw spirit of the car culture. Rock and roll was the anthem of their revolution. They birthed up a bad kid attitude that has fed the underculture since it's inception. While kids in California hit the strips and the beaches, teenagers all across the rest of country filled the drive-ins. They cheered the celluloid outlaw lifestyle created by Hollywood movie makers and projected against the dark night of repression. So thrill seekers in Florida, Texas, Indiana and Georgia all tricked out the old family car to see what it'd do. They watched *Rebel Without A Cause* (1955) or *Drag Strip Girl* (1956) and knew that the automobile could be the vehicle to their freedom.

The influences of hot rodding continue to split and create their own enclaves. Speed, style and art have been present since the beginning. Each category develops its own splinter groups and fans. Artists can view cars, people, and the race itself for the pure elements. Customizers come in all factions: classic, hot rod and lowrider. Music has ridden in the passenger seat since the beginning and, every now and then, comes to the forefront.

Sadly the effect of a thriving cultural scene attracts capitalist vultures. More frequently independent racers battle competitors with big money power supplied by multimillion dollar corporations. Ticket prices for races rise and suddenly you have to pay to attend a car show. Custom cars commissioned by millionaires, with all the expensive bells and whistles that practically assure top trophy honors, are rolled off of trailers and into car shows. When pinstripe artists' work jumps from cars to paintings, it quickly attains astronomical price tags. As already experienced with rock and roll music, film and sports, commercial interests threaten to strangle the soul of car culture.

Luckily, through low-dollar nostalgia races, cheap poster art, and free parking lot car shows, car culture participants find avenues for pleasures and win the battle over costs. Drag racing, hot rodding, custom car and lowrider cruising continue to bring the old folks back and build new audiences every year. And it will continue as long as each of us can explain to the world who we are, where we're going, and just how fast we're gonna get there. It's soul searching redefined, it's the endless search for purity of tone.

*A flag starter signals the beginning of the drag strip era. (Greg Sharp collection)*

(Rescue Photo)

(Rescue Photo)

# From 0 – 326 MPH

## CHAPTER 1

Pro Stock Driver Mike Edwards deals with the power of the modern engine. (Dave DeAngelis photo)

**W**ebster's Dictionary defines drag racing as "a type of automobile racing from a standing start covering a straight-away one-quarter mile distance." Sounds dull. Sometimes I describe drag racing as a battle of egos between two contestants using the track as a measure of competence. Or a display of metal, smoke and fury attempting to displace land and stop time. Drag racing means as many things as there are numbers of drivers and fans combined, but a definition doesn't describe what this chaos is all about. Cole Coonce, Southern California based writer and drag racing historian explains, "the excitement comes from the tweaked and crazed and absolutely nuts things people will do to get to the finish line first." Generally, the most exciting form of it involves people who fuel their cars with a class AA explosive to get to the other side. So maybe this is the reason novices don't get it. Because they've only experienced gas powered cars. The thrill is in the AA explosive—Nitro! It provides a bang like nothing else.

I prefer the fastest cars, but there are many divisions of the sport. Everything from the pro classes, where fuel spewing motors travel down a quarter mile track at 320 miles per hour generating 6,000 horsepower and getting to the other end in 5 seconds, to sportsman classes where gasoline powered small block engines crank up 470 hp that drags their metal hulks across a finish line at 100 mph in about 15 seconds. Then there are the wild folk out on the salts who drive any manner of internal combustion engine, modeled into a streamliner or a dragster, or, hell, even a Model T, and fly down dry lake bed flats to cross the lights 3 miles from their starting line and clock speeds of 200 mph. It's all a thrill and it all started in the same place.

Early 1930s streamliner at Muroc dry lake. (Greg Sharp collection)

Bird's eye view of the 1320 at St. Louis' Gateway International Raceway. (Author photo)

## THE STARTING LINE

You have to step back to see where this lunacy evolved from. Like so many bad habits, it came from the American need for more. We've always wanted to get more out whatever we have. More land, more speed, more weirdness. When the first cars hit the roads, displacing horses and buggies, you know some guy said "How fast will it go?." Kids in California were trying to answer this question as early as the 1930s when they took their roadsters out to Muroc, a dry lake bed in the Mojave Desert. They peeled away fenders and lights and set off in a straight line to see how quickly they could make it from point A to point B.

Racing at dry lakes, abandoned air strips or roads in open country stretches gave mechanics the opportunity to try anything just to see what would happen. The hot rod of choice was a '32 Ford, but vehicles strapped with aircraft engines and the low, sleek covered wheels of streamliners were also on the lake beds kicking up dust. The Southern California Timing Association (SCTA) was formed in 1937 to add safety, organize racing classes, and to have official recognition of the speeds and times racers were laying down.

World War II rudely interrupted the fun. Rationing was implemented on metal, fuel and rubber. Californians joined the ranks of the armed forces, where the wild tales of this racing madness started to spread. Soldiers from other parts of the country noticed that Californian GI's were whack. Instead of personalizing the barracks with pictures of their girlies, they put up shots of their "hot rods." That's all they talked about, planned on, and later, when they left the service and were settled into new jobs and houses in Southern California, that's all they spent their money on. Drag Racing.

The go-faster sport is a very logical extension of rampant outrageous capitalism that is at the core of America. It wouldn't have taken root and blossomed the way it has had it not been for the perfect circumstances of the late 1950s and 1960s Southern California experience. There was a surplus of everything. And everyone was emulating the American experience or more specifically, the Southland drag scene. It could be called the golden era. "It was flourishing," says Coonce, "Today the biggest race of the year features about 23 top fuel cars. In the '60s, there were hundreds and hundreds of top fuel cars, just in California. All of these guys were burning nitromethane in top fuel dragsters and a lot of them had decent paying jobs at Lockheed, or Bell Laboratories or any number of plants who were generating all this surplus war machinery. They were from Oklahoma or Texas or Louisiana or Maine. The government set them up in houses in California—Long Beach and LA

The flat wide expanses of Southern California's dry lakes were perfect for backyard mechanics to test the performance of their hot rods. (Greg Sharp collection)

specifically. These guys had the American dream; the house and the education was supplied by Uncle Sam. They had good gigs. And they were technically bent. These guys were trying to make jeeps run quicker in WWII and when they got back, the logical extension was to take a '32 Ford out to a salt flat."

Maybe these guys were a little careless because the military trained them that way. They were like the experiment-happy scientists that screwed around with stuff like B2 rockets.

Maybe those early speed seekers didn't stop to consider the ramifications of what they were doing. All they cared about was building a better rocket ship. And they did. They kept hammering at it until they came up with some absolutely wild arguments to the laws of physics, much of which was appropriated by early drag racing. Coonce figures that drag racers had charmed lives compared to WWII scientists, or anybody at NASA or Jet Propulsion Laboratories because "they get a very visceral, immediate bang. They get a rush, they get to stand next to bombs just vibrating, just waiting to climb out of the fucking motor and explode and obliterate everything. They have it both ways. They have the scientific challenge, and they get their rocks off. How can you fuck with that?" So, thanks to the war, Southern California was an abundance of spare military parts, and government trained technicians with damn good salaries and lots of spare time. And thanks to mother nature, Southern California's weather conditions allowed hot rodders to mix this stuff together almost year round. Car enthusiasts existed in other parts of the country, but they didn't have the zeal and bent of the SoCal boys.

These untamed geniuses dreamed up the unknown. Displeased with the Detroit output, these innovators knew they could make machines that were faster, more efficient, and in their eyes, more stylish. And they set out to prove it. The streets were full of sleek, fast, hand crafted beauties and more than a few badly built "shot rods." The term "hot rodder" became recognized slang and usually carried a bad connotation.

Film titles like *Hot Rod Rumble* (1957) or *High School Hellcats* (1958) may seem like over the top Hollywood creations. They're not. Those titles are an accurate reflection of teenagers gone wild. From 1947 to 1951, young men in their hopped up deuce coupes (and the high schoolers who sought to imitate them with their shop-class specials), took to the streets and created a rage of panic. Southern Californian newspapers and tabloids sensationally documented the period with headlines proclaiming: "'Hopped-Up' Car Kills Child" and "Police Cool Hot Rods."

In 1945, the average citizen knew all too well that these dangerous metal hunks were called hot rods, but the term didn't appear in print until after the war. Hot rodding wasn't exclusive to Southern California; but it grew here like wild sage. Dry lakes in the Antelope Valley in the Mojave high desert region were the testing grounds for these high performance vehicles. Typically guys would get into their souped up cars before dawn, race their way out the dry lakes, race while they were there, and race each other home as night fell.

*In the late 1940s, kids in fast and dangerous "gow" jobs menaced the streets and newspapers sensationalized their exploits. (Hearst Collection, courtesy Department of Special Collections, University of Southern California)*

Teenagers escaped adults' watchful eyes meeting at diners and drive-ins. (Greg Sharp collection)

At first it took technical word of mouth and mechanics by committee to transform a rusted $10 shell of a Ford T from field trash to race ready. But as enthusiasm for the sport gained, speed shops opened. Magazines such as *Honk!*, *Hop Up* and *Hot Rod* featured how-to articles on shifting, souping and striping. Automotive shop classes were added to high school curriculum nationwide as an option for non-college bound kids. With the schools' tools and their newly acquired knowledge, teenaged mechanics produced high performance engines as school projects. Funded by high schoolers' pocket money, getting these derelict mobiles on the road again took equal amounts of sweat and ingenuity. Spare parts could come from a neighbor's car parked on the street or late night, illicit visits to the junk yard.

City streets across the country showed the progression of hot rodders' enthusiasm. Each hot rod, or "gow" job showed off the ability and imagination of its builder. That freedom of expression must have been dizzying; to be able to travel where you wanted, in the car you wanted, at the speed you wanted. That was the power of being a teenager in the United States. How loud and fast your car roared spoke volumes about how cool you were. Some chose to carve out this image without much work. With a few simple modifications—lose the fenders, slap on some primer, put big tires on the back—and you, too, were a hot rodder.

Driving became a form of entertainment rather than simply getting from one place to another. As an enticement to these cruising teenagers, drive-in restaurants sprang up. Not only perfect for getting away from the watchful adult eye, drive-ins were ideal for making dates, arranging impromptu races, and admiring each other's cars. Car clubs adopted various drive-ins as de facto clubhouses. Drive-in movie theaters became popular for the same advantages of freedom from adult supervision. Dates took on a new dimension as visits to lover's lanes, make out spots and "submarine races" became standard. Whether they got bored traveling for hours to race or needed some mid-week release, these fast kids started using the flat, wide streets of the city rather than making the trek to the desert. The orange groves and oil fields of Los Angeles county were criss crossed with streets that hot rodders commandeered for speed contests. They'd pick a location with little cross traffic, block access, and race from two to six jalopies abreast. There were so many available roads that racers and spectators alike knew the circuit of five to seven straight-aways—Glendale Boulevard one night, Van Nuys Boulevard another. Local police were aware of the race circuit and would show up to block exits and sometimes break up rallies of 600 to 700 cars or ticket and impound as many as 100 racers in a night. Sometimes they'd catch no one as souped up cars fled the roads through SoCal's flat open spaces.

In 1947, the head of LA's traffic enforcement decried hot rods as "a mild form of anarchy (that) must be stamped out." Hell yeah! Not only were cops trying to regain control, but these rolling wrecks were dangerous. Kids weren't high on alcohol or drugs, they were high on their youthful immortality. Young boys thought plenty of going fast and little of stopping. Their jalopies had bad brakes and iffy steering. Crashes occurred while racing, getting away from cops and whenever some unsuspecting citizen happened into the middle of a speed contest. Rodders thumbed their noses at cops who were easily out-powered in their stock cars. They sped at night without lights. They shattered the quiet. They died in overturned cars and killed innocent occupants in other vehicles. And they gave hot rods a bad name. Any car without fenders was rightly or wrongly scrutinized as a lawbreaking hot rod.

Danger rose, tempers flared, and new measures were taken to curb the craziness. The California state assembly introduced bills requiring four fenders, mud flaps and outlawing the addition of after-market speed equipment. Anti-cruising laws were enacted and police enthusiastically enforced them. Films exposing the dangers of hot rodding

**'Hot Rod' Racing End Sought**

"Hot rod" automobile racing on valley highways is "a mild form of anarchy and must be stamped out," the head of the Los Angeles traffic enforcement division declared yesterday. Commenting on the round-up of some 50 youths who were racing in a marked-off strip near Van Nuys, Captain William Parker said:

"We will use every legal means to suppress these nightly race gatherings."

**50 POLICE SQUAD**

The 50 who were caught yesterday were given citations, ordering them to appear "within a week" to answer charges their cars were equipped with faulty brakes and lights.

They were caught when a squad of 50 motorcycle police roared up to their racing strip at Sepulveda boulevard and San Fernando road.

In a wild scramble, the "hot rodders" sought to escape with their cars. But their own barricades at the start and finish of the strip trapped them.

"In the future, more severe prosecution than the citations will be initiated," Captain Parker promised yesterday.

He said that complaints of Valley residents who were prevented from using their own highways were "growing."

Street racing in 1947 thrust "mild anarchy" on Los Angeles' residents. (Hearst Collection, courtesy Department of Special Collections, University of Southern California)

were shown in school, but *Hot Rod* (1950) and *The Cool Hot Rod* (1953) were better recruiting tools than deterrents. For the first time in American history teenagers were free to invent their own identities. Using their cars and their dress as a statement of style was fresh and exciting.

C.J. "Pappy" Hart, one of the first track promoters. (Greg Sharp collection)

The only effective efforts to completely contain speed vehicles were initiated by speed enthusiasts themselves. In a show of self policing, the Southern Californian Timing Association (SCTA) produced the first Los Angeles Automotive Equipment Display and Hot Rod Exposition so citizens could get a look at hot rods quietly resting in a safe environment. The 1948 show succeeded in calming fears and encouraging other positive moves, such as designating raceways with cooperation of the California Highway Patrol. Santa Ana became the first organized drag strip complete with an ambulance and accurate timing equipment. On July 2, 1950, racers were able to legally test their skills on the smooth surface of the abandoned taxiway at the Santa Ana Airport organized by promoters C.J. "Pappy" Hart, Frank Stilwell and Creighton Hunter. Following the success of Santa Ana, other raceways spread up to the Pacific Northwest and to the East. Police supported this turn of events as it got kids and their menace cars off the streets. Wally Parks formed the National Hot Rod Association (NHRA) in 1951 to create some boundaries for these loosely organized racers and clean up the image of the street racer. Cops were overjoyed and even assisted in finding locations for new drag strips. As one California Highway Patrol Officer, Clifford Peterson, put it, you can "do more with young people with law encouragement than law enforcement." Providing convenient, safe environments for regulated racing proved to be the antidote for the plague of street racing, and the roads soon returned to relative safety for John Q. Citizen.

As tracks opened, more and more hot rodders were discouraged from racing on the streets and encouraged to "run what you brung." Racers did and crowds starting showing up to see what the hell was going on. What they saw were vehicles that looked like nothing you could buy, traveling at unthinkable speeds. And not always safely either. Like an out of whack equation, each innovation brought another "accident" that needed another solution, that eventually brought another "accident" and so on. It got to the point that the looks of the car were being sacrificed for increased speed. Those gloriously painted bodies didn't fare well after banging other cars or the guardrail. And they were heavy. As the mechanics or "tuners" started achieving more speed, they headed for the track leaving cars with style to rule the street. Just as

C.J. Hart sets 'em off at his Santa Ana Drags. (Greg Sharp collection)

racers had dreamed of flying on the ground, designers, or customizers saw their cars as land based, space aged vehicles and they elongated the lines to create these visions. Racers and customizers parted ways. "Street rod" clubs were formed by customizers eager to drop the unsavory "hot rod" image.

## THE ROAD TO TODAY'S TECHNOLOGY

Those guys hauling ass out at Muroc in 1937 had no idea what they were starting. Their concept of limitations probably stopped at about 150 mph. Whodda thunk that by 1999 the great-grandsons of those roadsters would be pushing the envelope at 326? As drag racing progressed into a twisted world of its own, there were barriers to be crossed, factions to be won over, and the fact of consumerism to be dealt with.

*Utah's Bonneville Salt Flats offered a pristine surface for speed trials. (Greg Sharp collection)*

Roadsters looked less and less like the aerodynamic answer to speed. They were lowered to cut wind resistance and lengthened for stability. Racers experimented with all sorts of fuels: gasoline, methanol, hydrogen peroxide, anything that would burn or bang. Finally, the fastest drivers settled on nitromethane. But not without consequences. Nitro brings on speed, but its price in parts, and sometimes lives, is high. From 1956 to 1963, in a "sensible" move, the NHRA couldn't justify the risk, and banned nitromethane from their sanctioned tracks. That left the nitro innovators to run "outlaw" tracks. They stuck with the explosive, and a few people were killed before the fuel and its vehicles were made safe enough for public consumption and they were allowed back into the fold. The fuel experiments researched to tame the beast benefit us street drivers every day in fuel efficiency, seat belt design and chassis structure of our cars. So nitro was back and it was safer, but that doesn't mean that it was harmless. In its twisted fashion, this unreliability is just what adds a kick. You never know when nitro is gonna surprise you and put on a show. Fans turn up always expecting to see a crash but hoping that everybody will be just okay.

The Southeast experienced the learning curve of racer "Big Daddy" Don Garlits since 1952. With characteristic zeal and bravado, he brought his stuff from Florida and won West Coast fans' allegiance with his grit, determination and ingenuity. He and his ride, affectionately named the Swamp Rat, had a healthy following by 1970 when things went awry and he was reminded of the power of his fuel. Any race car with the motor in front, has got attitude. It's gnarlier and it's cooler, but it's also a much more dangerous ride that spews oil, smoke and fire in the driver's face. In a transmission explosion at

*The Beach—Lions Drag Strip—was a drag racer's mecca in 1957. (Greg Sharp collection)*

Lions Drag Strip, Big Daddy's car was cut in half, along with part of his foot. Following this incident, the racing world took a pause and said "Hey, maybe we oughta put those motors in back where they can't cause so much trouble." Most builders followed the trend. Except, of course, for funny cars—vehicles that have street-car bodies. They wanted to keep that motor up front where they could keep an eye on it, thank you very much. Funny cars also have plenty of attitude and so do their drivers. Except for "nostalgia" classes (which have a weirdo agenda of their own) and the aforementioned crazed funny car guys, everyone else took the hint and put the damn motor in a safer spot. And they continued on to make low E.T.s of 5 seconds and mph of 320 or higher. Without flying or blowing up. Usually.

## THE RACE

Two cars approach the starting line. The drivers hit the throttle and perform the ritual "burn-out" where fat rear tires spin wildly until they smoke and coat the track with a fresh layer of rubber. Then a crew member guides the driver back into a precise position in line with the heated tracks. The cars' front tires break the photoelectric beams and light the staging bulbs atop the "Christmas Tree," a pole positioned at the starting line with two yellow staging lights, five amber colored lights and a green light. Once the cars are lined up, or staged, the lights on the Christmas Tree are activated by the starter. Drivers do an internal countdown, launch with the pole's green light, travel one quarter of a mile through the electronic beams at the finish line and activate a win light. Nitro burning cars are built for peak performance in a quarter of a mile sprint and can go no further.

Florida's "Big Daddy" Don Garlits in his 1963 Swamp Rat V. (Greg Sharp collection)

The general goal is to try to beat the person in the other lane with a low "E.T." and/or a higher speed. An E.T., or elapsed time, is the electronic measurement of how long it takes for a car to travel from the starting line to the finish line, 1320 feet away. The speed is measured at the "top end"—the finish line. The difference between being quick and fast is that low E.T. often wins the race. If you can launch your car before your opponent, they have to pour on the horsepower to beat you at the other end. With today's top speed around 326 and the low E.T. about 4.50 seconds, blink and you miss the race.

In order to pilot these machines you must be 18, have a regular driver's license, pass a bi-annual physical and successfully complete a series of licensing runs down the track. Then you're ready to compete. Most racing associations keep track of their top drivers through a point system. Competitors earn points for qualifying and finishing in the top five slots in national events. By season's end, all these wins and losses and just plain making the field slots are tallied to determine championship status. It's a cut-throat race as more sponsors clamor for the first and second place takers than the no-name 10-20 spots down in the points list.

Don Garlits at Lions Drag Strip. (Greg Sharp collection)

Drag racing has evolved from basically moving a Ford flathead engine very fast, to any manner of motors. The professional racing organizations like NHRA and International Hot Rod Association (IHRA) define areas of competition, or classes. Keeping on top of these distinctions takes a mind geared for minutiae. Engine size, tire size, fuel used, weight, speed and body type all are considered in grouping who will speed down the

Don Garlits drove his innovations until his 1992 retirement. (Dave DeAngelis photo)

track with whom. Generally the professional classes are nitro burning Top Fuel Dragsters and Funny Cars, and the top of the line doorslammers, Pro Stock. The non-professional or "sportsman" classes include super comp, top eliminator, super gas, outlaw gas, top alcohol—basically whatever vehicle you build, you can find a class to race in.

Top Fuel Dragster: Don "the Snake" Prudhomme (Dave DeAngelis photo)

Fuel Funny Car: John Force (Dave DeAngelis photo)

Pro Stock: Kurt Johnson (DRM collection)

---

### *LET'S GO TO SCHOOL—Racing Classes*

**TOP FUEL DRAGSTER** *(TF)—0-300 mph in 5 seconds. This $100,000 convertible beauty features 5000 hp provided by a Supercharged aluminum 426 Chrysler Hemi engine fed by blown nitromethane—as much as 15 gallons per burnout and 1320 pass. The 280-300 inch frame weighs at least 2,025 pounds and is covered by a magnesium and carbon-fiber body comprised of nine pieces rigged for quick release. Sitting no less than 3 inches off the ground this baby keeps traction on two 18" wide (a big ol' 118" in circumference) slicks in the back and two littles in front and slides through its gears under the auspices of a highly calibrated clutch arrangement. Standard equipment includes a hand lever brake (which responds with five G forces of stopping power), parachute-release levers (to make sure it stops) and a top wing that produces 6,200 to 6,500 pounds of downforce on the rear tires to keep the whole shebang in touch with the ground.*

**FUEL FUNNY CAR** *(FC)—0-300 mph in 5 barely controlled seconds. Similar to a Top Fuel Dragster in fuel, engine, dual chutes, clutch and chassis, but features a 89 pound carbon-fiber graphite flip-top body (that looked a little off from the factory standard; it looked "funny"), representative of a 1993 or later mass-produced two-door coupe or two-door sedan. The same $100,000 buys you a shortened wheelbase (only 100-125" compared to a dragster's 300") making for a distinct "looseness" in the rear end. Rather than the rear wing on a TF/D, Funny Cars get their 5000 pounds of downforce from an aluminum and magnesium rear spoiler.*

**PRO STOCK** *(PRO)—0-200 mph in 7 seconds. These speedy kids are "stock" from body to engine—resembling 1993 and later 2-door coupes or 2-door sedans—but just try to get this doorslammer from your local dealer. The V-8 engine tops out at a maximum of 500 cubic inch and must be of same manufacture as body used. This baby runs on gasoline only—sure the engine costs $80,000 compared to the fulers' $50,000—but gasoline is a kinder, gentler fuel and only occasionally destroys engine blocks. Comprised of fiberglass, steel and aluminum components, and on a wheelbase of 99-105", this baby's weight breaks at a minimum of 2350 with the driver strapped in. Also comes with wheelie bars to prevent flip overs, two functional doors, stock lights with working tail lights, a braking system and a parachute. Hood scoops are an optional feature.*

**EVERYTHING ELSE**—*Alcohol Dragster, Alcohol FC, Competition Eliminator (Econo Dragster, Street Roadster Econo Altered and Econo Funny Car, Super Modified), Super Stock Eliminator (includes Super Stock, Modified Stock, Modified Truck and motorcycles), Stock Eliminator (for Stock Cars and Trucks), Super Comp, Super Pro, Super Street, Super Gas, Sportsman,—Classes populated by the masses run on alcohol and gas and generally turning in E.T. handicaps from 5.50—14.00 and slower. Much slower. Can be built in your garage. Classes break according to weight, power output per cubic inch.*

---

Consequently, there are a myriad of records to be set in each and every one of these divisions. Top speed for a track, an event, certain class or even personal best are always noted. Elapsed time can also be delineated for these categories. The first 16 drivers to cross into a new lowered E.T. is marked in record books. A lot of work and sweat and money goes into making the move from 6.0 to 5.0 seconds. The same can be true for crossing the frontier into 300+ or any other mph increase. For each of these impersonal numbers, there is a grinning face associated with it. The first woman to go 299 mph at a certain track. Someone bests a record for super gas at his home track. Assigning your name to a top speed record at the local track. Each of these numbers create a personal victory, making every statistic important.

The same search for personal best is exhibited in dry lake or salt flat racing, the older brother of the drag strip version. As opposed to a drag strip's asphalt, salt that's been hard packed for centuries or the dried mud surface of lake beds free from water for eons, serve as the racing surface. In as many as 100 categories, participants attempt to reach a top speed to smash the previous record. In these unassuming settings there are no

starting line theatrics, in fact, there's no staging at all. These drivers are racing the clock one car at a time. Competitors are often pushed by their tow vehicle and trip the timing lights with a rolling start instead of drag racing's dramatic, light-cued standing start. E.T. doesn't matter here, only the top end speed. Top end at a dry lake or salt bed is usually five miles from the starting line. Here automotive endurance counts. Unlike at a drag strip, having a motor blow up at 1320 feet means you hardly got out of the starting area. Drivers say that once you get out in the barrenness of the mid-track area, you have no sensation of speed, and no outside markers to tell you you're ripping butt down the track. The snap of the chutes makes you reckon with gravity and with any luck you've surpassed the last greatest speed for blown gas, blown nitro, hell, even motorcycles.

## THE GENIUS OF RACING

The result of this steady assault on records and physics is dropping E.T.s and gaining speeds. NHRA's done its best to keep a sort of sanity in this sport of acknowledged crazies. For every deterrent the Association implements, another spark of genius rises to beat it.

Chaos defies control. Stretching the limits of power and speed takes imagination and innovation. Sometimes you blow away established records and sometimes the shit just blows up. Sanctioning bodies have the dual responsibilities of keeping the sport safe and still allowing for the dramatic "controlled chaos" that attracts the ticket buying public. Periodically some major crash occurs and the powers that be mandate new limits on how much fuel can be carried or add more weight to the car or limit the size of the supercharger or something, anything, to make things safe again around the track. These sanctions actually dare the genius gearheads who live to overcome barriers and achieve higher performance. When you're used to bending the laws of physics, can the rules made by some administrative body be really insurmountable? In the late 1990s when NHRA didn't want cars going 300 mph, they mandated a gear ratio change to slow the cars down. It didn't work. The motors had to work harder, but the tuners still found ways to make them go faster. When 295 became a routine speed, the racing association backpedaled and starting selling tickets to see who would be the first team to top 300. There was heavy competition for higher speeds using these imposed specifications and finally the shit hit the supercharger. A very popular driver was killed and many people maintain that the rear end gear ratio change is the culprit.

But, not to forget, competition is what it's all about, so the faster you go with the most consistency, the more races you're gonna win. The lure of racing is that with a combination of driving ability, intellectual prowess and money, anyone can go fast. They say speed costs money, how fast do you want to go? Because of the excesses associated

Racer and journalist Wally Parks, founder of the National Hot Rod Association. (Greg Sharp collection)

(Carol Hakola photo)

Kenny Bernstein's 1992 record-setting 301.78 mph pass in Gainesville, Florida. (Dave DeAngelis photo)

In 1988, Eddie Hill was the first to run in the 4s. (Dave DeAngelis photo)

Beer and smokes—sponsors that fuel NHRA's drag racing machine. (Author photo)

with professional drag racing, people incorrectly assume that there's a pot of gold waiting at the finish line. Professional drag racing is one of the biggest wallet-emptiers ever. To add badly needed dollars to a race teams' war chest, many drivers augment their seasons with match racing. Tracks, usually ones far off the NHRA or IHRA circuit, pay racers to show up and perform a best 2 out of 3 run exhibition against each other or the local favorites. These racing forays are questionable as they are just as hard on parts as the pro circuit runs, but do help build a fan base to delight sponsors, along with the extra money. The average top fuel run is about $6,000 per 1/4 mile pass. That $6,000 includes normal wear and tear on the car, cost of tires, wages to the crew chief and crew, motels, and transportation to the track. That figures out to $6,000 for 5 seconds of dramatic and very expensive entertainment. One top team went through about eight $50,000 motors trying to winning an event. They runnered-up and probably spent $400,000 to win a purse of $20,000.

Account balances like these make professional performance dependent on self-made millions, or corporate sponsorship. The growth of logos on the cars require the drivers and crew members to rattle off sponsor names like a 10 second commercial and take way the individuality of the sport. Because there is a narrow margin of acceptable performance for winning cars, they don't take risks. Rides basically all run the same and all look the same. Flashy paint jobs and wild names like Swamp Rat, Bean Bandit or the Chi Town Hustler have given way to 320 mph billboards. Fans looking for a place to hang their allegiance have a harder time deciding whether they're behind the Budweiser King or the Skoal Bandit. What these corporate sponsors don't get is that they're dealing with a bunch of junkies. The competition-hungry drivers, the challenge-smashing mechanics and the nitro-sniffing fans don't care if our day's fun is brought to us by McDonalds or In-and-Out, just keep those motors running. Ultimately, whoever wows us with speed and dramatics is the hero of the day.

## WELCOME TO THE SHOW

Drag racing equals fat rednecks drunkenly gathered around hopped up Camaros, fighting over the outcome of a squealing tire display of speed. I mean, that's what I thought it was all about. One trip to a drag strip and one pass by a couple of nitro rails changed my mind. I got immersed in a world of sound, smell, vibration and even mental stimulation that was nothing like I'd envisioned.

As a neophyte I was led to a spot nearest a top fuel car where the need for explanation just doesn't exist. Positioned on the fence at Famoso Raceway in Bakersfield, not warned to cover my ears, not told that my world

was gonna shake, and without a clue that I may become addicted, my guide simply led and let the nitro speak for itself. Since then, I've learned to decipher the face of the novice. After a pass or two, they will: 1) look at the rest of us like we've taken leave of our senses and head for the nearest exit, or 2) join us as a new compadre in substance abuse. A new nitro fiend will eagerly stand along side us in the pits—nose wide open as a 6,000 horsepowered engine rumbles and begs to be let loose, spewing fumes that we willingly inhale until our eyes water, our eardrums nearly break, and our bodies instinctively try to escape.

Attending a major race is akin to going to the circus. The NHRA spectacle has no permanent home and each February to November it lumbers from location to location snaking semis and custom busses with its attendant vendors and side show acts.

Nearing the track is surviving an assault by buttloads of NHRA sponsor banners featuring oil, lubricant, gasoline, alcohol and tobacco products. After wading through a sea of parked cars you arrive at a mass of humanity. The crowds are huge and, in Southern California, diverse—an equal mix of accountants from Orange County, Hollywood hipsters, San Fernando Valley gearheads and East LA homies. They all dress in t-shirts whose florescent colors announce the name of their favorite race teams. Often in tow are kids in earplugs, wives and girlfriends with teased hair and a healthy number of video cameras. But the place to be is the "pits."

Fans pack the pits for drivers' autographs and to catch a whiff of nitro. (Nick Licata photo)

The pits are the sort of midway for this traveling circus complete with a human version of a moving sidewalk. Slip into a lane and glide through the carefully arranged semis and motor homes of the "stars," or the bigger sponsored teams—Budweiser, Skoal, McDonalds, and Winston. These cars don't drive to competition like the kids in the '40s. Now semis and trailers tow these specialty dragsters and funny cars—their shops on wheels, extra motors, extra bodies and their gang of mechanics—in multimillion dollar trailers. The low dollar race teams have to be hunted down as they're hidden somewhere on the far side of this arrangement. The onslaught of sound and visuals vie for immediate attention. Loudspeakers are everywhere blaring the voices of the announcers who are huddled safely in the tower—ringleaders guiding the masses to the next act. Consisting exclusively of endless babble, my heart (and stomach) always jumps when their insistent voices are drowned out by BAP, BAP, BAP.

That's my cue to rush along with the countless others, to the origin of the sound, an area of about 100' x 40' where some crew members have fired up the motor on a top fueler. While an ungodly sound pours out of this pit site, a crowd of spectators stands watching the crew work around a fire breathing, fuel spewing, ear drum splitting, mega-horsepower bomb. And we don't just watch, we breathe in the experience, and enjoy the ground fluttering like a predictable earthquake. This three minute session ends in one of two ways: the crew finds out what they need to know about their motor and it whines down to a shutoff or I get more than I can take, my eyes water a bit too much and I have to back off through the crowd. Either way, when I hear that BAP, BAP, BAP coming from another pit area, I rush right over with the crowd to get another snoutful. The fuel of choice is nitromethane—$CH_3NO_2$ to the chemists out there. Fed through a fuel pump at 50 gallons a minute, a funny car can slurp up 15 gallons (at $18 per) to perform its burnout and 1/4 mile pass. Like snake oil, nitro's good for a couple of purposes. In the best of circumstances, it'll cool the motor and fuel a light vehicle down a track. Or, without much warning, it can explode, sending parts and flames flying and testing a driver's ability and luck. I guess you could say that nitromethane always puts on a good show. It makes dramatic explosions because unlike gasoline, which burns, nitromethane won't ignite. But smack it, and it damn well will explode.

Flamboyant winner John Force brings healthy crowds to the drag strips. (Ron Lewis photo)

Neat. The fans love it. From firsthand experience I know that nitro is addictive; it appeals to every sense. You can smell it, it makes your eyes water, you can taste it and it runs down the back of your throat just like cocaine. It'll give you permanent ear damage if you're not careful. You can feel the pressure waves in your chest if you're close enough to a car when it goes by. Basically it turns a spectator sport into a participant event. You feel the action. Nitro appeals to fans over more efficient forms of propulsion. Hydrogen peroxide is a fast fuel, but it's quiet and unstable. Like Coonce points out, "it's not gonna make anybody's butt rattle when they're sitting on the grandstand." We know that nitro's brought us here and it's obviously true for the other fans. When sportsman racing starts, the stands empty out. Watching these gas powered cars tear down the track at a top speed of 90 or 120 or 150 mph, clocking an E.T. anywhere from nine to 14 seconds doesn't hold an attraction for me. For the average joe, it's financially feasible racing and they enjoy the competition. And for drivers in slower classes such as Super Street, Stock Eliminator or

Competition Eliminator there's a thrill in seeing a project to fruition. "You know what," says Coonce impersonating a race happy backyard mechanic, "I just bought a 1966 Dart and I think I can make it go quicker than any other Dart out there. And even though the quickest Dart out there is 11.55 seconds, I think I can do 11.54." Each time they dream up and build their one-of-a-kind racer, they scrutinize parts, finesse body design, coax fuel and clutch systems and attempt to eke out extra horsepower that will make them a winner over everyone else's individually designed racer. Competitors spend years and ignore their spouses to make it happen or not make it happen. This sport was born from this backyard enthusiasm, and it'll never go away.

From our standpoint, as clean and stress free observers, Coonce and I agree that we're elitist to bag on anybody who's not running nitromethane. Whenever we hang off the fence at the top end of the track, feeling a top fueler whoosh by like a low flying jet, we're looking for a thrill that reaches out and touches us. Sure nitro's far more expensive, far more crazed and far more explosive, with a much higher chance of things going horribly wrong. But sorry, horribly wrong can be far more interesting.

Okay, so now you're getting the clue that watching these things is like watching (barely) controlled disaster. There are plenty of explosions and parts flying, and race fans spend much time trying to get closer to these nitro bombs, to experience the thrill, and conversely obeying their bodies' urge for safety and moving out of danger. So what about the drivers, or the tuners (mechanics) of these monsters?

I talked to a couple of guys that could give me information from the wrenching/driving side. Pete Jensen and "Nitro" Neil Bisciglia run a car sponsored by Red Line Oil. Pete, who owned the car with his partner, the late Ken Castagnino, has been building and dismantling top fuel dragsters since he bought his first one at 17, a good ten years before "Nitro" Neil even got a glimpse at his first Hot Rod or Drag Racing magazine. Besides the talent for telling a good story, working overtime to live their dreams and making what they do look easy, they've both got it—the "sickness."

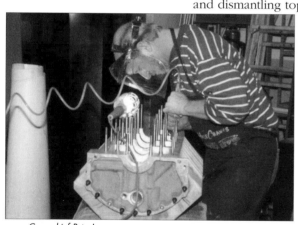

Crew chief Pete Jensen, an aggressive competitor on the nostalgia circuit.
(Mike Bumbeck photo)

## ADDICTION TO RACING

A self-described "hot rodder who drag races," Pete Jensen grew up in south San Francisco centrally located between Champion Speed Shop and Gotelli's Speed Shop. He didn't have a chance. In 1959 Pete's mom took him to the drag races to see Garlits run and, "I was just fucked from then on." He got nabbed by the normal stuff: the noise, the tire smoke, the parachutes and "the people, the racers. I grew up in San Francisco in the '60s, I graduated in '69, so I come from that kinda weird deal. I loved the people because they were real. You see Don Garlits, who's just greasy from head to toe from working all night long in a dirty lot, and just go out and run that son of a bitch. Especially when you hear the cars start going, the tone changes and they start gaining in RPM. And I just love that sound. It caught me real quick."

He started out as a gofer with Gotelli's team when they traveled to races in Long Beach, Irwindale and Pomona. Pete, Ken and about six or seven other kids were kind of raised by "Terrible Ted" Gotelli. Some racers remember "Terrible Ted" as a guy with a hellacious Italian temper, but Pete calls him "one the greatest guys that ever walked this earth."

In San Francisco the street competition was big. They used to race between the Park and the Great Highway. Says Pete, "unlike the Southern California deal, the Northern California deal, and especially the South San Francisco thing is a real tight knit group of people." Pete, of course, had the fastest car in high school, a '56 Chevy. Traveling to race was part of the fun. The races in Long Beach would be a mix of Valley guys, surfer guys, greasers, Latinos and Pete's hippie crew for Northern California. They didn't have time for tension—they all came there to run as hard as possible. It was an equal field because as Pete says, "You ran hard and that's how you gained your respect."

Pete's a competitive guy that doesn't like to hold back. Winning is it for him. He says what makes it better is "every partner I've had, and I've had a lot—Every partner I've had, I've beat them. At least the first time." Since his team first banded together, they've heighten their performance in a few ways. One is trying to encourage the best out of each team member. Pete does most of the tuning because fuel motors "kind of talk to me." He elaborates, saying "the motor's basically a foundation. And Ken built an excellent foundation and of course, Neil's a killer driver. So we feel like we've got it all." And something else too. "I've been racing with these guys out here all my life. I know their weaknesses. I know what you can pull on them. I believe in the psychological card real hard. The game of psyche and the mind fuck and the whole goddamn thing. Oh yeah, that's how we do what we do. We can't outrun most people, but we can fuck with you on the starting line like you've never even seen. Oh yeah, I'm very dirty like that. We're not all like that. I get guys who say, "That's not the way to race." But my whole team's like that. We have that reputation pretty good."

One skirmish was with an ex-partner who put "Pete who?" on the nose of his car. Fully aware of the slight, the driver was waiting for retaliation—he figured Pete would "burn him down," or get the jump at the starting line. But Pete had another plan, "I knew he was deathly afraid of being burnt down. So I used that against him. So I didn't burn him down, but I looked like I'd burn him down." Pete's driver RAPPED on the throttle and his opponent jumped the starting light, or, as Pete recalls: "Oh, he was hot. He red lighted low E.T. and top speed of the meet away." Mind games, luck—like the time on a different team, with another car and driver, when Pete's car ran out of fuel near the top end, and the PA-BOOM from their car's explosion shocked the driver in the other lane so much that he crossed the center line—an automatic disqualification. Pure luck. And talent.

*Pete "Race This" Jensen, burn down artist. (Mike Bumbeck photo)*

## THRILL TO THE DRIVER

When he realized that you can't pick up a book and learn how to build a front engine nostalgia fuel car, Neil Bisciglia was directed to Pete Jensen for help. Apparently a lot of guys can be secretive about this information, but Pete doesn't care, "I'll tell anybody. That's how you get it out there. Maybe more people will understand, maybe more people will do it and the sport will stay healthy that way." But that's how they met, and when Neil followed Pete's directions and his car ran in the 6.50s the first time he took it out. In exchange for the valuable advice, Pete insisted Neil tow his car from his home in Kenosha, Wisconsin to Sears Point, California so the two could meet.

This was their first meeting, and Pete had another dare for him: for Neil to drop some weight and drive Pete's new car. Neil got to work and Pete says, "he called me back two months later and goes, 'I weigh 162 pounds now, can I drive it?'" Neil dropped 86 pounds Rocky-style. He changed how he ate and exercised. At lunch time he set up a gym in some warehouse in American Airlines back there at O'Hare where he's an airline mechanic. He even made his own boxing gloves."

Neil, too, was bitten by the racing thing early on. The youngest of five kids, he used to work with his dad on the junkers they would buy to "keep them all in wheels." Although at six or seven when he was young enough to be rootin' around for beer cans under the stands, he remembers his first race—it happened to be the first tour of the Snake and Mongoose funny cars. It was enough to get his attention. The atmosphere of the whole day—loud cars, lots of people having fun, and a picnic with his family—made lasting impression. That attraction to racing really started kicking in as he got closer to driving age and ended up with a project '65 Mustang fastback, which he still has. He immediately tried to turn it into a racing car. Neil's dad saw what was happening to his son, and warned him "never to fall in love with metal." Neil remembers his dad would say, "even though you get a lot of enjoyment from it—to be completely focused on something that was made of metal—metal rusts and metal goes away and metal bends. There are more important values in life than chrome alloy and sheet metal." Neil listened,

*"Nitro" Neil Bisciglia debriefs fans following his fire at Bakersfield. (Todd Westover photo)*

but he kept wrenching. He did some low buck drag racing and then some enduro racing. The whole time he had a passion for front-motor top fuel cars. "It was considered a pretty crazy, or stupid idea," Neil says. You know how it is when you're in love, though, even the impractical seems sensible. Who cares that Big Daddy made the rear engine car work and even run competitively? Who cares that a lot of people got hurt and even killed in the slingshot? For Neil, it was "a real super, golden romantic era of drag racing. And the esthetics of the front motor car—I believe that the slingshot is the most beautiful drag racing car. At first I wanted to have one just to have it in my shop to look at it. I had no idea that it would grow into what it did."

He ended up buying a dragster from an old top fuel guy who had never completed his front motor car. The owner didn't want to sell, but Neil spent three or four months pestering the guy and convincing him that he "was going to turn it into this most wonderful, beautiful, completed front engine dragster with the early hemi in it and everything." Now Neil had never even seen one of these dinosaurs run, and that's when he started getting telephone coaching from Pete Jensen. Why was he so crazy about a

"Nitro" Neil Bisciglia's "most beautiful drag racing car," the front engine coupe. (Steve Collison photo)

car he'd only seen raced in pictures? "I knew, I definitely knew what the top fuel cars were capable of." Neil explains, "nitromethane is liquid horsepower. It's the ultimate internal combustion engine, in my eyes. It might not be the ultimate *efficient* internal combustion engine, but it's the ultimate displacement that horsepower ratio powerplant that you can get your hands on." And then Neil's gone—"I'd heard the stories—it was just crazy. Let alone, having the best seat in the house. I had a tendency to daydream and to me—I knew it before I had it, but now I really know it—that I can't picture a better place to be, as far as an intense, exhilarating, adrenaline raising ride, than in a front engine, blown fuel dragster. You've got the tires right next to you, you've got the pipes pointed right in your face and you can see the tune of the motor—If you're in love with the motor, I don't know how you could have a better ride. Even a funny car guy is covered by the body and the pipes are outside of the car. He can catch it out of the windows, what's going on, but in a front motor car, it's right in your face."

And I say to these guys—Pete and Neil both—it's a little nutty. Slingshots went out with, well, with the front part of Don Garlits' right foot. In response, Pete passes a Hemmingwayesque quote that his undertaker father used to try to talk sense into him: "'There are only three blood sports left: bullfighting, boxing, and auto racing.' The motor's supposed to be in front." Neil sounds more logical, but just as impassioned. He figures with the rear end under your butt, and the flames beside your head, you can keep a better eye on the motor, know what it's doing. In theory, you can avoid trouble before it happens. I say "in theory" because I was about 100 feet from Neil's blue coupe when it exploded into a fireball at a Hot Rod Reunion. I asked Neil why he didn't avoid that "trouble." He cites these factors: 1) they were amped because it was the last race of the season, and he was a long way from home; 2) even though the tires were "getting ahead of the car," he had faith that he could regain traction and overtake the car in the other lane; 3) even though they had "floated some valves" and ended up with an explosion and a fire fed by fuel and oil, Neil did not lift off of the throttle, because 4) "First I wanted to make damn sure that we didn't have a chance of winning."

*The exciting danger of a rear engine fire. (Dave DeAngelis photo)*

Now if this is you, and your first thought is not on winning, you are not a drag racer. My first thought was "Shit! I hope he's okay," and when the fire went out, I thought "Cool!" Neil says that, "because of that deep safety suit I had on, which was killer—really, to be honest with ya, I wasn't uncomfortable at all." That is, until he tasted it. Drivers know that the big problem in a fire isn't your skin getting burnt—rather it's breathing the flames and burning the interior of your lungs. Then pneumonia can set in and that's harder to deal with. So Neil held his breath, subconsciously he says. But even then, he tasted it.

Coonce explains from the laymen's side what it's like to drive one of these damn things. "Drivers actually are pulling things off that are pretty outrageous at five times the force of gravity," he says. "In other words, if you're trying to finesse something, and there is some finesse involved, like making decisions in literally a hundredth of a second. It can mean the difference between winning and losing, or living and dying sometimes. At 5 Gs, that driver who weighs 200 pounds, now weighs 1000 pounds. You have to get used to weighing five times your weight and finessing things with you're feet and your hands. Visualize 5,000 horses on your chariot and they all want to make a right turn and you want them to go straight."

---

### _SAFETY FIRST_

*Drivers must wear complete fire-resistant driving suit, gloves, helmet, 360-degree neck collar. They are secured into the cockpit with a five-point restraint system made of safety belts at least 3" wide and covered with fire-resistant material. Funny cars have a mandatory fire-extinguishing system with 15 pounds directed at the engine and 5 pounds provided for the driver's compartment (chiefly their feet). They have a handy working escape hatch on top and the side windows accommodate a fire hose.*

---

Okay, I think I get that. There's also a difference in how these horses handle, depending on whether they're pulling you or pushing you. In the modern rear motor top fuelers, it can be argued that the driver's being propelled and can only react to trouble, because in essence it's already happened before he's aware of the situation. That he can't see what's going on. Like Coonce says, "if the car quits pushing them back in the seat, that means the motor is eating itself up and the smart thing to do is just get off the throttle because you've probably lost the race and you're chewing up tons of expensive parts."

Like the nostalgia drivers, sometimes you gotta wonder about the brain power of a funny car driver. A "funny car" has the same motor as a dragster, but it sits in front of the driver on a shortened chassis—125 inch wheel base. It's also got a body composed of some sort of carbon fiber or fiberglass that's supposed to look like a late model Dodge Daytona or a Ford Mustang or something. And it never does. It looks like something from Mars.

Longtime racer turned team owner, Don "the Snake" Prudhomme, shares his expertise with driver Ron Capps. (Ron Lewis photo)

"The best rock and roll song you can ever hear" is how Ron Capps describes piloting a fuel funny car. (Nick Licatta photo)

## THE BIG BUCK TEAM

They may look extraterrestrial, but according to Ron Capps, funny cars are earthly. "They're animals!" Ron claims. I figure he knows. As the newest member of Don "the Snake" Prudhomme's Copenhagen Racing team, Ron's been learning about the tricks a funny car can pull. His drag racing rides have been an alcohol dragster, then a fuel dragster. Since early 1997 Ron's tried his hand as a funny car pilot—maybe both hands. "It's unbelievable how much of an animal they are." Ron describes that "after a few races I was driving the dragster with one hand. I had my other hand on the parachutes in case something happened. In the funny car, you can't to that. You really have to manhandle it. You've got to throw them left and throw them right."

Ron is a young guy in the early stages of his career. He's just happy to be doing what he's doing and learning from one of his heroes, the Snake. It's a little hard for him to believe sometimes, "I was a little kid playing with his Hot Wheels car and the next thing I know, I'm driving for him." Betwixt playing with his Hot Wheels and playing at being a pro, Ron spent time wiping the tires on his dad's race car then later racing go carts and motorcycles. By the time he was 23, he'd learned enough to be crew chief for a car run by his dad and a friend. He always wanted to be a driver, but he also wanted to learn all the mechanics. "I didn't want to be just somebody sitting in the cockpit with the pedal to the metal and not know much about the car."

A driver who can mechanically describe the changes in the car down that critical 1320 is a plus to any team. That ability might have gotten Ron the spot in the Prudhomme flopper's seat. Apparently the Snake had watched Ron and appreciated that he had a good head on his shoulders and was taking care of the parts of the car—then he offered him the job. Not that hurting parts is a major concern for a high dollar team like the Copenhagen Racing. Ron was a little unprepared for the difference a few million dollars can make in racing. Things like being able to take the car out between events and test it to improve performance. Or even in the media swarm and corporate responsibilities. And the fans. "Going to the track and all those people line up at the ropes to talk to me or get my autograph—that was me a few years ago." Ron's even getting his sponsorship lingo down. "The best thing you can do in an interview at the other end is describe how the run felt. If I can throw a plug in while I'm doing that, then, yeah that's great. I try to explain how awesome that run just felt." So I ask, what does it feel like—to be strapped in under the fiberglass body of a 6,000 hp animal and flying down the track at 300 mph? Ron says, "like when you're driving down the road in your car and you hear this awesome song on the stereo and you want to start rocking out. It's like that. It's just like the best rock and roll song you can ever hear." And for the first time in my life, I want to drive a fuel funny car.

## COURTING IMPENDING DOOM

All of this stuff is really exciting, and it's what both the drivers and fans show up for, but racing involves more than that four to seven second trip down the track. It's a lifestyle. For Pete Jensen, it's an outlet for his competitive nature, that takes dedication. "When we're racing, we work on this thing all the time. It's like another job," says Pete, who's first job is piloting behemoth semis down California's freeways. "I don't just come up and work on the weekends, or work on it for a few hours and I'm out drinking that night. I work my regular job 60 hours a week and working on this 20 to 40 hours a week. So it's a lot of time. You go there to win. That's what I like about what we're doing. I want to prove that I am just as good, or better, than these other people." By these other people, he means racers that can afford to put in about ten times as much money as people like Pete and Neil do. But they get out to the lanes, and it's all a level playing field. On each run, their pooled knowledge races down the track with that fuel burning beast. When I ask Pete what's at stake, he says, "I'm racing the people. The cars are just an extension of the people."

Neil faces a different opponent on the track, himself. "One thing good about racing yourself all the time is that you've always got somebody to beat. I feel good if we can leave the track either running quicker or faster than we've ever run before." Neil takes the whole deal very seriously because "there are so many people that help make it happen that when it comes down to the nitty gritty, it's all on your shoulders to make us all winners. I'm lucky enough to deal with so many good people that you just want to do good. You want to give them something to glow about for a couple of weeks." Pete describes Neil as loving the fray: "We'll be somewhere and he has a saying, "impending doom." Thunderheads are in the sky and it's lightning and half a crankshaft's hanging out the motor and we haven't got a chance, and Neil goes 'That's when I love it the best. I love that impending doom.'"

Driver "Nitro" Neil Bisciglia and crew chief Pete Jensen check their fuel. (Todd Westover photo)

Neil faces his "impending doom" in 12 to 15 match races a season. Match racing is, well let's start here—today's tournament style, NHRA sponsored racing is, as Coonce describes, "like Lollapalooza. You go to a drag race and there's 20 guys there, or 60 guys there who are touring professionals, and they're gonna pack up their tent and they're gonna load all they're shit into their semis and they're gonna go to the next Lollapalooza gig, which is down the road." Drag racing used to be a completely unorganized touring event where somebody with some prestige and outrageousness of showmanship would show up and just wow all the local yokels on a Wednesday night and 10,000 people would go out there to see them make a series of 7 second passes. This is what Neil does more than a dozen times a year, he mostly gets booked into smaller tracks that can't handle the semi circus of the pro circuit and he races whatever they put in the other lane against him. Sometimes it's late model funny cars with altered bodies on them, sometimes it's a jet car, and it's often the local hero. Coonce has a take on this too, of course, "it's basically the Harlem Globetrotters versus the Washington Generals. The Washington Generals change in each town. It's a hard lifestyle. You book all these little places across America and you load the car into the trailer, hit the road and the next gig is twelve hours away. And these guys are driving race cars with no sleep for weeks at a time, more or less."

Mr. "Atmosphere" Bisciglia likes it that way for its "smaller tracks which have demographics that are very interesting, like there's a river running right along side of it, or there're trees at the top or there're trees in the pits, and narrow tracks and grandstands right on top of the track and looser security for people—I found that the people there are a lot more personal—it appears that they feel very close to the track and very close to the racers. So they get really pumped up. Maybe it's because they are closer. The grandstands are smaller, they can pack them easier. Get a crowd going. Get them pumped up. They tend to get a lot more enthusiastic. You feel like you're someplace where something's really happening."

"Nitro" Neil, ready to dominate his field. (Todd Westover photo)

So of course Pete's goal is to stay in racing and "have a good goddamn time." Ron Capps says he wants to "have a great career and not hurt myself. And to have made a contribution to safety—or anything." I asked "Nitro" Neil when he would stop racing and I felt like I was telling a kid he had to take a nap while the other kids were still playing. Like all of these people who live the racing life, fun, family and employment are so intermingled, they can't imagine life without it. Working so closely and intensely for a common goal makes family of friends. They talk about marital problems and raising kids as much as clutch management or fuel combinations. Racing's history is littered with personalities who "retire" then return again not able to break away from the lifestyle. Because as long as you can race, you can win.

Neil's goal for this season? To dominate—and to step up from 232 to 320 mph—because nobody told him he couldn't.

(Rescue photo)

# The Other Who's Who of Drag Racing

## CHAPTER 2

I t took a crowd to start this sport and their names roll off the tongue like reciting the national anthem. NHRA founder Wally Parks and Hot Rod Magazine creator Robert "Pete" Petersen. Seminal track promoter C.J. "Pappy" Hart. Mechanical innovator and winning driver Don Garlits. Ed Iskendarian, Vic Edelbrock, Dean Moon, and Jim Deist—performance parts peddlers whose names show up on almost every vehicle that moves with speed. Stacks of documents have been written about them and hours of documentaries produced. There are other pioneers who had small successes and medium victories. Weighed against the pile of history, they may not reach so high. But taken in context of their time, their achievements against the zeitgeist was monumental. Rather than gush and golly one more time about the obviousness of early achievements of the loudest, the biggest or the most expensive, I'd rather acknowledge the sweeter, sometimes smaller victories of Malcolm Durham, Joaquin Arnett, and Barbara Hamilton—people without whom ex-NBA player Larry Nance, or sons of the "Flaming Mexican" Frank Pedregon, or the 300+ mph teenager Cristen Powell may not be racing today.

## JOAQUIN ARNETT AND THE BEAN BANDITS—Original Gangsters

Joaquin Arnett winged it and created from nothing, setting the pace for the racing world. Arnett's entree into the field of metal was a fluke; he was simply in the right place when things fell apart. While in high school, he had a weekend helper job at a welding shop. Because no one was officially certified, the shop got shut down and Arnett was chosen to go to school to learn the craft. In the mid-1940s, the 16 year old Arnett showed a talent and recalls the instructor telling him, "You're lucky. It's like learning how to blow a saxophone or a clarinet when you're as good a welder as you are." Back at the shop Arnett honed his skills building hearses. Hearses don't just roll out of the factory, they have to be special ordered and custom built. The bodies are cut and the extended rears are hand formed. His boss gave him a Buick, and the first thing he did was chop the top, or lower the frame between the roof and the body.

*Bean Bandits in 1951.*
*(Joaquin Arnett collection)*

Arnett's workshop for innovation was in his backyard. As they grew up together, Carlos Ramirez watched results of his young friend's innate curiosity. He and Arnett learned to drive cars when they were just 8 or 9 years old. Not that anyone let them. They would wait until their dads went to work then sneak the cars out. He watched Arnett as he figured out the wonders of automotive mechanics. As kids they'd explore Market Street in San Diego, California. Arnett would pick up car pieces, like an old carburetor—take it apart and see what made it work. Later he turned that research into winning races.

Arnett built his first "rail job" from scratch. He supplied it with a carburated 275-cubic-inch Mercury flathead that he powered with nitromethane loads as high as 80 percent. It was a 1325 pound, 134 mph dragster that set speed records throughout California in 1952. The Mark-II made history by winning Top Eliminator at the first meet ever sanctioned by the NHRA—the Southern California Championship Drags on April 11-12, 1953. He and his friends also turned top speed of the meet, 132.35 mph. Later

*Driver Andrew Ortega lends crew chief Joaquin Arnett his seat. (Joaquin Arnett collection)*

they modified this car to accept a second flathead V8 and either a dragster or sedan body. "At Pomona, I ran the dragster and it did 127. That was fast for a two engine flathead dragster," recalls Arnett. "This thing won 45 trophies so quick, we couldn't believe it." The sanctioning body couldn't believe it either; rather than let the team run in eight classes, they restricted them to four. That original dragster, restored to racing condition is on display in the Don Garlits' Museum of Drag Racing.

Not only was their car renowned, so too was the club itself the stuff of legends. Although considered a Hispanic group, they had a virtual rainbow of members. Ramirez ticks off the background of the group: Japanese, black, Filipino and Lebanese. "We had a mixture of guys that were all just great guys that loved the sport." At the drag strip they'd overhear "here comes those beaners." But they took those taunts as dares, says Ramirez, "We thought, "we'll show them. We'll leave our name on the tips of their tongues." The team made no apologies for themselves and took any hints of racism and turned it to their advantage. They even laughingly called themselves Beaners. Club member Billy Galvin heard it suggested that bandits like beans and thought, "Bean Bandits" and the name stuck. Hence the Bean Bandits became the official name for this young, innovative group from San Diego.

Early track records are commonly disputed. Outlaw tracks didn't even bother to keep records. Stopwatches and early timing clocks were often unreliable. Observers' memories are filtered by personal loyalties. Arnett acknowledges a degree of underreporting where the accomplishments of a group of Mexican-Americans from San Diego was concerned. But that's okay, they have a barn full of trophies and their memories.

---

### FOR THE RECORD—Joaquin Arnett and the Bean Bandits

- *January 18, 1953—Bean Bandits Class C Roadster won Santa Ana—135.13 mph*
- *April 1953—Bean Bandit Mark II (streamlined, modified Roadster/dragster)—won 1st SoCal Championships at Pomona Raceway—132.35 mph*
- *May 1953—Peggy Hart (Promoter C.J. "Pappy" Hart's wife) drove the Bean Bandits' roadster for top time of the day—112.95 mph*
- *October 1953—Joaquin set a new record at Santa Ana—142.95 mph with an E.T. of 1.08*
- *August 1957—Bean Bandits took Top Eliminator title at the Colton Anniversary race—154.63 mph with an E.T. of 9.78*

---

These numbers don't tell the complete story. As the old racers reminisce, long forgotten stories are retold. Sometimes it's about a race Arnett won without even trying. A racer from Sacramento recalled his first experience with Arnett's crew. "I'd heard of the Bean Bandits. When they came up here, I just kept my car in the trailer. After they made one run, I didn't take it out." Arnett hears lots of stories like this, "We knew we were heavy duty at that time."

The powerful fuel was new to the Bean Bandits and they'd arrive at the track with their nitro packed in rags. Nitromethane's not that volatile, but they didn't know it at the time. African American team member Harold Miller says they'd add to the mystique saying, "Don't go near it, it's gonna blow up." Paradise Mesa was their proving ground as Miller recalls, "These guys from LA would come down and make us look bad. Joaq would say, 'Okay, let's put the nitromethane in.'" Arnett finally settled for a 50/50 mixture because, as he told Hot Rod in 1953, "It's easy to mix this way. A gallon of this and a gallon of that." Arnett used an array of fuel additives to boost his team's performance.

Arnett's skills as a team leader were that he could recognize abilities in people and knew how to encourage them. He chose two alternating drivers for the team; Carlos Ramirez and the late Andrew Ortega. After Arnett chose Ramirez to drive, he taught him how to read a race. "He used to run me off and tell me to 'go watch those guys and see what they're doing. Pick up their mistakes.'" Studying their rivals taught Ramirez the best time to shift—before or after his competitors—the physical quirks of the track, the body language of the flag man who set off the racers. Then Ramirez put those skills to work. "The guys would tell me, "give it a ride" and they'd get away and let me concentrate on what I had to do."

Never big-budget racers, Arnett managed to make a little money and a lot of intuition go a long way. It was a necessity. When you're working on a budget, you can't afford too many broken parts. Long time racer Don Rackeman explains what the others respected in Arnett, "his mentality in the sport of automotive racing in the 1950s was far ahead of most people that were supposed to be know-it-alls and were equipment manufacturers." Racers weren't the only ones to take advantage of his skills. Local drug runners commissioned high performance engines to fit into their stock bodied cars. The cops never knew what outran them. Arnett just lived with it, "We never bad mouthed anyone. We were all from the same neighborhood."

Bean Bandits were consistent winners at their home track of Paradise Mesa. (Joaquin Arnett collection)

The club became local folk heroes. Their renown reached far south of San Diego into Mexico. Admirers in a poor town honored them by sending handmade peasant clothes "to represent the race." Arnett laughs remembering the white "uniforms." "We had all white pants that didn't stay white. Some of the guys had their shirts made out of sack material. Way down in Mexico they didn't have buttons or a machine to sew buttons, so they would tie them."

Success at their home tracks meant that the Bean Bandits could travel to challenge racers in other parts of the country. Coming from an area where all the domestic workers spoke Spanish, the guys were surprised by the difference of New Orleans where all the cooks and hotel workers were African American. As they traveled, the

The 1954 Bean Bandits were a multi-ethnic mix. (Joaquin Arnett collection)

reactions they faced ranged from ignorance in the South, where they didn't even know what a Mexican was, to outright racism. In Las Vegas in the 1950s, Sammy Davis, Jr. may have been the only black allowed in town, and even that was grudgingly. The black members of the Bean Bandit team were told there was no room for them in the gambling town's hotels. But for every racist remark or sour meeting, the San Diegans were also treated to people who revered them for what they could do, not their skin color. Arnett warmly recalls a man in Indianapolis who let the whole crew stay at his downtown Sears store in a furnished apartment in the basement. And he was honored to do so.

Race and ethnicity were often downplayed at the track. Photographs of the famous Stone-Woods-Cook racing team always displayed the car and Doug Cook, the white driver. You have to dig through a pile of memorabilia to find any shots of Fred Stone or the unassuming Tim Woods, the black owners. Conversely, the Bean Bandits were too raucous and too numerous to miss. Their pictures displayed a jumble of Mexicans, Japanese and blacks. Sometimes they slid past difficulty due to naiveté. When the Bandits arrived in Louisville, Kentucky, a hotel manager changed her mind about having room openings when she saw the crew. Arnett asked her why and she complained "some of the guys passed for black." Arnett explained they were Mexican. The befuddled manager asked, "What the heck's that?"

As gritty youngsters, the crew could hand out as much trouble as they received. Like 40 years ago when they put a T-Bird in a motel swimming pool to get back at fellow racer Don Rackeman. Apparently the Bandits were doing a late night thrash in their room, and Rackeman ratted them out to the motel manager saying: "these Mexicans are over there changing an engine." It was too late for the manager to stop them, but not too late to put Rackeman's ride in the pool. Now this anecdote only came to light as Arnett recently came clean with Rackeman. The response? Rackeman simply shook his head, but was still full of praise for the San Diego team.

Like many do, Arnett dropped from the sport to raise his family. Now he had his sons, Joaquin "Sonny" Arnett, III and Jeff to hang his comeback on. The kids had grown up with racing, and in 1988 they decided to take advantage of the growing trend in "nostalgia" racing and bring back the old Chrysler powered 1927 roadster. They got the club back together, had a fund raising reunion party and were able to rebuild a replica "Bandit" roadster that brought that NHRA win in 1953. In 1989 Arnett and his sons built a 20 foot

Proud supporters in Mexico made white peasant uniforms for the team. (Joaquin Arnett collection)

long streamliner—Bean Bandit Mark I—and ran it at the Bonneville Salt Flats. They went on to set a record at El Mirage dry lake of 202 mph in the Unblown Fuel Streamliner class breaking the old record of 185. In 1991 the same car had a pass of 317 mph at Bonneville.

The second reckoning of the Bean Bandits came to an abrupt halt in 1995 on the dried mud surface of El Mirage. Arnett's oldest son, Sonny, the man who convinced his dad to come back to racing, died in a dramatic fireball crash in the Bean Bandit streamliner that he was piloting at about 265 mph. The family, the racing club and the entire racing community felt the reverberations of the crash that day. Deaths are rare in dry lake racing and it's a small alliance that know and care for each other. After sitting out for a couple of years, Arnett decided he didn't know what else to do with himself other than to rebuild a car and make an effort to reach that 350 mph record that his son died trying to reach. The Arnetts still strive to make that record, now with the second-born son, Jeff, tightly strapped into the cockpit of the new streamliner.

People speak in hushed tones of the horrific crash at El Mirage that took the life of Sonny Arnett. When the elder Arnett and I first met at the 1997 SCTA Muroc Reunion, the Bean Bandit pit area buzzed with folks welcoming the group back to their first outing since Sonny's death almost two years earlier. Arnett was moved to tears as he talked about his son and the reasons they'd come back to the dry lakes. Later at his home in San Diego, I was surprised to find the tumbled wreck of a streamliner in the back yard. In some unsaid way, both the return to racing and that crumpled metal allow Arnett to get on with his day-to-day life.

It was hard for the team to return to El Mirage, but seemingly impossible for them to stay away. In May of 1997, Jeff drove the course for his first time. "Two years ago this month was when my brother got killed there. I was nervous about what my mom and everybody was thinking. We got there Saturday night and I don't think I slept 10 minutes, I was excited to be there. But once I drove on Sunday, it was great."

In 1992, Joaquin Arnett was inducted into the Drag Racing Hall of Fame for his innovations and significance to the sport. It's a major achievement and Arnett is proud, but it was never an easy path. Looking back, however, Arnett and his Bandits say they enjoyed the ride. You know it's true because they can still be found out on the dry lakes putting together cars with skill, spit and a prayer and going after records with all they've got.

*Jeff Arnett races in the memory of his late brother, Sonny. (Walter Cotten, Rescue photo)*

## STONE-WOODS-COOK

Maybe you know their car—that highly polished '40 Willys, famous for its consistent wins. Would you recognize the owners? Probably not and you're not alone. Tim Woods' and Fred Stone's black faces only show up in an occasional photograph. Yet these two men changed the path of drag racing. Before Woods and Stone hired Doug Cook to drive for them, doorslammers hadn't topped 150 mph or gone below 10 seconds and they basically raced for free. The Stone-Woods-Cook team built beautiful cars that became nationally known speed demons and created a furor that paid for their cars to travel.

Early in his real life, Tim Woods had already started attacking record books. He built his business to be the largest black owned construction company on the West Coast. Erecting 30 and 40 unit apartment buildings wasn't enough challenge for the man, so he took to racing his brand new Oldsmobiles on the drag strip. He'd drive them off the showroom floor and straight to his mechanic where he'd have a Cadillac engine dropped in. His son, Timothy Leonard Woods II, recalls that changing gears in the powerful cars would make it sound like the engine was gonna jump out.

Eventually Woods started building race cars and toned down the family car, but as Leonard says they were always "faster than fast." His wife, Velma didn't worry, because as fast as the family car driven by Tim was, every other year he bought her a brand new Cadillac or Lincoln of her own. That's part of what kept them together for 56 years. She appreciated her husband having a hobby that didn't involve smoking, drinking and chasing women, but she didn't appreciate the "hillbilly" drag racers. Mrs. Woods probably never realized exactly how expensive her husband's hobby was. But that's okay, because in short order it grew from a money hole to a money making proposition.

Along with their white family friend K.S. Pittman, Stone and Woods built a car that soon became a popular and quick racer, the Supercharged Gasser. Prewar Fords and Oldsmobiles were leaving the unblown cars in the dust. K.S. Pittman, Stone and Woods built the first

*Tim Woods and the Swindler A, aka the Black Widow. (Velma Woods collection)*

*K.S. Pittman (second from left) was Tim Woods' (far right) first driver. (Greg Sharp collection)*

Leonard Woods and Fred Stone
flank new driver Doug Cook.
(Velma Woods collection)

Swindler, a beautiful '42 Studebaker that got up and down the track until the day it leapt from its tow trailer into a ditch on the road from Bakersfield. They recycled its parts into a '41 Willys coupe, and the Swindler II was born.

The Stone Woods B/GS car murderized the competition with K.S. Pittman at the wheel trading off to drive his own C/GS car. Both cars did well at the Winternationals, that in those days featured an all around elimination at the culmination of the event. "K.S. drove the Swindler and won, he drove his car and won, then it became apparent it was going to come down to the two having to race. K.S. made it clear that if it came down to that, which car he was gonna drive," Leonard Woods remembers K.S. Pittman's choice—his own car. "My father was pissed and Fred was even madder. They wanted Doug Cook to drive the car, because he had already gotten beat. As fate would have it, K.S. got beat in his own car before that decision had to be made." K.S. Pittman ended the day winning the meet in the Stone Woods car, but his lack of loyalty created division and the team split. Because he had been such a close family friend, Leonard remembers being devastated by Pittman's departure.

---

### A/GS, B/GS, C/GS—Supercharged Gassers

*In 1960, NHRA presented rules officially establishing a class for stock-bodied, gasoline-fired blower cars. These blown cars were separated by the weight per cubic inch of engine displacement: A=0-8.59; B=8.60-10.59 and C=10.60 and up.*

*Should an A/GS racer decide to compete in B/GS, they would add weight to the car, allowing teams to class jump and creating a media frenzy. Tire manufacturers provided improved traction and Gassers upped their performances thrilling crowds with uncontrollable lurching that sometimes put the cars into the stands. So much so that NHRA changed the weight rules several times before the class finally died an unnoticed death in 1975.*

---

But the racing went on. Stone and Woods brought Doug Cook on to wrench and drive their car. Although he was from the land of Jim Crow and racial inequity, Cook had been in Los Angeles long enough to know that joining up with these black men should pose no problem, especially considering they had plenty of money to make their cars competitive.

*Stone Woods "Cookie" Willys.*
*(Velma Woods collection)*

Like the Studebaker they'd built earlier, the Willys was a coupe manufactured for a short period, that could be acquired cheap. Because it looked like a boat, and weighed like a tank, putting a supercharged motor under its hood turned it into a "sleeper." Fans loved the Willys look—jacked up in front to throw the weight in back—and the innate impression that it moved like a turtle. Tires weren't "all that" back then, and with the displaced weight, Gassers put on a tire smoking, clutch lurching, short wheel base bearing, guardrail-to-guardrail running show. Fans loved that too. Particularly Tim Woods' clean, highly polished, highly chromed and highly stock looking show car. Even stripped for speed, this race car featured fine blue and white tuck and roll upholstery and sequential T-Bird lights that lit up at night under all the smoke of a burnout. Needless to say, the crowd loved that as well. A man all about speed, and damn the chrome, Cook thought all this flash slowed him down. But their style drove up their popularity, and as a fastidious man, Woods wanted his cars to look good first, and be fast second.

NHRA once again revised the weight restrictions of the classes and in 1964 Stone-Woods-Cook built a new lighter Willys A/GS, the Swindler A. A relative first at the strip, they could afford to campaign both the new car and Doug's brother, Ray Cook, drove the older B/GS. The success and beauty of their cars attracted the Revell Company, who turned the Swindler into a popular selling plastic model kit for kids. Part of the genius of the kit was you could build either the A/Gas or the B/Gas car—they were almost identical.

---

### FOR THE RECORD—Stone-Woods-Cook

- *First A/GS car into the 9s—9.79, 142.85 mph*
- *1962—Won NHRA's Nationals A/GS class*
- *1963—Set B/GS record of 10.60 (down from 11.03)*
- *1964—Won Winternationals at 10.03, 142.85 mph; ended season with 9.57, 149.25 mph run*
- *1965—Won NHRA Nationals at 9.53, 152.54 mph*
- *1965—Fastest A/GS running 157.78 in Rockford, Illinois*

Swindler A at Capitol Raceway.
(Velma Woods collection)

Competition, marketing and showmanship encouraged a mid-1960s "war" between gasser teams...
(Velma Woods collection)

A former Secret Service agent from Detroit (Leonard points out, "Black folk ain't been taking no shit from white folks in Michigan for years"), Fred Stone was a piece of work himself. In contrast to Tim Woods' quiet strength, at a burly 270 pounds, Fred Stone offered flamboyant power. He had a zest for promoting and was largely responsible for their biggest money making venture of the 1960s, the Gasser Wars. The Willys was a more competitive car than its predecessors. The new A/GS "Swindler" mostly brawled with Californian Gassers. The car's wins were intimidating—it's rumored that one time at Long Beach, Cook ran the car at a record setting pace, and visiting competitor "Ohio" George Montgomery packed up both his cars and skidaddled.

Bi-weekly racing papers such as *Drag News* and *Drag World*, allowed fans from coast-to-coast to keep up on records and achievements. Parts makers were the chief advertisers, and as their racers started to bring home trophies, self-promoters such as Ed Iskenderian and Jack Engle knew they'd sell parts by pointing out winners who used their stuff. Iskenderian had highlighted the Swamp Rats' performance which helped earned Garlits a paycheck for some non-exhibition runs in 1958. Then in the 1960s, ads showed up in the rags proclaiming Isky, Engle or Howard Cams as the pivotal feature in a car's performance. These "Camgrinder Wars" evolved into the "Gasser Wars" in 1963 as Fred Stone took to writing open letters that ran as ads in the drag papers. He'd question records set at far away east coast tracks and offer up challenges to their competitors, who recognized the value of the spotlight. Stone-Woods-Cook's ads were answered publicly and the gauntlet was thrown. Interest on the east coast was piqued and a pro match racing circuit rose up to satisfy the public's curiosity about these record setting Gassers. And each one of the screaming participants yelled all the way to the bank.

The open letter brags and dares reached a peak in 1964 as competition grew between Stone-Woods-Cook and their closest rivals—Big John Mazmanian, "Ohio" George Montgomery, K.S. Pittman, and Junior Thompson. There was mild name calling— Pebble, Pulp and Chef, Big June and the Easter Bunny— veiled accusations of lying, cheating, stealing and in-your-face

*...and the weekly papers were the perfect showcase. (Velma Woods collection)*

affronts at the track. But the cars toured nationally from spring to November picking up appearance fees of $500-$750, which gave them more money to drop on parts, more experience at building, and resulted in better performance at the track.

In 1964 one of the cars that the team built varied from their trademark blue, to Cook's color choice, a deep, dark black. Although the gold leaf lettering on the back fender read Swindler A, Cook called it the Black Widow. The team ran the black car, the blue B/GS driven by Doug's brother Ray and sometimes a third car to races across the country, trading wins with Montgomery and the other Gassers.

By 1965, car manufacturers caught the racing bug. The new cars at the starting line were Detroit-manufactured Factory Experimental (F/X), Super Stock Experimental and Supercharged/Factory Experimentals that packed a punch and ran on exotic fuels. Cook found himself competing against factory sponsored superstars like Arnie "the Farmer" Beswick, "Dyno" Don Nicolson, and Jack Christman in his supercharged Mercury Comet. In a blink, those experimentals went from stock looking doorslammers to full-bodied, flip-top vehicles with shortened wheelbases, where the driver sat over the rear tires. They looked different and were quickly named "funny cars," or "floppers." They were unusual, but clearly had performance potential. The average S/FX started 1965 with speeds of 130 mph and Don Gay's F/X Pontiac GTO finished the season with an astounding speed of 170.45 mph and destroyed the Supercharged Gas Coupes' claim of fastest stock bodied cars on the track. Funny Cars devoured promotional dollars, drew fans at the gates and instantly became the new big boy in town.

The Swindler, along with the other bigger slower Gassers were no match for the new Funny Cars, and got kicked downstairs into non-paying sportsman categories. After turning in an E.T. of 8.9 and running 158 mph, the Swindler was retired in 1968. Ready to join the fray, Stone-Woods-Cook built a '66 Mustang Funny Car, dumped the Willys' engine in it and ran the darn thing on a 50/50 mix of alcohol and nitro. The Funny Car's rudimentary technology was still being explored when Cook ran the car in Alton, Illinois. Running a mixture of nitro and alcohol and going out the back end at 189 mph, the Stone-Woods-Cook Funny Car got air up under the body, flipping the car end over end. The Mustang flew, crashed, and Doug Cook survived with 49 broken bones. He had a lengthy recovery and never drove another race car.

Beginning with changing his dad's tires at 6 years old, Leonard Woods grew up on the race track. Polishing chrome, keeping quiet and learning were his specialties. Later he toured the cars with Doug Cook during school breaks—but school came first. Tim Woods was a believer in education; his son possesses a masters degree from University of Notre Dame and his daughter is an attorney with two masters to attest to that family rule.

Looking back, Leonard can clearly see the lessons of his youth. California was a haven for the Stone-Woods-Cook team in many ways. As the home of drag racing, competition was geared against the clock. If you raced hard, people didn't care that you were African American, Asian, Mexican or Caucasian. Stone-Woods-Cook may have faced some jealousy because their successes—a famous team of two to three cars, a model car contract, their name sold products for sponsors, hell, they had sponsors. It was a big deal for that time, and these accomplishments became the brass rings for other Southern Californian racers. That same West Coast ease of integration didn't fly in the Southeast. There, the Swindler traveled without its black owners and Cook was even seen as a black man's lackey.

Leonard's other lessons were the bumps and bruises that every competitor deals with. You win some, you go home with your butt kicked on other days. "I remember the first major defeat—my dad teased me about the way I took it for 30 years, until the time he died." They were in Indianapolis, nemesis George Montgomery's territory, but Stone-Woods-Cook were considered most likely to win. Montgomery got the better start and beat their quicker car by mere hundredths of a second. The 16 year old Leonard was devastated as the fans cheered as loud as they could for their local favorite winner. "When I got back to the pit, my dad said I tucked my head. It was a hurtful thing." His

dad simply built a new car and challenged Montgomery in Indianapolis the next year. It so happened they lost this event as well, but Leonard left knowing that it just goes with the flow of the game.

Some of the things learned had more sweetness to them, like the happiness of a well oiled team. Simply picking people for their abilities and not for the color of their skin was impressed upon the younger Woods. Those lessons he learned as a kid are evident today in the current success of his Ford dealership where he has a mixture of employees—blacks, Hispanic, white, female. "We all work as a team, and we respect one another and treat one another like human beings. It's a tribute to my father and things that he learned; that he taught me. I want to encourage more people, there are a lot of things that you can do when you try." Leonard's simply owning the dealership made his car-happy dad proud.

Fred Stone stayed in the fray until it became more of a job than a hobby, then passed away in 1982. Tim Woods had other drivers run his Pinto and Mustang Funny Cars, but never again achieved the success of the Swindlers. He died in 1985. In 1997, the Stone-Woods-Cook team was inducted into the Drag Racing Hall of Fame, making the stylish Woods and burly Stone the first blacks invited in. And when you go to the track, you see enough Stone-Woods-Cook t-shirts, you'd think that clean, highly polished Willys was still loudly challenging competitors today.

### MALCOLM DURHAM—FUNNY CAR FOREFATHER

Another man who helped broaden the world of drag racing was alternately known as "the Lip" and "the Cassius Clay of drag racing." Malcolm Durham was also called the first black drag racing legend. The nicknames were invented by a promoter to entice the press and draw a crowd. Durham was, and still is, a quiet man. What was flashy was his win record and his inclination toward beautiful, late model Chevy doorslammers. Now in his late 50s and mostly retired from racing, Durham encourages his racing sons Bernard, Raynard and Bryon, and lends them his extensive knowledge as they try to crack the sponsorship nut.

Durham's seen a lot since he started racing at 16 back in North Carolina. He had an urge to drive fast and the competition of the sport held his interest. He won the first race he entered at Easy Street Dragstrip in Newton, North Carolina and took home a "little ole teeny" trophy. Stepping on the gas in his 225 hp '56 Chevy was a far cry from plodding around on the family tractor that he'd learned to drive. He went on to "road race" or meet up with other kids to run the country thoroughfares, then moved to Washington D.C. in 1957 and raced at Aquasco Speedway.

Racing's lessons are sometimes harsh—like not competing in your daily driver. After blowing an engine, and hoofing it to work, Durham never again raced his transportation car. He learned that a low buck racer can get ahead with good technique as opposed to expensive mechanics. And he learned how to build Chevys to run competitively with Fords and Chryslers. The full bodied cars Durham raced in the 1960s are direct precursors to what we know as Funny Cars today. Durham drove doorslammers that, although hopped up, looked like cars sold off the local lots.

Malcolm Durham signing autographs. (DRM files)

His "Strip Blazer I" (named for "trail blazers," the western pioneers) was a result of Chevrolet entering into the specialty car market. His 1963 Z-11 Impala was one of only 50 of the aluminum frame, aluminum bumpered cars. He "blueprinted," or rebuilt the motor and won 90% of the races he entered. Strip promoters soon offered money for Durham to race at their tracks. His high win record along with his desire to race cars that looked like those that regular folks drove, made Durham a popular draw at the strips.

He raced Tuesday nights, Wednesday nights, Thursdays—whenever the crowd would come out. Tracks resorted to special mid-week shows because Durham was fully booked for the weekends. At one point his team was racing three cars and putting away the competition very consistently. He picked up lots of fans, particularly outside of Washington DC, at tracks frequented by blacks. His face stood out among the mostly white competitors because there were no other minority drivers.

Teammates Bernard Butler and Malcolm Durham's 1971 visit to the Capitol. (DRM files)

### FOR THE RECORD—Malcolm Durham

- Beat 1964 Winternationals winners Sox & Martin with his '64 Chevelle Strip Blazer II at 75-80 Drag-a-Way on Friday night and Cecil County on Saturday night
- 1965—Added injected nitro and instantly ran 9.56 at 150 mph
- 1966—Entered 8 second field and won UDRA Nationals
- 1968—Won UDRA Funny Car Nationals
- 1969—Broke 200 mph at Aquasco

And he set records as well. What Durham didn't do much of was race at NHRA's national events. "In other words, come Labor Day Weekend, they had the Nationals down in the Indianapolis area, but I was usually somewhere else on a three day deal for a guaranteed purse that was more than all their purses put together. So, I just couldn't afford to go to NHRA." He would often race all week, getting paid an average of $800 per appearance.

His Race Car Automotives shop turned in okay money, but it was the match racing that paid for the cars. Each season when it started snowing on the tracks, Durham was shut out of his extra income, and spent the winter waiting for spring and more money. Finally in 1975, Malcolm parked his Strip Blazer and settled down to the business of raising his family. Racing was good to him and fit into his family life. But like any other drivers, when it's time to raise the family, it's often time to climb out of the cockpit. He and Darleatha, his wife since 1961, had sons Bernard, Raynard and Bryon to get through college. Only after school, did Bernard decided he was interested in racing one of his dad's cars that was still lying around.

With Bernard, and now Bryon racing, Durham has reason to look at the motorsports industry and take note of the changes. One thing that hasn't changed is the lack of blacks. Nearby Maryland track, Budd's Creek is one of the few tracks in the nation where the black spectators outnumber whites on any given day. Budd's Creek offered comfort where other tracks offered strife, as Durham recalls of one Southern drag strip: "There was a problem down there in Virginia one time when we won. They didn't have an electronic system back then and the track man gave the win to the other driver. The spectators were ready to riot, so they judiciously changed the decision." All the fans were on his side, "I had as many white spectator friends, more, than I did black friends." Still, the usual racial slurs and minor tensions were evident in the north as well as the south.

Malcolm Durham's Strip Blazer.
(DRM files)

His oldest son, Bernard, is attracted to the sport because he likes the athletics, complications and problem solving of racing. "Technology is a good marriage because of computers and the engineering aspects of it. When I got older I began to appreciate it more from just racing." He's currently running in the super gas class, and he's way into competition. Same with Bryon, the youngest son who uses some of his dad's parts that are older than he is. Both sons recognize that having dad as a crew chief who knows the ropes and has years of experience is a giant plus.

Building a car and seeing what kind of performance he can get out of it has always been the attraction for the elder Durham. When he first started, cars were going relatively slow. Toward the end of his professional career, he was going over 200 mph in less than 10 seconds. He says now, "I get in something now that doesn't run 150-160 mph, it seems like I'm waiting for something to happen." And even if racing on the straight track seems risky to most, Durham says he felt safer in his race car than his street car. Safe, even though he's had his bell rung a time or two. In fact, upon his return to racing in 1985, his '84 Pro Stock Camaro got airborne at Rockingham, disintegrated and put Durham in traction and out of action for six months. It took him five years to get back to racing.

The sons learned reasonableness and consistency from their dad. Keep to a racing program that makes sense, don't overspend, and consistently come back and show folks what you can do. Currently there's no African American drag racing superstar—perhaps another Durham can fill the vacancy.

Barbara Hamilton Advey with her restored B/GS Willys.
(Barbara Hamilton Advey collection)

## BARBARA HAMILTON—GASSER GAL

Older now, and humble as ever, Barbara Hamilton Advey spends much of her time trying to reconcile her name being engraved in granite alongside her idols at the Drag Racing Hall of Fame. She doesn't quite understand it, and she's a little embarrassed, even though "Big Daddy" counseled her not to feel that way. "Big Daddy" Don Garlits got around lots in his youth, and he knows that when she competed as Hamilton Racing, she stood out as "a gal that not only drove her car, but wrenched it, built it and did all the tuning on it." Unlike 95% of the other inductees, this one cries when she thinks of her name in stone.

Hamilton got hooked on racing in 1958 when her gang of high school friends attended the local tracks. She also hooked herself a drag racing boyfriend, John Dunlap, who let her pilot his B/GS supercharged '34 Ford Coupe. From then out, there was no question what the 19 year old wanted to do—race.

By her sophomore year in college, Hamilton had convinced her folks to help her out with a loan toward a car of her own. She spent the next three years sitting on her garage floor trying to decipher a Chilton's auto manual well enough to assemble her short block. Her dad was alongside, helping her decode the mystery. Hamilton was determined to finish this supercharged motor—it was what her boyfriend had raced, and all she was familiar with.

In the 1960s journalists didn't quite know what to make of this woman racer—one racing article reduced her hard work to a sacrifice of "clothes and dates" to build her newly acquired '37 Willys. Even then, the money from her secretarial job couldn't go far enough to finish. Luckily Hamilton picked up a partner—Nancy Leonello. Together they formed a then unimaginable two woman team. It was particularly wacky because as a woman, Hamilton was not even allowed to drive a supercharged car at the strips. Hamilton points out that supercharged cars were prone to fires and NHRA was always afraid of bad press—especially concerning women drivers. Ohio's Dragway 42 and other local tracks let her drive, but she was aiming for NHRA's national tracks. Following two years of pestering and petitions, the sanctioning body finally relented, hoped that nothing awful would happen to this gal, and in 1964 Hamilton became the first woman licensed to drive a supercharged car.

Newly legal with the NHRA, she registered for one of the most prestigious events in the sport, the NHRA Nationals in Indianapolis. It took her a few years to get the skills down, but in 1968, Hamilton and her B/GS Willys left the track as runners up in her class. During that learning period, the "gal in a Gasser" did well and was known to trade records with fellow competitor and good friend Bill Linder out of New York.

The AA, BB and CC/GS (revised from NHRA's earlier A, B & C/GS class) club was small back then, and the members were what Hamilton calls "a special group of selected people." They put on the great show of East Coast vs. West Coast, and the drivers loved it as much as the fans. Hamilton was the only woman who ever drove in that class. Long ago phased out, she will go into the books as the sole shoe of her gender who managed the monster cars. The tuning she and Nancy Leonello worked out functioned well; at one point they produced 118.42 mph and an 11.83 E.T. in the heavy steal behemoth.

*Barbara Hamilton at Irwindale Raceway in 1967. (Barbara Hamilton Advey collection)*

Barbara Hamilton's Willys on display at Don Garlits' Drag Racing Museum. (Barbara Hamilton Advey collection)

She was a member of another group that she didn't ask to join. One day in 1967 Hamilton's mail included a returned entry form and refunded entry fee, and no explanation as to why NHRA would not let her race. She and four other drivers had their licenses yanked because Shirley Muldowney applied for a license to drive a supercharged dragster. Hamilton, Paula Murphy, Della Woods and Virginia Graham all were ousted while the NHRA tried to find a logical way to keep Ms. Muldowney from the driving the car she hungered to pilot.

Rather than sitting around and waiting for an explanation, Barb's dad made a sign reading "Race Car In Tow," and she and Leonello quit their jobs and headed out to California to press NHRA for a face-to-face reason. At that meeting, the powers that be simply told her to stay away from any lawsuits (like the one Muldowney and Paula Murphy's sponsor STP threatened) and also stay away from the track. The lawyers she could do without, the racing had to go on.

There was a highlight in this six month period of darkness for Hamilton. Bones Balough, who put her up, was one car short in his match racing schedule, and slipped Hamilton into the open slot. Veteran track operator, C.J. "Pappy" Hart had no problem with allowing the unlicensed driver to race (or the extra spectators a female Gasser driver brought in) and Hamilton drove in the hot rod Mecca—Irwindale and Lions.

Just as mysteriously as it was taken away, NHRA returned the license to Hamilton, and she went back to the track. Reporter's recognized a good story, and started peppering the mostly male mags and rags with profiles of the Willys driver. Statements like "blonde behind the steering wheel of race car," "blonde takes on triple engine trouble at Dragway 42" and "lookout men, it's all over" didn't make her happy then and still sting today. If not for the reporters, or the announcer's voice booming over the p.a., fans often didn't know there was a woman in the Willys. The car had no name, Hamilton and Leonello's names were absent from the meticulous surface of the car (she only wanted to race, she didn't care if folks knew who was driving).

While she tore up the local tracks, Hamilton never fared as well at the national events. That fact makes winning at the Springnationals in Bristol and runnering up at the Nationals in Indy stand out in her mind. Or perhaps it was how she didn't win at Indy that stands out. Hamilton's strength as a racer was being a "good leaver"—cutting a quick start at the green light. Somehow she got outside of her game in Indy. Fellow racer Bill Linder still relishes the win, and still goads Hamilton asking if she still sleeps at the light. Even with the kidding, it's a loss she accepted gracefully. She was fiercely competitive, but never lost her temper, shouted or threw parts. At least one opponent shied away from her competitiveness, claiming that his car broke at the line both times she staged against him. All that "car trouble" kept him from competing against a woman, and kept him from looking bad if she had kicked his ass.

Leonello and Hamilton figured out as much as they could about improving their performance, but when they hit the rough spots, Hamilton was never afraid to go to the top for advice. Often "Big Daddy" Don Garlits was a phone call away with the answers to why she was eating so many pistons or how to stop the engine from detonating. Because of his generosity, it was an even greater pleasure that "Large Father" was the one to introduce her at the Hall of Fame ceremony.

---

### FOR THE RECORD—Barbara Hamilton

 First woman licensed to drive a Supercharged car
 Only woman to drive in the Supercharged Gas Coupe class

It was also Garlits who asked after Hamilton's Willys. Although she was reluctant, he convinced her to take it out of storage and let him house the historic vehicle at his museum in Florida where it could be admired by others. Hamilton decided to relish the final summer with her beloved car—she took leave from her job, and took time to get the beauty into running order. Finally she was able to turn it over, and had fun doing burnouts after 20 years of retirement.

Her husband, an ex racer himself, saw how much pleasure his wife got out of rebuilding her car. He suggested she build a new one, and that's just what she's doing. Stuck on the Willys design, she's switched to a newfangled fiberglass body. But she still derives pleasure from spending the hours of work, then hearing her engine turn over from the life she's breathed into it.

So, although she was not a pro, and simply a weekend racer like untold others, the effort and passion for driving are well justified with her 1992 induction into the Drag Racing Hall of Fame. If given the chance to do it again, she would change nothing, except maybe that loss at Indy.

South Central Los Angeles street racing scene in the 1960s. (DRM files)

## BIG WILLIE ROBINSON—RACING FOR PEACE

Willie Andrew Robinson III is a true believer that "If you're racing, you're not killing." He learned that back in the 1940s, where as a black youth in New Orleans he was accustomed to segregated schools, eating places, neighborhoods—even segregated seating at the race track. The only time blacks and whites played together peacefully was racing their cars on the local side streets. In the spirit of those well spent youthful hours, Robinson and his wife of 35 years, Tomiko, fight to maintain a dragstrip close enough to the city of Los Angeles for folks to race their racial tensions away.

Perhaps it was weeding his way through a violent world that led Robinson to seek peaceful times. As a pre-med student at Louisiana State University, he dealt with Jim Crow laws and hard stares. One school day he returned to the parking lot to find his '53 Olds with flat tires, totally dented, windows broken and upholstery cut up. He left the racial hatred of Louisiana behind to move to the relatively calmer environs of Los Angeles.

Robinson tried pre-med again for a short while at UCLA, then found a place where he could really learn something. He joined other students of speed, racing from midnight to dawn on the streets of South Central LA. Just as Robinson had found in the outlaw racing circles of New Orleans, the late night LA speedsters were a cooperative group where Mopar vs. Chevy was more important than white vs. black.

The confrontation in Vietnam heated up and in 1964, Robinson was drafted to do his part for his country. He did, and came back wounded in 1966. Back home, protesters and veterans had a hatred brewing all their own, and Robinson was hurt that the Army

International Brotherhood of Street Racers' "colors." (Author photo)

recommended vets not wear their uniforms. A bowler hat, leather pants and a leather vest became his new uniform. Robinson also filled his time with weight lifting in training for Mr. America competitions.

While Robinson was away, the Watts section of Los Angeles was the scene of 1965's violent race riots where 500 square blocks were looted and burned, destroying an estimated $40 million worth of property. Some 15,000 police and National Guardsmen are called in and 34 folks (mostly blacks) lost their lives before it was all over. Yet when he returned, the only place where he found complete racial cooperation and comfort was racing the streets near the epicenter of the previous year's violence. So effective at keeping the peace, Robinson was able to hold a combined purse of $54,000 while two rival gangs—one from Compton, the other from South Central LA raced their two 9-second Camaros. With the big man's arbitration in effect, the losers—the south central kids—simply nodded and the gangs peacefully went their separate ways.

A reporter for *The Los Angeles Times* wrote a story on the outlaw racers and nicknamed Robinson "Big Willie" for his 6'6" 330 lb. bulked up frame. The article informed folks that half of the racers were white in South Central LA, and there was rarely any violence associated with the racing.

The nation's first drag strips were created by hot rodders teaming up with the police department to keep racing kids off the streets in the 1950s. Mirroring that earlier period, Police Lieutenant Frank Beeson read the *The Los Angeles Times* story on Big Willie and sought him out to talk about the possibility of organizing street racers to keep kids out of trouble. The Brotherhood of Street Racers was created on November 20, 1966, with the combined efforts and good will of the street racers, Big Willie Robinson, the local police officers and mayor Tom Bradley. Anxious to keep the peace in the area, local police

Big Willie Robinson greets crowd. (DRM files)

helped block off streets and seemingly ignored all night racing. To be a member of the Brotherhood, you didn't have to pay dues or have any special equipment, but there were rules: no drugs, no alcohol, no fighting and no showboating. The "club" had their own "colors"—a largish embroidered patch sported on every member's vest or jacket. (By this time Robinson had traded in his bowler for a beret, his leather pants for military camouflage and his leather vest sported the Brotherhood colors with the word President spread across his broad shoulders.) Robinson's goal was to show the benefits of legal outlets for racing. He wanted local strips to extend their hours to satisfy the late night racing needs of the kids and allow anybody to run what they brung—not just professional racers.

An imposing figure on the street racing scene, Big Willie spent a lot of time without a ride of his own. Famous engineer Keith Black built a great Hemi engine for Willie's '69 orange Dodge Daytona four speed. With the new mill, Robinson beat local competitor

Bo Peete, and named his car "King Daytona." His wife, Tomiko, had her own '71 Hemi Daytona named "Queen Daytona." (Tomiko once rolled her race car four times, before coming to a rest. She sat in the car upside down for 15 minutes before the distressed Big Willie ripped the door off its hinges to free her.) From 1971 to 1973, they toured the country making appearances at races and on talk shows pushing the National Brotherhood cause and opening chapters in over 38 states. The Robinsons—President and Assistant President of the Brotherhood of Street Racers—were media darlings during this time. Willie was in the Paul Newman film *W.U.S.A.*(1970). He was also in the opening sequences of the zen-like street racing film, *Two Lane Blacktop* (1971), where he raced his King Daytona, and he and Tomiko appeared in various TV series. Even today, he has a contract with HBO to bring his huge life story to the little screen.

"Run what you brung" was indeed the motto of Brotherhood International Raceway. In 1974 the city's Harbor Commission eventually leased Big Willie a tract of land on Terminal Island—a peninsula bordered by a dump and a major industrial dock—for $1 a month. Up went a POW-MIA flag alongside the American flag, indicative of the high veteran membership in the Brotherhood. $10 got you in, and once in, you could choose to just watch, or to race whatever you have. Diesel-spewing big rigs, Jr. Dragsters with their little 4 hp lawnmower engines, flame shooting jet cars, ground shaking front engined nostalgia dragsters—even Big Willie's mom's Cadillac—anything could race at Brotherhood, and everything did. There were even scraping and bouncing competitions for the lowrider aficionados of Brotherhood. The track ran 24 hours a day through the weekends.

It was available and offered racing for everyone, but Brotherhood Raceway Park was not exactly a premier track. It featured a gnarly bump that encouraged wise top fuel drivers to get off the throttle at 1/8 mile instead of racing an entire 1/4 mile sprint. Jet cars were prone to burning the back fence at the foot of the announcer's tower. Betting was a large component of the atmosphere at Brotherhood. Big Willie's voice could often be heard booming over the loudspeakers wagering for "hot dogs" (their weird jargon for dollars) on his favorite car. Bold evidence of the widespread betting were the many late model Nissans and Hondas staged at the starting line without the usual shoe-polished dial-in times on their windshields. Their handicap times were a secret between the driver and the officials who set the timing light, leaving competitors to guess at the times the car was capable of running. It kept the mystery in racing and the stakes high for wagers.

Street racing's been an acknowledged fact in LA since the 1940s—long enough for police to recognize that violence decreased noticeably when Brotherhood Raceway was open. Big Willie lives to help cities like New Orleans, New York, Philadelphia and

Detroit with their violence problems in the same way—by increasing the peace. He once told a *Sports Illustrated* reporter how mixed up the environment at Brotherhood was: "Black, white, yellow, brown, skinheads, Nazi party members, Muslims, we got 'em all. They're all here at the track, and they're communicatin'. And once they start communicatin', they start likin' each other, and once they start likin' each other, they forget about the hate." Rumors of black and Hispanic street kids racing at all hours and betting to boot frightened off some suburban race fans. If they put their fears aside and visited Brotherhood, they would have noticed the family environment. Young kids played peacefully while their parents got together under the hood of the family car to try to eke out some more go power.

Whenever it dreamed up alternate plans for the land, or for any other seemingly petty reason, from 1974 to 1984, the Harbor Commission closed Brotherhood Raceway 11 times. Since the mid 1990s it's been closed indefinitely. Most people who raced and played there say it's closed permanently. But Big Willie Robinson has another view; he says, "Until the powers of the universe tell me that it's not gonna happen, I'm gonna keep pushing forward." He is a frequent visitor to city offices, expounding the numerous reasons why the track should be reopened. For a period he seemed to have succeeded— some funding was found to reestablish Brotherhood Raceway in the high desert. To Big Willie this seemed reasonable, but a majority of the Brotherhood did not want to travel an hour away to visit their "local" track. Robinson had to carry the "no" vote back to the city and continue his quixotic quest to regain the land on Terminal Island.

Robinson's dream is shared by his large number of street racing brothers and sisters. They want to reestablish a legal, safe racing venue to bring kids off the streets. They want to again sponsor events that rock like the nitro spewing Thunder Island Nostalgia top fuel invitational were folks saw a jet car race a Jr. Dragster and got to thrill to the rumble, smell and glow of cars sending up flames at night. They want, just like Big Willie, to Stop the Violence and Increase the Peace.

## SHIRLEY "DON'T CALL ME CHA CHA" MULDOWNEY

Shirley Muldowney, drag racing icon. (DRM files)

Shirley Muldowney, in a fire suit, prepares to race. (DRM files)

She was not the first woman in racing—Peggy Hart holds that distinction. Nor is she the fastest woman—that record belongs to Cristen Powell. But, the longest driving, the winningest and the best known woman in drag racing is Shirley Muldowney. She was the first woman to win a NHRA national event, the first woman to win a NHRA points Championship and the first of anyone to win the Championship three times. Standing tall at just over five feet, Shirley Muldowney was also the first driver to survive the worst non-fatal accident and come back. She helped break the gender barrier and withstood discrimination and hostility to feed her passion to drive. You'd think that a senior member of the National Hot Rod Association tour, whose been named to the Auto Racing All-America Team five times, had her career documented in the feature length movie, *Heart Like A Wheel* (1983), and is one of the most recognizable names in the sport, might slow down. Reconsider.

While still in a Schenectady, New York high school, Shirley Roque was introduced to the world of racing by her future husband, Jack Muldowney. Her reaction?—"The winning, performance, competing bit me in the early days." She saw Garlits in a top fuel dragster, and said, "uh-oh, this is it." She wasn't sure she could handle all of it, but she fell for the sound. The determined youngster quit school, married Jack and had a son. Her first car was a 1940 Ford Coupe that Jack beefed up with a Cadillac V-8 engine. She street raced that thing from red light to red light—getting up to 120 mph and plenty of tickets. They raced a gas powered front engined dragster and did well at the local tracks. They very nearly qualified at the Nationals in 1970. The Muldowneys bought a funny car from fellow racer Connie Kalitta and for the first time, Shirley was under the hood with the motor, match racing to beat the band.

*Shirley Muldowney turned a short stint as a funny car driver. (DRM files)*

Eventually, Shirley changed teams—she split with her husband and raced with crew chief, and lover, Kalitta. Soon they had a match racing tour as the his and hers "Bounty Hunter" and "Bounty Huntress." Muldowney and Kalitta had public "love spats," that probably fueled her desire to win even more. Shirley was highly visible and perhaps from either her quick tongue or her quick driving, she got labeled "Cha Cha." Often promoting herself in hot pants or knee high boots, Muldowney was the rage at the track.

It seemed go to well until "Cha Cha" had a serious fire in the Funny Car, and wanted back into an open cockpit. Having fought to be allowed to race a supercharged car, the NHRA pulled her license when she climbed into a Top Fueler. In response to an under-thought decision where the NHRA suspended every woman's license in the association who was driving a supercharged car, the women all protested but none louder than Muldowney. Within six months NHRA reneged, and by 1973 Muldowney got her wish and was piloting a Kalitta run Top Fuel dragster.

Moving to a dragster put Shirley head-to-head with the Big Daddy of racing. Her quick leaving ability and growing win record probably made Don Garlits wonder why he'd ever vouched for Muldowney and facilitated her getting licensed to begin with. Promoters played off their conflicts holding "Battle of the Sexes" extravaganzas peppered with Garlits and Muldowney's insults. They fought verbally, but then settled arguments in the seats of their race cars. "The promoters jumped on it like you can't believe," says Muldowney as she laughs at the drama that came from the real life tension between she and Garlits. "It filled the stands for a lot of years." Garlits would get Muldowney going by pitching darts at a target made of her picture proclaiming "Somebody has got to stop Muldowney, and right now, it looks like I'm the only one standing between her and glory." Well, he must have stepped aside, because the woman charged on. And she met his match. Excluding Muldowney's AHRA win, she and Garlits are tied 3-all in winnings of national championships. Many races later, twists and turns of straight track racing found the pair transformed from fierce competitors to easy co-workers. For a period in the late 1980s, Muldowney hired Garlits as an "advisor" to give her team an extra edge. For a period, the man she called a cheapskate, an old fool and a creep was the one consulting with her team for getting her down the track faster.

Her former partner, and lover for seven years, Connie Kalitta knows the harsher side of Muldowney, once calling her a "gutsy little bitch." Like Garlits, Kalitta used to give the fans a show, but theirs was a more intense relationship, which featured either spats or kisses on the starting line. Portrayed by Beau Bridges as a womanizer in *Heart Like A Wheel* (1983), Kalitta will long be remembered as the man who got "Cha Cha" in the driver's seat of a dragster. As if to signal a change in her life, Muldowney left the "Cha Cha" off her car and wanted to be known as "just Shirley." Just to antagonize her, guys at the track laughing referred to her as Shirley "don't call me Cha Cha" Muldowney.

Her reign as Queen of Drag Racing was temporarily interrupted in 1984 by a crash that left Muldowney near death. At over 250 miles an hour, an inner tube in the front tire of her dragster snaked out and wrapped itself around an axle, pitching, rolling and tossing Muldowney and her disintegrating 26 foot car into a gravel pit. What followed was a 90 minute ambulance drive to the hospital and six hours of wire-brushing grit and grease from her wounds. The crash left her with broken bones in three fingers, a broken pelvis and mangled legs—her left foot and right thumb were nearly severed.

Following nine weeks of hospital recuperation, she married her crew chief, Rahn Tobler, and convinced him to get the car going again. The hope of returning to racing helped her to endure bone and skin grafts, then pushed her through 18 months of rehabilitation. In 1986 she climbed back behind the wheel of a 280 mph race car. As she said, she missed everything about racing—her friends, the lifestyle, and she needed the money—"Cha Cha" had to get back to racing.

*Shirley Muldowney and Connie Kalitta raced two funny cars as the Bounty Hunter and the Bounty Huntress. (DRM files)*

The crash was so severe, others in the sport thought she'd retire. There were times when she cried from pain and she thought she'd never return. Muldowney faced reality and got rid of 60 pairs of beloved high heels in exchange for her specially made athletic shoes that allow her to walk with a fused foot and a right leg 5/8 of an inch shorter than her left. (A true fashion plate, she still wears oversized glasses to cover the scars her smoldering goggles left on her face in an earlier crash.)

Despite her lengthy convalescence, Muldowney never showed signs of apprehension when she climbed behind the wheel. In fact, she finished in the top 10 ranking of NHRA for several years before trimming back her racing schedule. Muldowney retains her place with the best in the business as elapsed times have shatered the five second barrier. In 1989, she joined the elite four-second club with a 4.974 elapsed time at the Keystone Nationals. She immediately went on to become the first driver to post sub-five second runs in three consecutive national events.

---

### FOR THE RECORD—Shirley Muldowney

- First driver to win NHRA World Championship three times—1977, 1980 and 1982
- First female fuel driver to win a national event—1972 IHRA Southern Nationals
- First woman to break 6 second barrier—5.98 on August 24, 1975
- Survived worst non-fatal accident—1984

---

The only woman ever to have won the Labor Day NHRA U.S. Nationals, the sport's foremost event, Muldowney has made a career of defying the odds. She's intuitively flexible and that's one of her driving strengths. "I am not predictable to the point where they get complacent when they see the car. I am versatile on the starting line; you've got to be because every race is different." And she follows her husband's directions to a T, because she knows his skills are what help to keep her winning.

Muldowney took the flack long ago, so drivers like Shelly Anderson and Cristen Powell don't have to. She's done much for the sport, particularly women in racing, and she's quick to remind you. And Muldowney legendary sharp tongue can usually find

*The cool beauty of a determined competitor. (Steve Reyes photo)*

time to talk about those Jane-come-latelies who don't seem to understand the barriers she had to destroy. Take for instance the bleached blonde racer Shelly Anderson—"(She) speaks highly of me, but she's changed," says Muldowney. "At first it was, 'If not for Shirley, we wouldn't have…' Now her deal is, 'Well, she was the first.' The first, Shelly? The first to do what, Shelly?" Muldowney says she doesn't have any hard feelings—"A very pretty girl and very good for drag racing. But can she win world championships? That remains to be seen."

Her defense for her words—well, they're true for one thing. And these women can say nice things about her because she left NHRA and races safely tucked away in another association, IHRA. Muldowney knows it'd be different if she were a factor for these women, "If I were out there, they probably wouldn't be saying all the things they say. I don't think there would be a war of the words, or there'd be any bad feelings, but women are women, aren't they? You know they are, and I didn't fall off the pumpkin truck yesterday."

"I was there to beat the boys," says Muldowney of her determination. "When I started touring, I fully intended to kick ass regularly. From New York to California and back. I have not yet, in any form of motorsports, ever come across another woman that thinks like I think."

That's just a peek at the legendary frankness that defines Muldowney; she doesn't suffer fools. She's raced long enough to recognize what's wrong and what doesn't work at the track. When NHRA was slow to fix safety regulations in the sport, Muldowney leapt over to IHRA, an arena she feels is more respectful of racers and their opinions about the race tracks were they spend their working hours. Her rift with NHRA spreads into every category, from safety issues to fun for the fans. The sanctioning body's imposed rear end gear ratio contributes to more parts breakage, and crashes, according to Ms. Muldowney. That breakage leads to higher costs (recouped in fans' ticket prices at the gates) and slow downs in racing. She calls the carnage at the tracks unbelievable. "The fans in the stands don't see full runs. They see tires smoking, they see breakage," says the disgruntled racer.

NHRA's desire to cram racing down the television audiences' collective throat is a whole 'nother problem if you ask this veteran drag racer. She feels it's just not a live TV sport. Much to the detriment of the racers and the fans, sessions are rushed or held to fit into the televised time slot. "There could be a monsoon coming over the mountain and they will hold that last final round, even if there's a threat of rain. I'll tell you, it robs the fans sitting in the stands, and I have a real problem with that."

This seasoned racer recognizes yesterday's racing as different: "We did stuff together. All those people do is argue and try to steal each other's sponsors." She misses the camaraderie of the earlier days, but there's still a lot of good out there. Enough to make her want to stick around.

So they've gone to IHRA and she and her husband, Tobler, like working there. The budgets are smaller, and the team runs without major sponsorship. They are able to keep costs down by running their own mechanical set-ups. Tobler does all of this with help from a heap of part time, revolving crew members. Friends that come in to work on the weekends and go back to their jobs during the week.

It's a good thing she's got a place to be herself, because if there were a 12 step program for drag racers, Shirley Muldowney would have to be a member. It's what she does. There are options, of course. She could give up driving and own a team like other

popular drivers—a la Don Prudhomme—but no way. Ms. Muldowney is no schmoozer. "I don't have time for that. I've got to do the fan mail, I've got to do the books, I've got to do the errands. Maybe that's why I don't have a deal because I don't go out and rub elbows and tip glasses." Another option is sitting on her haunches and becoming a grand dame, perhaps commenting on races. That wouldn't work either, Muldowney figures—she's way too honest. "If there's a moron in the left lane, I will probably point that out. Not like that, but they want everything nice. 'You love everybody, everything's great.' That's not the way it is out there. It's real life out there."

Basically, Muldowney plans to drive until it's no longer possible. She likes to drive, and she loves to win. But for the foremother of drag racing, it's more than that. "It is my business. It's what I do for a living. I feel that because of what I have contributed over the years, I have every right in the world to be out there. Probably more so than most of them."

## PAULA MURPHY—Miss STP

As she sat in the staging lanes at the Winternationals, some wise guy cracked, "Hey lady, don't you think you ought to put the slicks on the back?" Well, if anybody knows where the fat racing slicks belong on a car, it's Paula Murphy—if it has wheels and a motor, then she's raced it. Since first being goaded into driving in a "powder puff" race in Santa Barbara, California, Murphy has competed in a myriad of motorsports. When female racers were delegated to events of their own, Murphy raced like a girl, setting women's records behind the wheel of a stock car, a fuel funny car, a jet car and even a rocket car. The only thing she regrets at this point, is no longer going fast. And yes, she knows that to do a good burnout, you need the slicks on the front of your front wheel drive Datsun.

The native Ohio resident didn't see any racing until she'd moved to California, where she was dragged to a sports car rally. The sport looked boring, and she didn't think the female drivers could be called "ladies." But taking a trophy in the first contest she entered made her reconsider the racing stuff. Sometime in 1956, Murphy became a Sports Car Club of America member, gained a '54 MG and lost a husband. In 1963 when separate races for women were quickly became a thing of the past, Murphy raced with the boys.

Murphy's first promotion for the fuel additive, STP, was a 1963 coast-to-coast, border-to-border four record setting tour in an Avanti with fellow drivers Barbara Nieland and Bill Carroll. She raced at Indy twice, setting the women's closed course record each time. Her mechanics didn't think she had all the equipment she needed, so they strung a set of hushpuppies from the steering wheel to give her those badly needed balls.

When she debuted on the drag strip it was in an Olds 442 tuned by Dick Landy. Quickly hooked, she convinced her sponsor to back her venture and for two seasons Miss STP, as Murphy was billed, drove stock eliminator, with a 12.46 E.T. and 110 mph best. In 1966, she stepped up, and stepped behind the wheel of a Chrysler powered Mustang, making her the first woman licensed to drive a fuel car. She had a couple of

Paula Murphy at Rockingham.
(Paula Murphy collection)

other nitro Funny Car rides, a '69 Barracuda that hopped end to end in 7.17 seconds, and a '71 Duster that took the top speed at the 1973 Bakersfield March Meet, at a womanly 218 mph.

Miss STP was not the only moniker for Murphy—she was also called "The Fastest Woman on Wheels." And for Ms. Speed, racing competitively in the formerly all boys clubs was fairly problem free. She even held licensing with the NHRA to drive a fuel Funny Car. That is until Shirley Muldowney applied for a license to drive a fuel dragster and you know the rest: the NHRA called all of the women out of the pool; the women made noise and within six months, they got their right to drive back.

Fully licensed and majorly sponsored, match racing became the game of choice for Murphy, and she played it with gusto. Racing IHRA, AHRA and NHRA, she found herself booked for as many as 3 and 4 appearances a week. Crowds came out to see Murphy challenge the guys, and on odd occasions, another woman racer, Della Woods. For a brief period, Shirley Muldowney was driving one of Connie Kalitta's Funny Cars, although she and Murphy had bad fortune every time they were to face off—one or the other of them broke, so there are no good head-to-head races for the history books. The fashion side of her disliked the unflattering fire suits and helmets that destroyed her coif. Her own designs—a red ruffled fire suit with bellbottoms, earned her comments. One kid asked if Murphy was really a lady, because "you look like a clown in that suit."

First Miss STP funny car in 1966. (Paula Murphy collection)

Still fans flocked to her to get signed t-shirts and photographs and to take pictures with her holding their babies. And the big question was always, "how do you get into racing?"

In 1973 all this came to a resounding end when she took her maiden run in her Pollution Packer rocket dragster at Sears Point in Sonoma. The throttle stuck and the rocket ripped away from its parachutes. Murphy went out the back end and into the hills at over 230 mph. She's seen pictures of that ride, her car free flying end over end, way up in the air. Had that ill-fated run taken place at any other track rather than Sears Point, Murphy would not have had a chance. As it was, Sears Point's rolling hills that replace freeways or turnaround roads at other tracks, gave her more than a mile to finally bounce down in relative softness, and luckily not blow up. What she thought was a bad whiplash, turned out to be a neck fracture that qualified Murphy for a head-to-hip cast for four months. For a period of time, she worked on rebuilding the beast, then realized she didn't really want to get back in the thing. Later, another driver, Dave Anderson died in a crash in another version of that same Pollution Packer. The irony of the crash is that the negative press and "tarnished image" that NHRA had always dreaded in association with a woman in a serious accident never happened following her misfortunes at Sears Point.

Her 1976 comeback, per se, was another record setting drive, but this time it was at much lower speeds. She and Indy winner, Johnny Parsons, drove in the U.S. Bicentennial Global Record Run, where they attempted to drive around the widest part of the earth in as short a time as possible. The effort resulted in Murphy and company driving and flying 38,786.43 miles through 29 countries over 5 continents in 105 days. The trip is what Murphy smiles and recalls as the highlight of her career.

Having been inducted into the Drag Racing Hall of Fame in 1992—perhaps that, too, rates up there with Murphy's fondest memories. But Murphy, who still loves competition, soothes her need with dog shows. And if somebody offered the chance, she'd be right back in the seat of any fast moving car.

Photo op with Pollution Packer dragster. (Paula Murphy collection)

Della Woods with funny car.
(Carol Hakola photo)

## DELLA WOODS—FUNNY HONEY

Squealing, smoking and speeding down the drag strip in a fuel Funny Car, Della Woods is a woman of many fast firsts. She was crazy to drive—at 9 she was doing burnouts in the gravel on the family tractor, at 12 she was driving a car and at 14 she was street racing near their Michigan country farm. She enjoys the sport for every aspect—the competition, the speed ("I had this need for speed and it hasn't died yet"), the teamwork, even the traveling.

Woods and brother Bernie ran a team ("Bernella") starting with a '63 Dodge Super Stock and moving up to match racing a Funny Car in 1965. Like Muldowney, Hamilton and the others, Woods felt the wrath of NHRA's chauvinism. While waiting for women to be reinstated, Woods raced the outlaw tracks. "On some of these tracks, the car would literally leave the ground it was so bumpy." At one track up in the mountains, they showed her where to take the car if she got into trouble—it was the bottom of a ravine. At another strip, she and her brother had to pit on the track, because the locals had shotguns and were liable to shoot any driver that lost them money on a bet.

Bernella frequently raced both with and against Paula Murphy. Fans turned out to see the women cat fight each other, or take the tar out of some men in dual Battle of the Sexes match ups. They always had a crowd as the local papers were constantly interested in relaying another "woman in racing" story. Maybe because of this added attention, the men were a little touchy. Woods says they all gave her a hard time. Back in 1966, they wouldn't even run against her. Track operators had to pay Woods to take her funny car on single passes, because the guys had met and decided that if she beat any of them in the South, it would ruin their image.

The team came to an end when Bernie got married and moved to Arizona and Della quit racing as well. Eventually she, too, married, finding De Nichols, who used to race top fuel dragsters on the UDRA circuit. Nicols understood her, and in 1981 when he asked if she wanted a new addition on the house, or a race car, he was not surprised by her answer. They did all right as a new team—finishing 29th, then 21st and finally 20th in the points finals, before Woods had a severe crash in 1986 and had to sit a few seasons out.

Before Cristen Powell's 1999 entry into the fuel funny car world, Woods remained the fastest and quickest woman in a full bodied car. There are constant comparisons to the other first lady of drag racing, Shirley Muldowney. Woods says it's needless—there's no woman that's gonna meet Muldowney's record—few men who can. For Woods, her need for speed will not be quelled until she's won a national event in her funny car— no woman's done that—not even Shirley.

Della Woods with Funny Honey.
(Carol Hakola collection)

(Rescue photo)

# Thrills, Chills and Paying the Bills

## CHAPTER 3

One thing that doesn't sit well with racing is subtlety. Smoking tires, loud motors and engines exploding into mushroom clouds don't slip by unnoticed. For some spectators the shared excitement of someone "smashing" an E.T. record by shaving off 2/10 of a second, or besting a mph stat by an extra one-point-five-oh miles just isn't enough to bring them out to the track on a warm summer's night. What these folks crave is a little excitement. Fortunately the drag strip can be just the right place for that action.

I find entertainment in peculiar little ways—reading t-shirts proclaiming "Will race for food" or "No man with a good car needs to be justified" helps me pass the time during oil downs. Trying to gauge my beer drinking time to be proportionate to my wait in line for a port-o-john also takes my mind on a journey. But for others, maybe they need a little more. Race promoters want to keep those turnstiles clicking, especially when we're talking anywhere from $15 to $70 a head. Those kind of figures make it worthwhile to find something for everyone.

Drag racing is inherently a hurry up and wait sort of proposition. Nitromethane is rough on the engines of dragsters and funny cars, and crews generally have to pull the motor and replace parts before they can return for another pass. Even alcohol or gasoline burning cars need to cool down in the pits before they can make a follow-up run. Competing cars can make as many as 12 passes in an event and need down time between runs. When drag racing first found itself on a track, that was the only reason

Motorhead—fan at Pomona Raceway. (Author photo)

Left: Exhibition entertainer Jim Brewer, the only African-American wheelstander. (Paul Rosner photo)
Right: Hemi Under Glass driver steers while gazing at the track through a hole in the floorboard. (DRM files)

to be there. With a little luck a roach coach would be hawking drinks and hot dogs. As racing enthusiasts got older, got married and had kids, they started bringing them along for a few hours of pleasure. And then the funny stuff started. In order to keep those wallets within the grounds, promoters found all sorts of distractions.

American flag-toting, smoke-streaming parachutists land in the middle of the track to the sound of country mega-stars twanging the "Star Spangled Banner." Stealths and other war planes perform military fly overs. Cars kick up for spark shooting wheel stands that stretch a full 1320 feet. Motorcyclists dismount and ride their protective metal shoes, pulled by their bikes traveling at silly speeds. Any number of non-racing, yet automotive, stunts keep the fans in their seats and catch the attention of the little ones.

During the early years, the grandstands ran higher in testosterone levels than today's mixture, so flaunting some female skin would keep those slight male butts plastered to the wooden bleachers. Trophy girls abounded with a kiss for the winners and a smile and a wave for the fans. Linda Vaughn made a career as the Hurst Shifter girl riding down the track nuzzled against her giant phallic partner. She later turned her skills to hang-ins with the drivers and then commentating. Women worked their way onto racing teams and were seen as crew members spinning wrenches and backing cars down the track. All this softer action held the attention of the guys in attendance. None better than Jungle Pam, the "better" half of the Jungle team.

Jungle Jim Liberman takes a moment. (Jere Alhadeff photo)

## JUNGLE JIM LIBERMAN—Sex & Drugs & Flaming Burnouts

Jungle Jim wasn't sure how he acquired his nickname. He guessed it had something to do with a wild man swinging on vines. His friends just called him Jungle. His parents knew him as Russell James Liberman. Unfortunately for Liberman, on September 9, 1977 he swung his Corvette too wide on the street and fatally ran head on into a bus. But he will always be remembered as a drag racing legend from the era when nitro burning funny cars were new and still looked like the cars regular guys drove on the street.

Too much was never enough for Liberman. He required too much speed, too many women, took too many risks and probably had too much fun. To racers and fans, he was an ordinary guy that rebuilt regular cars and invested regular sums of money in them. Somehow he managed to extract extraordinary amounts of power for his work and won against inordinate odds. "Match racing," or being booked by a track to run a series of passes against a competitor, was a new wrinkle in the drag racing world. Jungle Jim found a way to push it to the limits.

From age 19, Jungle Jim was a hard working one man band—he built the cars, the engines, tuned them and did the body work. He also booked and drove the cars from place to place. Within three years he had three cars and two other drivers criss-crossing the country and pulling in money match racing for paid appearances. Other drivers like Don "the Snake" Prudhomme may have won more races than Jungle, but no one was a better crowd pleaser. A match racer is only as good as the number of fans he brings through the turnstiles and Jungle had a three ring circus full of entertainment. Like he said in the 1970s radio ads—"Drag racing is f-a-a-a-r out!"

Left: Jungle Jim Liberman performing his trademark track-long burnout. (DRM files)
Right: Jungle Pam Hardy backs up the Liberman funny car. (Jere Alhadeff photo)

In a video interview, Jungle Jim talked about his fear of fire. "A driver's worst enemy" is what he called it, saying that once you had one, it was always on your mind. "…All of a sudden it's all around you and you panic in a thousand different ways. You still maintain to drive the car, but your main interest is in stopping the car in any way, shape or form … and get away from the heat." Even so, his neatest trick was his fire burnouts at the starting line. Liberman was also the king of long burnouts, sometimes smoking his tires the entire 1/4 mile of the track. He also offered burnouts on the return road, after finishing his pass. Did the fans love this? You know they did. In 1966 he made a full pass while competing in a match race with his front tires up in the air—at 165 mph. During a race in New York in 1975, when Jungle's competitor hit the guardrail and crashed through the scoreboard, Jungle simultaneously blew his motor and flew through the top end, narrowly missing a stand of trees. While every spectacle was not planned, Liberman strove to make the race as exciting as possible for the paying spectators. He would have preferred to give up driving, but like any other practical wrencher, Liberman knew sitting behind the wheel was the best way to judge the performance of the car.

Parents don't nickname their daughters Jungle. The Hardy's named their's Pam and thought that she would be a regular child, which is what she was until she ran into her future. To Pam, her future looked like a wild red-headed man piloting a fast Corvette through West Chester, Pennsylvania. Jungle Jim caught one look of the long haired, well proportioned and very pretty 18 year old, flipped a 180 and suggested he show her his car—his funny car that is. Pam went along, took a look at the race car, dumped both her boyfriend and her plans for college, and moved in with Jungle the very next day. As Jungle Jim's new girlfriend she was quickly christened Jungle Pam and they went out to entertain the racing troops nationwide with displays of sex and power.

The addition of Jungle Pam to Liberman's wild show was like icing on the cake of excess. The attention of the mostly male audience followed her every move as the bra-less lass ran onto the track to back up Liberman's car following his burnouts. Wearing a mesh halter top or crotch length short-shorts, Jungle Pam was the first woman to make an appearance on the track at many race venues. They ran into problems at Atco in New Jersey, where the NHRA "no chicks allowed" rule kept Pam off the track. Jungle simply refused to race, saying "No Pam, no run."

Once things really got hot, Jungle kept a crazy schedule juggling cars, tracks and driving. He and his team ferried his three cars like puzzle pieces between New Jersey, Connecticut, Pennsylvania, South Carolina. It got to the point where they would pass each other out on the road, one car headed in the direction that another car just left. Keeping to a schedule this wild was near impossible—one crew member credits amphetamines for helping them make their schedule—Jungle also relied on overbooking dates. By some estimates, Jungle Jim ran as many as 120 dates in 1970 and averaged more than 100 for most of the 1970s. There's a story of a weekend where Liberman match raced in nearby towns on Friday and Saturday, then arrived at a NHRA national event, pulled the car off the trailer, made a pass and qualified in the last possible session. Promoters faced a test with Jungle. Usually he was late. The other times he just didn't show. Match racing paid the bills so Jungle would take chances, sometimes he booked all three cars to run on the same day. Sometimes it worked but other times he found himself in an all night thrash building a car for the next day's race and paycheck.

---

### FOR THE RECORD—"Jungle" Jim Liberman

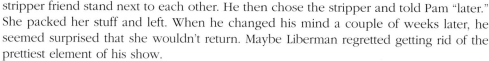

*1968—Won Funny Car Eliminator at ANRA's Winternationals at Lions*
*1975—Won NHRA Summernationals*
*1976—Won March Meet in Bakersfield, California*

---

It's a good thing that match racing existed, because the "professionalism" of NHRA wouldn't have tolerated too much of the Jungle Jim show. He was not above staging a fight at the starting line with another driver, yelling and tumbling, to get the fans going. While racing one night, Jungle's steering wheel came off in his hands. Instead of doing the prudent thing and stopping the car, he opted to stick it back on and drove full throttle to safely finish the pass. While money was his goal, he did take time out of his busy match racing schedule to win trophies at two NHRA national events—1969 Funny Car Eliminator and 1975 Summernationals. The closest anyone comes to the Jungle Jim personae today is John "Brute" Force. He's what Jungle would have had to become—wild, yet tame. Today it's mandatory that racers spout thanks to all their sponsors; Jungle Jim would not have been up to the task of kissing all that butt.

*Jungle Jim Liberman's grave marker. (DRM files)*

Jungle did what he wanted and he did it a lot. Whether it be playing harmonica to pass time or shooting pool on the table in the middle of his living room or firing up his funny car on the streets of his neighborhood, he lived without considering consequences. His bank account showed the results of this lifestyle choice—it was basically empty. He loved to gamble, and had been known to lose his track winnings at late night dice games in the pits or at the tables in Las Vegas. He also paid the price for being a notorious womanizer. Before Pam, even when he was married to "Jungle Bobbie," Liberman always had a woman or two in the wings. That was what finally did in the relationship between he and Jungle Pam. Maybe himself as well. The story goes that one day he said he needed to make a change. He had Pam and a new stripper friend stand next to each other. He then chose the stripper and told Pam "later." She packed her stuff and left. When he changed his mind a couple of weeks later, he seemed surprised that she wouldn't return. Maybe Liberman regretted getting rid of the prettiest element of his show.

Pam Hardy says now that she thought the end was close for him. The Corvette he died in was one that he had previously owned—he had checked out a "for sale" ad, and was surprised to be reunited with the car. Some people claim that he was despondent over Pam's refusal to come back to him. Others say that his career was at a low point; which wasn't true because he'd just signed a big deal with Revell and had money pouring in. Still other stories contend that he'd been taking pain killers for having some teeth pulled and was on his way home from a bar. It's also said that he had a steering problem with the Corvette, but why didn't he fix it? We'll never know exactly what was going through Jungle Jim Liberman's mind, all that's known is that he's missed and the sport will never be as wild.

John Force borrowing Jungle
Jim's track-long burnout stunt.
(Dave DeAngelis photo)

## JOHN FORCE—I RACE THEREFORE I AM

He said it and the fans believe it, "I have no life without a race car." That statement spurted by John "Brute" Force carries as much power as his record breaking fuel funny car. Staying in the cockpit of that funny car takes money, supplied by sponsors that love owning fans' attention. Consequently, Force courts his fans like nobody's business. He's been called the biggest name in drag racing, and from the crowds he draws, you have to believe it.

He's got all the stuff to make him popular: wins, competitive nature, huge line of collectibles; but it's his ease with drama that makes him so visible. The simple act of warming his tires for a pass, or his burnout, becomes theater as he thunders from the starting line nearly all the way down the track. He drives each race like it's for the big money often spouting engine-devouring fire at the top end. Reporters spring to interview Force at the top end of the track as he pops from the cockpit of his flopper. He prattles almost as fast as his car runs and sounds like what he is, an overexcited truck driver, high on nitro and the thrill of the ride. Following a hairy fire at a track in Memphis, Force swore he "saw Elvis at 1000 feet." The quip became the name of a NHRA published book of quotes from a myriad of Force's quote worthy, yet incomprehensible monologues.

Fire is Force's friend and he knows it. He once said, "you can talk about money, fishing trips to Mexico, bonuses, anything, but nothing brings out the best in a good racing team like an old-fashioned engine explosion, a fire and a 280-mph flip into the sand pit." That's experience talking because Force has been on fire so many times, it's not worth counting them. Lots of drivers have quit due to fear of fire; Force knows the trick is to outlive it. Following the simultaneous engine fire and Elvis sighting in Memphis, he and the crew paid special attention to singe protection. They added extra fire bottles and metal wheels to take over when the rubber ones burned off. Some people claimed that he went overboard in protecting himself, but Force countered that if his crew chief Austin Coil was gonna make so much power and continue to set him on fire, they could do something to keep the driver from getting charbroiled. Just as drivers dread it, Force knows that the drama of fire keeps the fans paying the big dollars to see seemingly fearless drivers risk their lives with every pass. TV viewers who watch all that smoking, flaming action from home are likely to come down to the track the next time Force is in town.

John Force excites his fans,
which thrills his sponsors.
(Nick Licatta photo)

The only other fire protection option would be to have Coil to hold back, but that's not why Force hired him. Force had been taking a funny car down the track for ten years with more losses and second place winnings than he'd care to think about. In 1984 he called Austin Coil every 20 minutes until he agreed to leave the champion ChiTown Hustler team to join up with Force. After a short 3 years the Coil/Force combo came into its own and won a national event in 1987. Since then it's been non-stop amazing,

Force put together a team with two crew chiefs, and another funny car, piloted by another competitive non-stopper guy, Tony Pedregon. The fans go wild when the two actually have to face each other. They race in earnest, and Tony may fear losing his job, but he has beat the boss. In 1997 they had the pleasure of posting side-by-side 4.94s, and Force's underling raced so hard, that Force turned in a record setting speed of 313.15 just to beat him. Talk about entertainment.

Almost any Force fan can tell you about his humble beginnings—a poor kid, raised in a 40 foot trailer, sleeping head-to-toes with his brothers, four to a bunk bed. His father was a truck driver, and Force followed in his footsteps, even becoming the spokesperson for Wally Thor's School of Truck Driving. While still in high school, Force and a brother began toying with drag racing. He had saved his ambitions for the strip, he never street raced, and at 16, his first trip down a track in his '55 Chevy in 1967 simply whetted his appetite for more. He had his introduction to fire early. His uncle once said, following a engine disaster that destroyed Force's car, the only thing left to sell was the fire and a picture of the fire.

Wanting to race and be a champion, (because as Force says, "Second place is first loser") has meant giving up on the other parts of life. His Castrol GTX, MacTool, Ford and Action sponsors—yes, it's a mouthful, but repeating those magic names pays the bills—get their money out of Force by sending him to autograph signings when he's not racing, which is hardly ever. While other drivers run around 20 races a year, Force sometimes adds as many as 10 match races to his schedule. That's ten extra opportunities to gain seat time, try different tunings on the car, add money to the budget, get the sponsors' names seen, and 10 extra opportunities to please the fans. It's a win-win-win idea and Force's smile slides wider with each new championship.

Offering memorable quotes like a motor mouth on speed; signing autographs on t-shirts, hats, pictures, arms and stomachs; driving burnouts that reach almost to the finish line; and going into the crowd even when he loses, may appear to be simply sound business practices. For Force, it's the real deal. In his 14 years without a major win, he learned that the fans were always there. Fans backed him even when he lost because he stuck around to tell them why. These days fans crowd in to celebrate following a win. Right now Force is riding high—he's won the fuel funny car national championship an unprecedented eight times since 1992, currently holds top speed record, and in 1996 he was the first drag racing driver to be voted Driver of The Year by the International Motorsports Hall of Fame. He knows that success can be fleeting, getting there slowly taught him that. Like he says, it took him 18 years to become an overnight success.

*John Force's successful career pays off in a garage packed with spare funny car bodies and engines and a sizeable paycheck. (Nick Licatta photo)*

*The winning Castrol-GTX-Mactool-Ford-Action John Force funny car. (Ron Lewis photo)*

---

**FOR THE RECORD—John "Brute" Force**

- *Lost first nine final rounds before earning first career victory at 1987 Le Grandnational at Montreal*
- *Only driver to win 8 NHRA Funny Car championships (1990-91, 1993-1998)*
- *One of only three NHRA competitors to appear in more than 100 final rounds*
- *Set speed record of 323.89 making a funny car faster than a top fueler for the first time in history—1998*

---

Force loves racing so much that he wants to build a house adjacent to the track in Indianapolis just so he can look over and get motivated. Force loves racing so much that he'd encourage his four daughters to get into racing for its education in respect, responsibility and driving skills—and the fun. The thrill of beating the other guy and outrunning the fire is the only life for him. He can't even contemplate retirement. Force would like to race until he's so old they have to pry his arthritic fingers off the wheel and bury him with the throttle pedal in his casket. The fans just hope none of that happens too soon.

## JET CARS—HIGH SPARK OF LOW FLYING CARS

A jet dragster takes out the back fence at Brotherhood International Raceway. (April Hazen photo)

Fire is a known factor at the race track. Often uncontrolled, usually exciting, always an attention grabber. Using the drama of fire and ear blasting sound, promoters have seduced patrons through their turnstiles during the bleakest periods in motorsports.

Crowds flock to see jet cars for the novelty of watching a ground-based vehicle with a flaming flight-based apparatus strapped to its back. Incongruous in idea, clumsy in execution, it's excitement in the making. Walt Arfons dreamt up the odd combination of car and jet in the late 1950s. He and his brother Art, Craig Breedlove, and Romeo Palamides struggled through the infancy years with these Frankenstein children. Always constructed from surplus military plane parts, keeping the post WWII jet cars in extra parts was nearly as easy as picking up Chevy parts at the local junkyard. By 1960 the Arfons brothers got their Green Monster off to a rolling start on Bonneville's salt flats for a record 342 mph. The brothers split the team, but Art Arfons continued to run the Green Monster at the drag strips. At a 1961 meet in Fort Worth, he drove 209 mph to break the 200 barrier for standing starts. And in 1963, Arfons easily upped his mph to 238.

It wasn't easy to convince sanctioning bodies to let jet cars run in competition with fuel burning dragsters. Like dragsters, jet cars had an extreme learning curve. From the get-go, jet cars delivered exceptional speed. Stopping them was harder to control. Jet cars used the same equipment that slowed pickup trucks, along with parachutes for backup. But they were prone to crashing; the cars' structure wasn't up to snuff with the power of the jet. And because they were built with used parts, people were afraid of them. In 1962, NHRA took stock of the situation, and said "no way." That decision sent the jets to the outlaw tracks.

Jet wagon. (Author photo)

By 1963 NHRA ended its self-imposed nitromethane ban and welcomed fuel cars back with open arms. Mechanics had worked out the bugs at the pirate tracks and crowds wanted to see the speeds they could turn. Now newly safe, fuel cars ran at speeds of 200 mph in 5 plus seconds. Tickets sold. Jet car drivers, too, thought they could return, but NHRA still thought otherwise. After a taming period, jet drivers considered themselves to be as safe as the average fuel car. After all, fuel cars were known for propelling parts into the audience. Claiming insurance woes, NHRA begged off from the jets that often could not stop, and could get into the crowd.

*Doug Rose's Green Mamba incinerates a wagon. (DRM files)*

Naturally there's lots of grumbling by the jet car drivers about the NHRA's ban. Most feel it has more to do with letting the fuel cars be the darlings than with safety concerns. Also, wherever the local press shows, they focus more on the drama of jet cars, than on the actual racing that the piston driven models provide. Even with speed limits, and lacking handicap racing or prize money, jets draw a crowd. But it's not the real deal. NHRA lays it out this way, "Jet cars are considered exhibition vehicles only and direct competition is prohibited. Jets may not compete for prize money. Jets may run against other jets or other NHRA standard drag race cars on a heads-up basis only." That means no handicaps for jets' relatively slow starts. Jet dragsters are not to surpass 320 mph and jet funny cars, 305 mph. NHRA is serious about this stuff, too. Disregard the rules and exceed the speed limit by 1-10 mph, you pay $500, exceed by 11 mph and higher you fork over $2,000. The next time around, it's $1,500 for 1-10 mph over and break their speed limit by 11 mph and up, and you get a $5,000 fine and a six month suspension. Do it three times and the penalty's $5,000 plus an indefinite suspension. And NHRA feels it's within their rights to fine both driver and/or owner.

Although not allowed to race on the majority of drag strips, Utah's salt flats witnessed fierce competition between the fire machines. Drag racers disown jet cars because the vehicles are pushed by thrust and not pulled by an engine, but the jet pilots ignored the nay-sayers and Breedlove and Arfons spent time trading records. In 1963 Breedlove went 407 mph in his Spirit of America (SOA). In 1964, Arfons' Green Monster went 536. Then back to the SOA with a 555. Four days later Arfons turned a 576, but almost died due to a rear tire explosion that gave him an uncontrollable ride. Not afraid of the upped stakes, Breedlove went 600, and held the record until a rocket took it away some five years later. Arfons tried to take that record too, but crashed going faster than 600 and never made another Salt Flats pass. He kept racing the tracks, but in 1971 he lost control of the Super Cyclops and killed his TV personality passenger (yes, passenger) along with two track employees. That was enough for Arfons and he got out of it at age 45.

*Craziness of Bob Correll's jet bike. (DRM files)*

As the fuel guys spent more time at the growing number of NHRA sanctioned events, promoters at small venues felt the pinch. For the high dollar racers, the little tracks were inconvenient to pull in huge semis and besides, the races were basically money losers. Pro drivers who had cut teeth on match racing, had to charge podunk tracks an arm and a leg to cover the expense of dragging out their entire dog and pony show. Breaking parts at a small track doesn't add points for the national circuit, and to compensate, big teams charge the small guy plenty. Jet cars are much less likely to have things go wrong and consequently charge less to the promoter.

*Exceptional craziness of Jack McClure's 215 mph rocket cart. (DRM files)*

Not willing to give in to the NHRA stronghold, Roger Gustin moved from nitro funny cars to driving a Walt Arfons-built jet funny car—a lot of power for a short wheelbase. His car, the Time Machine had to be rebuilt to meet NHRA's high safety standards. Gustin, with Romeo Palamides, built a "new age jet dragster," they called the Daily C Special. He then became the first driver licensed by the sanctioning body to pilot a jet dragster in 1974. That wasn't enough of a victory for Gustin, so he built a jet funny car and somehow got that sanctioned in 1980 as well. Although Arfons; Al Hanna; the sole African American driver, Fil Smith; and some other jet car drivers got into the game, NHRA still sticks to their guns about the tough rules.

The thrill of fire up your butt was experienced by at least five NHRA licensed women as well. The best known was Aggie Hendricks, who drove the "Odyssey" and Marsha Smith, wife of Fil, was the only black woman.

In 1963, Doug Rose started driving Walt Arfons' Green Monster, where the cockpit is in the nose of the vehicle. In 1966, he and the Monster were in a low speed run in Virginia where Rose crashed and lost his legs. A mere three months later he was wearing prosthetics and back to sitting in the front of the car showing what it could do. Rose built his Green Mamba in 1968 and steadfastly refuses to conform his car to the regulations laid down by sanctioning bodies. Since he won't move his seat to the mid-section, he's relegated to sideshow status and prohibited from racing. Instead, he keeps a full calendar of monster truck shows and events where he burns old cars to the ground.

---

### FOR THE RECORD—Andy Green

*The current landspeed record is held by British driver Andy Green who drove the Thrust SSC across the Black Rock Desert in Nevada at a speed of 763.035 MPH on October 15, 1997. Green broke Richard Nobel's 1983 record of 633.468 and also busted the sound barrier at Mach 1.002.*

---

Al Hanna keeps the jet car dream alive booking acts for his Pro Jet Association. His drivers don't perform servile tasks like track drying or over-the-top car burning stunts. They want to be taken seriously, dammit. There are drawbacks however to taking the dignified route. If racers win the lower priced purses, they'll miss out on match money dollars. Jet cars don't have the brand appeal of the "Chevys," "Chryslers" and "Fords" driven by top fuel and funny car drivers—you can't go to your local dealer and pick one up. To race competitively, they have to lose the extra fuel that produces the popping afterburners and huge fire shows that attract spectators. And being more competitive, as any veteran nitro racer can tell you, costs more money. Heightening the prize stakes will take deeper pockets for competitive equipment. That means a new jet turbine at $80,000 as compared to $2,000 for a previously owned model. Companies like Boeing or McDonnell Douglas have yet to see the benefit of sponsoring these land based jets.

So do you call vehicles like the Green Mamba or Bob Motz's jet powered Kenworth truck, racers or sideshow acts? Most fans don't care, they just call it fun.

The Untouchable machine and driver "Jet Car" Bob Smith. (Robert J. Snayko photo)

## "JET CAR" BOB SMITH

Getting into a jet car, then getting the runs on NHRA tracks is how Bob Smith spent the 1960s. In 1962 he'd already been powering fuel dragsters down the 1/4 mile at about 185-190 mph, but like any other speed jockey, he wanted to go faster. Jet cars could turn in 200 mph easy, and that's where Smith went. Smith's first car was built by Romeo Palamides, and as soon as he stepped into the cockpit of the Untouchable, he was clocking 220 mph. "When you're driving a fuel car," he reasons, "how much more dangerous could a jet car be?" Anybody who wanted to go really fast, took the chance. He soon became known as "Jet Car Bob." The Untouchable was a 30 foot long, four ton monster that was powered by a Sabre J47 engine that put out 10,000 pounds of thrust. In 1962, that was a lot of horsepower.

Because they were so fast, spectacular and easy on the wallet, Smith thought these new buggies would be the stars of drag racing. He was shocked when NHRA imposed the ban, but he wasn't immobilized. Instead, he stood in the faces of the officials, stating his case. Any West Coast track where NHRA took the fuel dragsters, gassers and floppers, Smith would show up with his jet dragster on a trailer, exciting the fans and irritating the officials. Sure, he wasn't allowed to compete, but he sure could remind everyone of the excitement they were missing. He explained that he'd add every safety feature they wanted, but the sanctioning body would have nothing to do with it.

While unable to break into NHRA's environs, Smith did his best to delight the country. As a West Coast driver, he was one of the first to take a jet racer to the East Coast. He is probably the only guy to have piloted his fire breather down a major city street. Smith did just that to show Mike Douglas' TV audience what the Untouchable could do. And he did about 120, thundering down the main drag in downtown Cleveland.

He was a serious racer, but also liked to thrill the fans. The cars cruise so smoothly, that Smith could take one hand off the wheel and wave at fans when he passed. Says Smith, "It was okay as long as I didn't get it up in the air stream." People were unaccustomed to the cars and would run out to the track following his pass to feel the heat on the asphalt. While "weenie roaster" drivers today burn cars and pop their afterburners, Smith chose to show off with feats of excess. He'd often have track owners shut off the lights

as he slid his car down the track in the dark. The 30 foot flame out the afterburner lit the scene like daylight. Once he attempted to clear a painter who had set up his gear at the back of the track—the painter said, 'Arfons brothers had been there and he'd seen their cars run, so he wasn't worried.' So, Smith hit the afterburner and blew the guy, his ladder and a 6 foot chunk out of the fence. Not only was he coated with paint, but he reconsidered the power of the cars. But Smith, stepping as far away from side show stuff as possible, says he never burned anything that wasn't "natural"—generally meaning the already standing protective fences behind the staging lanes. Unfortunately he couldn't get that safety for himself. Due to the inherent danger in racing any car, Jet Car Bob's had his own brushes with disaster. While it took three years for him to recover from one such incident, he claims the cars are still no more dangerous than the fuel cars he once raced.

Jet dragsters are easier to keep in a straight line, but braking can be more of a problem, as they gain more thrust on the top end, they rely on chutes for fully stopping power. Smith can tell you that better than anyone. The normal procedure is to turn off the engine, pull the chutes. One awful time at Broadway Bob's Great Lakes Dragaway, the Untouchable II slammed a bump at about 1000 feet that kicked Jet Car Bob's chute out to be incinerated by the afterburner. Smith didn't find out until some 300 feet later when he pulled the lever to stop and got nothing. The Untouchable ran out of track, jumped a road and ended up straddling a car in a ditch on the other side of the county road. Fortunately Smith escaped with a broken finger and a cut lip, while the driver of the Nash Rambler came away with a broken collar bone and a hell of a story to tell the folks.

Since they only run on kerosene, explosions are not what jet car drivers worry about, it's "getting into the crowd." Smith avoided one such incident by aiming for empty stands rather than hit some photographers shooting him. Thanks to the ban, Smith spent much of his career at non-NHRA events. Savvy strip promoters would drop their NHRA insurance and put on a show with the jet cars that drew a few thousand people. It was money in the bank for the smaller tracks that couldn't attract an audience for a grocery getter going maybe 160 mph. Smith match raced, making either three single runs, or blowing the wheels off of the local track's favorite fueler.

Denied for much too long, "Jet Car Bob" Smith was duly remembered in 1994 when he was inducted into the Jet Car Hall of Fame. Unfortunately, the group is so loose, they didn't know where to send his invite to the induction ceremony. The next year they figured out how to contact him and finally Smith got his due. More recently Smith was recognized by a larger group of racers and inducted into the International Drag Racing Hall of Fame. It may have been for rattling the windows in downtown Cleveland, or holding the world's record of 287 mph for 13 years, or maybe for bugging the NHRA to consider his work with the respect that other drivers received. But probably because "Jet Car Bob" did what all those guys did—he just wanted to go fast.

Paula Murphy's rocket car
at Bonneville.
(Paula Murphy collection)

## ROCKET CARS—UNSAFE AT ANY SPEED

In an ironic twist, lethal rocket cars were a welcome addition to the same drag strips that banned the safer, more predictable jet cars. In the 1970s, NHRA sanctioned rocket cars for racing on any and all tracks. Two years later, a handful of drivers were dead and rocket cars were banned from racing. Their speeds were incredible; the hydrogen-peroxide fed vehicles clocked over 300 mph with low E.T.s in the 4s. Like the jet cars, rockets brought too much attention to the circus atmosphere of the drag strip. Journalists looking for the spectacular would report on Evel Knievel's jumps or four fuelers or jet cars running side-by-side.

This sensationalism didn't sit well with drivers who had fought furiously for their sport to be taken seriously. Over the course of two seasons, crowds watched 12 rocket drivers, six of whom were killed by their exhibition vehicles. Paula Murphy did what Wally Parks of NHRA always feared—became the first woman in a serious accident at the track. When she broke her neck in Pollution Packer in the 1973, it signaled the end for the rockets. At the Dragaway in Wisconsin, a catalyst blew up on the starting line. Fortunately the pieces only hit one person—the starter, who's arm was torn off. There were rocket powered skateboards that guys rode at speeds up to 70 mph. There were two go-karts where the drivers laid on their backs with parachutes strapped on. If they got out of control or if they lost it, they'd pull the chute and it would slide them out of the kart. At one race the go-karters crashed and one of the guys slid under the guardrail and was decapitated. For obvious reasons rocket racing was short-lived.

## BROADWAY BOB METZLER—THE FANS' FRIEND

For the 45 years he ran his Great Lakes Dragaway, Broadway Bob Metzler had two favorite stations—greeting the fans at the gate, accepting a beer from almost every one of them, and riding the nose of a jet car, also with a beer in hand. He was easy to spot, in his flame- or skull- or car-painted pants, wearing Batman or star sunglasses. The crowd always greeted him with applause, sometimes more than they doled out to the racers. His "extravaganzas" and being the only promoter who allowed the jets to run in heads up competition earned Broadway Bob a spot in the Drag Racing Hall of Fame, and a warm spot in the hearts of Wisconsin fans.

Broadway Bob and car clubs like the Milwaukee Motoring Association needed a place to race, so in 1954 he took his kitty (earned gambling in the Marine Corps) along with his money from a successful business, and built a drag strip. Metzler had been a modified stock car driver, but switched his allegiance to the straight track and opened the Great Lakes Dragaway in 1956.

Trademark "Broadway" Bob Metzler, beer in one hand, jet dragster in the other. (Dave Milcarek photo)

Once the jet dragsters started attracting national attention setting speed records, Metzler brought them to Wisconsin, for the first match race. The featured event was "Jet Car Bob" Smith in the Untouchable against Art Arfons' Green Monster. Predictably, the crowd went wild for the flaming speedsters. The extravaganza was extended to two perennial weekend events, the Olympics of Drag Racing for Memorial Day (the sport's oldest single event still staged on the same track since 1957) and the Jet Rocket Nationals thrilled the workers on Labor Day.

As if the flaming cars weren't excitement enough, starting in the late 1960s, Broadway Bob would climb atop the jets for a cruise. "I'm the only person in the world that's ever done it. I did it mainly when the jet was being fired up and during the wild burner pops and the big fire show with the flames." The driver inside wore all the regulation protective gear, but Metzler was the bigger daredevil. He wore a t-shirt, maybe a sweatshirt. Never a fire suit, never a helmet. As Broadway Bob says, "If you're not living on the edge, you're taking up too much space."

Don't believe him? Often as not, he'd have a can of beer in one hand, leaving only one hand to hold onto the beast. "I'd wave to the people and show them the beer and take a swig. The Untouchable, the USA 1, the Green Mamba, the Chicago Fire, the jet limousine... I rode about 7 different jets."

While other track operators lived in fear of the wrath of the big daddy NHRA, Metzler did whatever he could to entice the fans. He never got his hands slapped or his insurance canceled or his sanction revoked. At most they said "cool it." As E.T.s dropped, speeds increased and the range of the pro circuit widened, small tracks like the Dragaway had to fight to stay in business. The sanctioning bodies understood and looked the other way as Metzler continued to explore outrageousness. His arena was quantity, not necessarily quality: "I'd hire a bunch of jets and a lot of low dollar dragsters and people didn't care. They'd see a lot of cars, a lot of monster trucks and a lot of car burning." From the nation's only combine demolition derby in the nearby farming community of Kenosha, Metzler would appropriate crashed combines. "I'd trade 'em passes to come to the track, have the jets melt the combines. I'd have tank trucks and monster trucks crush the combines." The rest of the season you could take out your daily aggressions and "grudge" race against your buddy or your boss in your street car.

Metzler brought in big drag racing names too: The Snake and the Mongoose in their Hot Wheels cars, Don Garlits, "TV Tommy" Ivo, Shirley Muldowney and Connie Kalitta

Don "the Snake" Prudhomme and Tom "Mongoose" McEwen's "rivalry" enticed crowds to their match races. (Jere Alhadeff)

during their boyfriend/girlfriend let's-have-a-fight years. He had floppers driven by women: Paul Murphy, Shirley Shahan, Della Woods. The wild and unpredictable fuel altereds raced there. Minority racers like the "Flaming Mexican" Frank Pedregon and the first black drag racing superstar, Malcolm Durham were also featured at Metzler's track. When the Factory Experimental cars ruled the strips, they all made appearances at Great Lakes Dragaway—the Ramchargers, Arnie "the Farmer" Beswick, "the Lawman" Al Ecstrand, Bill "Grumpy" Jenkins—all the "names" making the circuit. Broadway Bob handed out discount fliers for return visits and plastered the town with print ads and radio spots for the weekend shows, then freed the track for sportsman racing the other five nights.

Like much of the United States, the mid to late 1970s wasn't a good economic time in Wisconsin. Fishing the depths of his creative pool, Metzler came up with events that compelled fans to part with their hard earned dollars. Advertising his little heart out, Metzler brought in his biggest crowd ever to see Evel Knievel jump two trailer trucks. There were van-ins where two vans would tug-a-war with other until the transmission popped out of one. There were Harley shows where a crowd pleaser was the Honda drop. A Japanese car would drop 700 feet from a crane onto a Honda car, then jet car drivers of the Green Mamba and USA 1 melted entire stacks 30 or so Japanese motorcycles with a couple of import cars thrown in for good measure. On the adjoining motorcross track, half sized tanks raced stuffed with girls in brief red, white and blue outfits and an Uncle Sam look-alike fired blanks from ack-ack guns. There was always 24 hour live music, beer gardens and wet t-shirt contests.

"Broadway" Bob booked the Snake and Mongoose Hot Wheels show for his Great Lakes Dragaway. (Steve Reyes photo)

Putting on a wild show isn't the only thing Broadway Bob is known for; he's also a friend of his fans. "Never once did I try to get their last dollar. When I stood out in front, I'd see people turn and walk away and they'd only have the $15 for the show not the newer price $20. I'd say, pay $20 for one of you and keep the other $15 for beer and food and I'd let them in." He once got a call from a guy inviting him to a party—years earlier Broadway Bob had let the police officer and his wife into the track for half price. They remembered and wanted to pay him back when they hit the lottery for $40 million.

The racers, the spectators, the track—he loved it all. So much so, that Broadway Bob and his wife of 45 years still live at Great Lake Dragaway. "I can look out and see a scoreboard and the stands. Every time this track is open, five days a week, we have company that stops in to see us. I walk out 100 feet and I'm surrounded by people." For that love and innovation, and throwing great parties, Broadway Bob Metzler has his name on a plaque in the Drag Racing Hall of Fame.

Smoking slingshots have been delegated to "nostalgia" races since the 1970s. (Steve Reyes photo)

## NOSTALGIA RACING—THE NEW NAME FOR EXCITEMENT

Some people only feel alive when they're looking to the past. Luckily for them, there's nostalgia racing. But ardent fans explain that those old cars may be the future of drag racing.

The word "nostalgia" generally brings up ideas of Norman Rockwell's warm and cozy paintings, or Lawrence Welk's sleepy time tunes, not smoke-belching, fire-breathing, asphalt-eating, front-engined race cars. Time to readjust your ideas. As mechanics grappled for speed, the first group of racers eliminated were the granddaddies of car classes— the four bangers. In the early 1960s the "X" classes that had been specifically created for four-cylinder vehicles were cut as six- and eight-cylinder bad boys took their places at the starting line. Moving to Californian tracks in San Gabriel, Colton and Fontana that weren't so well attended (and are now all gone), the Forever Four still raced their "antique" cars at an event that became the Antique Nationals. The initial race was at the now gone Lions Drag Strip. Then the Nationals tried other disappearing tracks like Orange County and Irwindale Raceways, before becoming a stalwart event at the still existent Los Angeles County Raceway in Palmdale. The race continues to welcome any 1948 or earlier muscle machine.

Time went on, innovations moved forward and more cars were left outside of the "legalities" of the track. The most significant shift occurred when Don Garlits mounted his motor behind him and won. Nearly every other racer followed course and sanctioning bodies decided it safe and was the only way to go. Suddenly racers who still sat behind their engines and who had been thinking independently since the beginning of the straight track fun were shit out of luck. All fueled up and nowhere to race. Bitter and often not having the dollars to reconstruct their cars, they stayed home.

Not willing to miss out on all the fun, history-steeped cars like Ed Cortopassi's "Glass Slipper," Art Chrisman's "Hustler I" and Big Daddy Don Garlits' "Swamp Rat I" made tire smoking track appearances during the 1970s that excited old-time racers, fans and promoters alike. Now cars out of the past were located, rebuilt and raced in their former glory. By 1981 racers could participate in side-by-side racing at the annual Nostalgia Nationals held at the Baylands Raceway in Fremont until 1988. Organizers Brian Burnett and Tom Prufer handed out cash prizes and trophies and watched as more and more "obsolete" cars knocked at the door requesting admission.

Front-engine dragsters bring out the best in drivers and crowds who love the drama. (Steve Reyes)

Nostalgia races, like Famoso's March Meet, bring slingshots back to the staging lanes. (Walter Cotten/Steven DePinto, Rescue photo)

NHRA's huge change in sanctioning rules sharply decreased the numbers of cars seen at the national events. Where it was usual to feel/hear/see 100 top fuel dragsters beating their motors out to qualify for 24 spots on the racing day, events dwindled to 16 cars looking for 16 spots—not the picture of dramatic competition. A few smart entrepreneurs decided to make sour grapes into wine, and organized a sanctioning body where the slingshots where welcomed. Burnett and Prufer started the Nostalgia Drag Racing Association (NDRA) in 1985 and opened it up to cars with 1964 and earlier body types.

All the innovations that had kept the older cars out of competition at NHRA started arriving at the track in the form of replica cars. They looked like the old guys, but had modern chassises carrying Hemi engines that spun new wrinkle-wall Goodyear slicks and left no smoke as they often charged the top end at 225 mph. Just as they had in the other car clubs, guys with more money had found a way to come in and take all the trophies from the guys who were having fun with their hobby and couldn't or wouldn't sell their houses in exchange for extra horsepower.

This disillusion led to the dissolution of NDRA and like mushrooms in the wake of cow shit, other short-lived groups sprang up—Nostalgia Timing Association (NTA), West Coast Timing Association (WCTA), Vintage Racing Association (VRA) and American Nostalgia Racing Association (ANRA). It was great that racers had had options on where to race. What was not cool, was that they each had different sets of specifications to which racers were expected to adhere. NDRA went so far as to say that cars would be disqualified if their tires did not smoke during their launch. The sentiment was for keeping the old cars, but the means were harshly under-thought.

Finally Bob Webber and Jim Real stepped into the fray and purchased ANRA. They joined with a street rod organization, the Good Guys, and created a points circuit. Good Guys feature six points races and ANRA has four—and just for good measure, NHRA puts on the California Hot Rod Reunion and Good Guys the Hot Rod Nationals in Indianapolis, neither of which gain points for racers, but both are heavy in prestige.

The two groups have been able to agree on specs that the racers can deal with—quite well, thank you very much. E.T.s have dipped to 5.96 with the exclusion of computers (except data recorders), even with the use of regulation tires and a single fuel pump. Even with the cost cutting measures of disallowing high-tech on-board computers and early 1960s body types, there's still in influx of big time rebuilts—out of 18 fuelers running in California, only three reckon back to the old days.

Cars and drivers alike have personality on this circuit, like "Nitro" Neil Bisciglia or the "WW II" car. Original steel body, supercharged funny cars are now making their way back to the track for serious audience identification, just like when they first appeared in the early 1960s.

While the drivers appear iffy and on the greasy side, so do the spectators—but then, it's not the multi-billion dollar dog and pony show of NHRA. And that's the attraction for racers and fans alike. The rules are made by racers who own or race front engined cars—they understand that fun and not necessarily dollars is what the show's all about. Fans, too, take advantage of the low key atmosphere. The admission price is affordable and often you can walk right up to the people who made history and chat 'em up. And for fans and racers alike—it's still all about nitro; it makes pulses and cars race at about the same speed.

## FUEL ALTEREDS—GUARDRAIL TO GUARDRAIL ACTION

*Fuel altereds' explosive power on short wheelbases produce plenty of sideways action. (DRM files)*

*Nostalgia meets offer the only venue for the AA/FA class to race. (Steve Reyes photo)*

Jet cars provided speed and fire, making them a brilliant and scary sight. Rocket cars had an unpredictability that, though thrilling, got them banned early in the game. Then there's Fuel Altereds. They're fiery, unpredictable, and as scarce as the American bald eagle. Old timers wax poetic relating the bygone days when the fuel altereds bounced along the track. Their class description AA/FA was often called Awful Awful Fuel Altereds.

The idea must have been conceived by someone not planning on driving one: a front engine coupe with a wheelbase shorter than a dragster, precariously perched on a high chassis powered by nitromethane. All of these components make the supercharged babies smoke their tires and zig zag across the track in a way that had the NHRA quickly saying "no way." Fuel altereds first showed up at the track around 1953, when Jazzy Jim Nelson piloted his Fiat-bodied racer.

Drivers of these cars are given their due, but also a befuddled look—why would anyone risk their life in this wild ride? Drivers had names like Dennis "Bing-Bing Ricochet" Geisler and the cars were named Groundshaker Jr. and Pure Hell. No one got stranger looks than "Wild Willie" Borsch, who campaigned the Winged Express. A Model T body with a blown Chrysler and a 90" wheelbase provided such a wild ride that Borsch often found himself pointed at the guardrail. He was famous for his "casual" driving style— right hand on the steering wheel and left hand on the door. Truth is, that the "Stab and Steer" maneuvers of an altered required that you hold on for fear of dying. Drivers of "safer" fuel dragsters often refused to compete alongside altereds knowing the car would just as soon go sideways as straight down the track. Anyone who's watched a AA/FA make a pass knows it can take them a mile of swerves to travel the 1/4 mile straight track. Borsch's Winged Express was the first altered to get into the 8s, then the 7s and the first go over 200 mph.

The Winged Express impressed fans across the country from the 1960s, until Borsch and the car's builder, "Mousie" Marcellus parted ways. They never raced together again,

but did bury the hatchet before Borsch passed away from cancer in 1991. The renewed friendship is evidenced by Marcellus bringing the Winged Express to car shows with Borsch comfortable in his old driver's seat—although now as ashes in an urn. Marcellus so loved the old wild days that he's currently trying to corral others like him and create a class called the Nostalgia Fuel Altereds. See, altereds can still be found at the track, but they've changed a bit. Marcellus wants to restore them to their previous unpredictable glory.

Left: Wild Willie Borsch
in his funny car days.
(Steve Reyes photo)
Right: Wild Willie Borsch's
urn of ashes in the Winged
Express driver's seat.
(DRM files)

## HOT RODS FROM HELL—A RIDE SO SCARY, IT REFUSES TO GO AWAY

Fuel or not fuel, Scott Jezak is still gonna run those short wheel-based altered demons down the track. Jezak slowly built his way from Hot Wheels, to soap box cars and model building to the strip racers he now drives. His first altered was built in 1984, a '23 T. Later he match raced Wild Thing, a '32 altered he campaigned with Camp Stanley's Wild Bunch. Stanley decided to move onto the new world of pro modifieds, and Jezak stuck with the altereds. He continues to offer the excitement of watching these supercharged vehicles slide their way down the 1/4 mile, just like in the old days.

Getting together a gang of individuals and asking them to function as a group may have been the toughest challenge. Hot Rods From Hell is a touring group of two to 12 alcohol altereds that can be booked into a show at a track and are guaranteed to perform. The rules are stringent: Jezak requires meticulously kept cars capable of making 6 second, 200 mph passes. What he offers to the strip promoters is sure starts, fast speeds and long side-by-side burnouts (sometimes reaching half track).

Some critics argue that a car running on alcohol cannot be a "fuel altered" as these cars are billed, but the Hot Rods from Hell persist. Fans don't even seem to mind the longer wheelbases these cars are built on. What they long to see is that nearly forgotten thrill of centerline to guardrail racing that Hot Rods from Hell saved from the past to enjoy today.

Hot Rods from Hell. (DRM files)

Linda Vaughn congratulates Surfers driver Mike Soronin in Bakersfield in 1966. (Greg Sharp collection)

## LINDA VAUGHN—MISS HURST SHIFTER

Excitement for a bunch of guys at the track can stray beyond fast times and fast speeds. Sexy women are a perk to a sea of testosterone, but they don't often grace the track. When they do, it's with a husband or boyfriend in tow. Promoters know guys like that cheesecake sex appeal and do their damnedest to provide it. Tool and parts calendars featuring scantily clad women have decorated garages since the 1950s and promoters do their part to have these same babes jump from the page to the track. Women in bathing suits, sunsuits, hot pants, pedal pushers and bikinis have smeared their lipstick on winners since records were kept. Spotting these women at the drag strip has been good sport for the fans.

In the mid-1960s, a company that made floor mounted gear shifters for racers put their dumb sticks together and found its best spokesperson. Not a racer, or even a women racer, but the Queen of Speed, Miss Linda Faye Vaughn. Vaughn's 42-25-35 numbers are more obvious than her more than 50 years, making her a popular autograph signer even today. Known as much for her southern charm as for her swollen figure, Vaughn has kissed many a winner in her 32 years as queen of the drag strip. Vaughn isn't the only trophy girl to grace the track, but certainly the biggest name.

Linda Vaughn's Hurst Shifter "float" on parade. (DRM files)

Brains got her out of high school at 16 and her beauty was the vehicle for Vaughn to arrive at the track. She made a career of beauty contests; her first title was Miss Dalton—Georgia that is. The next, Miss Poultry of 1961, was won with the assistance of a lie. She added two years to her not quiet legal 16 and gained entry to the contest where she bested the other 199 contestants. Along the way she won the Miss Atlanta International Raceway title, and was also awarded the nickname of Queen of Speed. When the Queen and "Fireball" Roberts did the Twist on the track as a PR stunt, they got mounds of press and attention, making Vaughn an instant celebrity. Her biggest coup combined her intelligence, looks and vibrant personality to land the job of a lifetime.

Hurst Shifter Performance Company knew how to grab customers with sex appeal, and had successfully sponsored beauty contests for a while. Because she'd been touring the early stock car circuit, Vaughn knew she liked cars and even knew a bit about marketing.

On the eve of the Hurst beauty contest, she met with company owner George Hurst and contest co-sponsor, *Hot Rod* magazine editor Ray Brock to suggest ideas for the shifter's campaign. She won the Miss Golden Shifter title handily and held onto it for 13 years.

The new Miss Golden Shifter's first day on the job was at the Winternationals in Pomona, California. She witnessed 100 fuel cars attempting to qualify for 32 spots and described her introduction to the power of drag racing as "all the rock and roll bands rolled into one." The Mae West of racing represented Hurst from 1966 to 1983 (when she "retired" to a VP position at the company). Generally she wore outrageous outfits: usually bikinis, sometimes bras fashioned from parachutes, and often gold lamé—lots of gold lamé. Vaughn rode, prominent breasts leading the way, with a giant 8 foot replica of a Hurst shifter mounted on the back on an old convertible. Penthouse and Playboy wanted her for their pages, but the "sexy, not sexual" symbol turned them down. Miss Shifter's been down the track so many times and kissed enough winners that she's now considered experienced enough to co-announce the Pro Stock rounds at NHRA events.

Demand ran high for the full figured spokesperson for the company. To help fill requests for her appearances—as many as 135-200 a year—Vaughn put together a dozen "similarly equipped" voluptuous blondes; the Hurstettes. Her love of chatting up the guys was obvious, particularly when she spent 5 years meeting and greeting American troops at bases and hospitals across country and in Vietnam. Unlike sex kitten Ann Margaret she'd let the boys know she didn't sing or dance, and they didn't mind. Hurst's wily rep would simply get the ball rolling by asking what their favorite car was and they'd be on the best of terms. During a period, Vaughn was all over the place, at the track, in print ads, and even in the movies, such as *Cannonball Run* (1981) and *Stroker Ace* (1983) with Burt Reynolds where she played Linda Vaughn, Queen of Speed.

The race track has been more than a workplace for Vaughn. It's where she achieved royalty, it had been her dance floor and when she got married, the track was her altar. She'd dated many racers, but lucky speedster Bill Tidwell wed the Queen at Lions Drag Strip's "Last Drag Race" on December 2, 1972. Fans feared that she would turn in her crown, but her job had more staying power than her marriage, and she continued to make appearances.

More than a knock out figure, she's the face of drag racing, the embodiment of motorsports. She has a PR talent for remembering names. As she told George Hurst and Ray Brock in her tryouts for Miss Golden Shifter, Vaughn's goal was to get the Hurst name to be a household word; she succeeded fabulously. Vaughn still makes up to 200 appearances a year and is considered the most recognized face in motorsports. Yes, face of motorsports, because as the Queen of Speed said, stealing a quote from Dolly Parton "I don't sing with my boobs."

*Then... (Robert J. Snayko photo)*

*... and in 1996, Linda Vaughn still entertains the fans. (Steve Collison photo)*

(Rescue photo)

# Me, Myself, My Car

## CHAPTER 4

The surge of American self-expression through the hot rod nearly died when the British invasion attacked in the 1960s. Kids, our purveyors of popular culture, had their short attention spans whipped from the West Coast to the far east. Suddenly all things foreign were cool including music, clothes and cars. The surface desire of hot rod stuff was lost. But the roots, the racing, went on. Guys addicted to speed and power didn't need wide audiences to continue. The whole culture rode its undercurrents and never disappeared. It weathered its strongest followers being whisked off to Vietnam, the influence of drugs, gas wars and environmental threats. But when baby boomers wanted to be baaad and return to their blue collar roots, custom cars and drag racing were there with open arms to welcome them home.

Artist Dan Collins. (Andy Takakjian photo)

## CULTURAL IMPLICATIONS

While drag strips and chop shops aren't considered mainstream, they're still very real aspects of American society. So cultural historian, Sara G. Parker hung at the track and frequented car shows to research her book entitled *Mortal Culture*. Parker examines the car's place in society and its roots as an expression of personal identity.

Anyone forced to toe the line all week long gets weary of obeying the status quo and starts taking another look at the weekend getaway of cars as a means of self-expression. Anybody can own one, with a little knowledge you can work on it. Owning a personalized vehicle is a common denominator for car clubs and outings. Cars are an extension of our identities and a huge banner describing who we are. When I sold my dual heaps of a '63 convertible Dart and '63 Falcon to buy a much more reliable Volvo wagon I was afraid I'd be seen as a yuppie/boring/old woman. Maybe that's just a Southern Californian neuroses, but it illustrates how strong our identification with transportation is in these parts.

Cultural historian, Sara Parker. (Zuika photo)

Much of our wild car decoration is rooted in the Chicano or Latino culture or what Parker describes as how we "move through the landscape." "Whether you go fast or slow, it has to do with the use of a vehicle decorated to suit one's personal taste to move through the landscape of California and the Southwest." Parker has traced this tradition of decoration from the Sicilians of Southern Italy and later Chicanos picked it up from their Gypsy roots from southern Spain. In an extreme evolutionary way, these trends for stylized transportation are reflected in lowrider art. One of the first celebrated customizers, Nick Matranga most certainly brought his Latino background into his work.

*Sides...*

*Hood...*

*...and all over, a car that doubles as a gallery. (Author photo)*

Although there are subtle differences, customizers and hot rodders are part of the same world—but then there are "lowriders" to consider. Lowriders stand apart with their addition of hydraulics, use of late model cars, and abundance of chrome. But the paint is similar to that on custom cars; it's one of the things that brings all of these branches together. They may paint in different styles to get different effects, but they're using the same materials.

When guys started bucking back against their stale existence by creating their own visions, they used 1930s and 1940s late model automobiles. It must have had been a shocking reflection for normal people to see these radically cannibalized cars that used to look just like their own. It must have struck fear into their hearts and made them envious as hell. By bending metal, welding frames and removing chrome, you could express your creativity and customize your personal view of perfection.

As for the style of custom rods, the way back machine got turned on and seemed to be stuck around 1955. Models past that date aren't cool to chop or customize and '32s are often rodded in a 1950s style. Lowriders are slowly breaking out of this trend, using 1960s cars or even late model Nissan cars and trucks. Music and clothes, too, got cycled in the same time machine. The 1950s rockabilly and girls in Betty Page bad girl outfits abound. What could be frightening about this romantic look back is the return to the mores and ideals of the time. Like Robert Williams says, those times sucked, who wants to go back to them? Certainly not blacks or women – we had to fight hard to get out of the kitchens and take a seat at the front of the bus. We damn sure ain't gonna go to the back of the dragster.

For all of its detractions, the 1950s were a period of cool style, which can't be disregarded. Everything during that American era of power was strong—photography, fashion, wealth—we were admired worldwide. In our current environment that values efficiency over identity, style has gotten lost. We have to live with highly dispensable cookie cutter designs. In a new form of rebel stance, Southern California says, "wait a minute, what about style or individuality?." Hot rods and customs are the essence of what America is about. Freedom to do what you believe in. Ability to innovate. A platform to shake stuff up. We could say that the Pilgrims fled persecution to be able to come to a country where they could chop, channel, and soup their cars to their hearts' content. And you can see that it's striking a chord—when advertisers pick up on it, you know it's true. Flames, pinstriping and the Prowler are showing up in the most respectable commercials.

In another departure from the 1950s style regulations, multiculturalism struggles to exist. Lowriders in particular are a vibrant mix of Latinos, Asians and African-Americans. This stands in strong contrast to the hot rod, customized or racing world that is essentially white. There are always strong protests that racism doesn't exist, but as they say, if it walks like a duck and quacks like a duck…

Participants are slow to join the racing game because of how middle class American sees motor racing and the mechanic classes. Parker explains, "You've got this strange dissonance because it's other, it's outlaw, it's dangerous, it's in that forbidden territory. "Momma don't let your babies grow up to be race car drivers." And yet there are all of these other people, working class Americans and upper middle class and very wealthy Americans that absolutely love motor-racing." The "lowbrow" aspect of hot rods and custom cars attracts a heavily bohemian crowd as an environment where the combination of outlaw individualism and artistic freedom are expected. Artist Robert Williams and *Gearhead Magazine* publisher Mike LaVella are showing folks the way to get back to their greasy, trailer park roots—even if they never had any to begin with. When you embark on the project of building your own car, your hands get dirty, you often race illegally, and you learn to feel comfortable with your automobile's sinister profile and big, big sound. Suddenly you find yourself on the other side of what's seen as correct and proper and you're living in an enjoyable, self-made party.

*Seen in "Running Wild" (1956) and on the streets of LA, Sam Barris built this award-winning '51 Merc for Bob Hirohata. (George Barris photo)*

## CUSTOMIZERS

Artist/hot rodder, Robert Williams explained the hot rod, custom dichotomy to me: "A hot rod is the first cousin to a race car. It appeals to the testosterone of a male. A custom is a car for a lounge lizard. A custom car is for getting pussy. A hot rod is for keeping your mind off of it."

To customize a car is to change its looks, sometimes radically. The motor must run, obviously, but its performance is secondary to the looks of the car. In the same way that speed is about pure expression, lengthening, lowering or smoothing the line of a car is another form of communication. Simple customizing began with add-ons purchased from the local hardware store—a foxtail, some mirrors, lights, hood ornaments. Just as hot rodders took off any extraneous metal, customizers took off any extraneous details. They made Frankenstein-like creations by swapping bumpers, fenders and rear ends. Experimentation then continued with paint finishes and upholstery.

And just as going fast brought the wrath of the law, so did recreating a car. Stories abound of cops testing car clearance by having low cars drive over cigarette packs. Windshield height, license plate placement and any other modification outside of the ordinary was heavily scrutinized. It varied from the norm and therefore something had to be wrong. No matter that thousands of dollars were put into these cars, they looked too outlaw. Like race cars or hot rods, customs have attitude.

Customizers are not a singular group; there were many attacks and divisions. East Coast vs. West Coast, chrome vs. clean, classic vs. radical. And there are heroes. Two names closely associated with the beginnings of customizing are George and Sam Barris.

## SAM AND GEORGE BARRIS—KUSTOM KINGS

Want a car to match your socks? You can have that. How about removing all the chrome, extending the front end about three feet and installing a hidden bar behind the seat? Child's play. Imagine the mixture of real life and fantasy coming together in the automobile of your choice. Combine the childhood remembrance of your favorite uncle's car with your vision of space vehicles. Sometimes you see a hero's car in a movie equipped with the coolest features that just don't show up on the dealer list at your local shop. If that superhero is Batman or Dick Tracy, chances are his wheels were individualized by George Barris, the King of the Customizers.

Brothers Sam and George Barris were the first notables to re-design Detroit's output, establishing their personalized spin on every auto they touched. A 1936 Ford convertible was the first car the brothers enhanced while still high-schoolers in Sacramento, California. The Barris' restyled the car using parts from other cars. Their use of unique details—skirts over the rear tires, frenched license plate and push buttons replacing the door and trunk

George Barris and his most famous custom, the 1964 Batmobile. (George Barris collection)

handles—earned them customers. Like so many young men at the time, World War II interrupted their lives. Sam entered the merchant marine in 1943 and George moved to Los Angeles, opening a small shop the following year. Customizing was a growing trend, and upon Sam's return, the Barris brothers opened a new shop together. On the street, heads snapped to watch Barris beauties like Bob Hirohata's Mercury, Nick Matranga's coupe and the Golden Sahara show car cruise around the neighborhoods and freeways. Their work made Detroit car makers stretch to stay ahead of the brothers' vision of the future.

Innovations such as frenched details, floating grills, and Sam's early recognition of the Mercury as "the" car to chop are the Barris brothers' legacy. Functioning as a "talent agent," George managed cars for other owners to provide movie and TV productions with specific period vehicles in accurate styles and colors.

Frank Monteleone's Ford was featured in Allied Artists' "Hot Car Girl" (1956). (Allied Artists)

Since first supplying a custom '56 Ford convertible for the motion picture *Hot Rod Girl* (1957), George Barris delivered hot rods, customs and trick cars to keep movies and TV shows rolling in style. For an accident scene in Alfred Hitchcock's *North by Northwest* (1959), Barris replaced steel parts with easily crunchable panels in Cary Grant's Mercedes-Benz sports roadster and Eva Marie Saint's 1947 Ford. For *The Patsy* (1964), Barris designed a remote controlled car whose trunk, hood and doors all matched Jerry Lewis in a battle of the wits.

*The Many Loves of Doby Gillis, The Beverly Hillbillies, Daktari, Mannix* and even a modified Volkswagen for the kids' show, The Bugaloos featured Barris customized vehicles. Herman Munster drove the Munster Koach, a combination hot rod and stage coach. Later Grandpa Munster had his own ride, the Drag-u-la which Barris styled as a dragster/coffin/hot rod combination. For the first supercool Batmobile, Barris reworked the caped crusader's hot rod from a 1955 Lincoln Futura. Built in Italy, the Futura already boasted an unusual look that Barris modified by making it more bat-like. The interior held all the Bat stuff—laser gun controls, radios, TV, Batphones and the entire body could be slowed by Batchutes. The Batmobile was a highly visible and successful design for Barris. He made a mold from the original and built five copies which toured internationally. More recently Hollywood offerings *Dick Tracy* (1990), *Jurassic Park* (1993) and even *The Flintstones* (1994) have relied on Barris' automotive stylings.

During the past forty years the Barris operation has been a showroom for talented artists. "Jocko" Johnson, Bill Hines, Von Dutch, Dean Jeffries, and Larry Watson all spent creative time employed in the North Hollywood shop. The quality of Barris' work earned awards at events like the prestigious Oakland Roadster Show and put numerous cars on the covers of *Rod and Custom, Hot Rod* and *Car Craft*. The combination of magazine covers and entertainment contacts attracted luminaries to Barris looking for something special. Elvis wanted his Cadillac plushed out. Cher wanted her car to match her dress. They all got their dream cars, as did Liberace, Nancy Sinatra, Glen Campbell, Clint Eastwood, and many other people with a vision, but not necessarily a big name.

Customizers can pull a car's shape to match any vision. (Andy Takakjian photo)

The Barris' fame grew and extended to other products: model kit companies Revell and AMT distributed high selling plastic, do-it-yourself versions of the Barris' customs. In the height of the 1960s hot rod era, George even produced a record, *Kustom City U.S.A* by the Kustom Kings. The album cover featured award winning Barris customs, as did the album cover of *Little Deuce Coupe* by the Beach Boys and the Deuce Coupes' album, *The Shut Down*. In his free time, George formed a car club, Kustoms of Los Angeles, which later became Kustoms of America. Although his brother Sam died of cancer at an early age, Barris continues to assure the quality and innovation that earns the Barris crest in the window.

## JIM AND JIMMY BRUNS—A BRIDGE FROM 1950s TO THE FUTURE

I walked into their backyard shop knowing practically nothing. Since it was only nineteen days before their D-Day—the Paso Robles custom show—Jim and Jimmy (the senior and junior) Bruns were frantic in their backyard shop. There were several cars in different levels of progression; at least three were supposed to be completed before the trek up north. Within a couple of hours, the Bruns had given me the righteous knowledge that I could distinguish a chop from a channel, a suede from a metal flake, and most importantly, what's cool, from what sucks.

Jim Sr. first lived the hot rod style as a kid in Ohio. After his Marine Corps stint, he wandered out to California and got into the hot rod frame of mind all over again. His son, Jim Bruns, Jr. (Jimmy), is usually found alongside his dad in the backyard garage chopping, painting and dropping Mercs and other bodies for their customers. So far their business is part-time, but Jimmy loves to work on the cars for the "thrill" of catching the appreciative eye. Working together is also a huge bond between the two Bruns generations. Jimmy calls his dad his best friend who's taught him everything he knows.

Showing that some tastes run in a family, the Bruns built and drove matching '41 Fords. Jim Sr. had his first, and Jimmy liked his dad's convertible so much he went out and bought the same model in a coupe. After watching pro Gene Winfield chop the top on his other car (for a measly $4,500), Jimmy bought a welder and went at the Ford coupe himself. For the most part, the custom community is supportive; folks will tell you when your shit looks good, or when you have to go back

The Jims—car artists Jim Bruns, Jr. and Jim Bruns, Sr. (Sam Painter photo)

to school. They share tips with each other. It's work that the younger Bruns feels he'll never tire of. "When I get frustrated, the shop is where I come," explains Jimmy. "I like having these ideas and transforming them onto the car." He also has ideas of becoming a good metal man along the lines of Winfield or Barris. He wants to reach the level where his name is on a little logo on someone else's gracefully shaped car.

Jim Sr. had a chopped Ford he was getting ready for Paso. They kept telling me it's a custom, but that car looked like a hot rod to me. It was equipped with a full race motor because, "He likes to go fast," said his son, Jimmy. I'm still convinced that Jim Sr.'s car is a hot rod: rake, or not, I asked him why he named his car the Black Dahlia.

*Waiting for a makeover in the Bruns' backyard. (Author photo)*

"You know how they found that girl all chopped up?," says Jim Sr. in reference to the infamous Los Angeles murder case of 1947. "That's what this car is. All chopped up."

The elder Bruns looks like an outlaw from the past. He used to race at the now-defunct San Fernando Drag Strip. "I had a '37 Buick. I did no good," says Jim Sr. "All the guys with money beat me. A little guy can't do anything." Customizers face the same limitations racers do. If you have the money, you don't have the time, and visa versa. It takes dollars to whittle a car into the shape you dream about.

According to these guys, if you've see one hot rod, you've pretty much seen them all. That's what turned the Bruns into custom fans. They felt hot rods look more or less the same, maybe they have different paint jobs but the traditional T bucket, highboy stylings were too limiting for them. With custom cars everybody wants something different; they strive to out-imagine the other guy. These days you'll find customizers on the high tech track; they add air conditioning, power steering, well, according to Jimmy, they want too much of that. "I like to keep my '36 all pretty well original," says Jimmy. "I just put a '50 Merc motor in it. I like everything the way it was in the '50s."

Just as the '32 Ford was the car of choice for hot rodders, the Merc is the shit for customizers. The Barris brothers showed folks what could be done with they built their first "right" model in 1949, and since then Mercurys became the customizers dream for their futuristic, smooth look. Chop the top and remove the chrome and you're in business, daddy. That ultimate evil looking Mercury body was only produced for a short while—1949 to 1951, to be exact. Oh, there're some Mercurys sitting around—in fields and old ladies' garages—but folks don't want to get rid of them. That was their husband's car, or their grandfather's car and they want to keep it. Since the preferred Merc body is near impossible to find, some people buy the sedan model, remove the two rear doors and shorten the entire car to make it into a coupe. Some folks, either tired of the look of chopped Mercs, or disgusted with the lack of availability of bodies, have taken to customizing anything else, like Oldsmobiles, Buicks, Chevys or shoebox Fords.

Simply take a photograph, or a book or an idea to an artist, and your dream car is on the way to becoming a reality. The artist puts it on paper, which gives the customizer plans to work by. Be it extending the rear quarters to accommodate Packard tail lights or taking different parts off of different cars, it's all kosher. This tendency to switch fenders, grills, motors or rear ends is a telling difference between customizers and traditional hot rod fans. Those lovers of the big and littles, tuck and roll upholstery and louvered hoods on their '32 Highboys can be sticklers about matching motors to bodies to gauges to paint color, and on and on till yer sick of 'em. That and the size of the engine. No sense in dropping a race motor into a car that rides two inches off the ground. Here's a novice's tip to instantly tell the difference between the two styles—Does it lean forward, or does it lean back?. "A hot rod is jacked up usually, it's got a rake to it, big and little whitewalls, a loud motor," explains Jimmy. "A custom's the other way around. It's draggin' in the back, it's laying on the ground. It's got a sleek and evil look to it."

*Jim Burns Sr.'s Black Dahlia gets new paint for the Paso Robles show. (Author photo)*

It may sound easy, but there's a lot of work to get lowered to the ground. You've got to cut the whole center out of the car—that's called tunneling. By putting a V notch into the frame, a space is made to accommodate the drive shaft, so it doesn't rub against the lowered frame. Then there's channeling, where you cut the floor out and cut the body over the frame. Then you slide the body down. Another favorite is sectioning, but

*The Bruns, Special Guests of Honor at the 4th annual Blessing of the Cars. (Author photo)*

not too many people section a car anymore. That's where you take a piece out of the middle of the car and bring the front and rear pieces together to shorten the body.

These steel bodies take a craftsman's trained hands to coax futuristic shapes from 1950's ideas. Says Jim Sr., there aren't too many people who've mastered the fine art of metal work. "Anybody can put the bondo on. But if you've got to add metal here or there or take it away and put another piece on it…" I get it, you're in trouble. Especially when it comes to finding lead. Due to the environmental poisoning attributed to lead, state law requires a license to get it. This, of course, bugs the custom guys. "They outlawed everything we need," complains Jimmy. Jim Sr. adds that because of the lead in lacquer paint, you can't get that in California either. Although customers want wide choices in paint, the Environmental Protection Agency has restricted the use of lacquer and polyurethane. Which is almost a death knell to the classic Kandy Kolors, which require a toxic base and a color coat. They're adjusting, of course, says Jimmy, who's just finished his first paint job with new water borne paints, "Now you've got to buy a base and use a concentrate that you mix in with the new clear coat that they're using. None of the old guys like the new stuff that's coming out, so they stick to the old stuff." The outlawed paint is still available out-of-state, and at a much higher price. If the demand exists, it'll be used more often than the slower drying, new alternative.

As in any other division of automobile fanaticism, trends are fully embraced or recognized as passé with regularity. Sueding (which uses various colors of preparation paint—primer) is enjoying its popularity as I write this, and may be considered terribly late-90s as you read this. It's really a clever idea to cover your car in primer paint. Once your baby's primered you can drive it around and not worry about it. If you get a dent, oil primer is easier to touch up. Any of the fancy paint techniques can be done in primer—scallops, flames, two tones—it all looks good. Then, when you're ready to change for a glossy paint job, you don't have to go back to do a lot to get paint on it— because it's already primered!

Lack of bodies, lead and paint are not the only current differences in creating a classic custom car. There are innovations as well. On the East Coast, cars that have to deal with salt in the winter and rust in the summer are pleased as pie to be constructed of fiberglass. Although that shit don't fly out here in sunny California. The snobby, trained eye can immediately tell the difference between 'glass and metal.

Some of these lead (or 'glass) sleds are everyday drivers, and that two inch clearance doesn't work well on the road. But airbags help. Not to protect your life, but to protect your ride. "If you get a flat tire, you'd be stuck on the ground," explains Jimmy. "The police don't want that because you're stuck there and you're gonna back up traffic."

Some people put in airbags and hydraulic suspensions to avoid such a catastrophe, others do it in a pseudo-attempt at being law-abiding (in California that legally equates to your car riding as high as your wheel rims). Like the lowriders in East LA, they arrive at a car show, and lower the car, when they leave they simply raise the car again and have a legal and cushioned ride home. Add your disc brakes and power steering and that 1951 Merc will cruise with all the luxuries of a new car.

Another difficult task with the car of your dreams is to keep it street legal. Actually, if you have anything that's a variation of a 1955 or before, you're in good shape. Just go to the DMV and register it. So tiny windshields, or even no windshields, don't worry; you've got time on your side. Unless you go to Downey, California, as Jim Sr. says. "The cops escorted me out of Downey. He couldn't get his foot under my running board." I guess hot rods still have a bad reputation—wherever you go.

Add chrome, a suede finish and a lowered profile, and that classic ride becomes a sinister custom. (Andy Takakjian photo)

Once you're chopped, lowered, painted and flamed, you've got to go show off somewhere. That's why car shows exist. One of the coolest is the Oakland Roadster show. It's existed since 1949, and is the place to see and be seen for a custom car. When big name customizers charge folks $50 an hour, and you spend as much as $80,000 on a car, you want folks to see and admire it. If lookers like what they see, that pays too. Jim Sr. says, "If you get some top honor at the Oakland Roadster Show, then the value of your car automatically jumps up to $25,000 or $30,000." But to get into Oakland is a process. You send in pictures of your car, then a committee decides if you're good enough to enter and if you're good enough to sit in the main arena. If you get into the main arena and you win something in Oakland, it's a big deal to a lot of people. With that winning trophy, you can get paid endorsements, or your car can end up in ads. When a builder's car wins, then people think, "hey, if this guy is good enough to win in Oakland, then he knows his business." "All the big custom guys build a car almost every year," explains Jimmy. "A new car for somebody. Even if it's not their car, its got their name on it." People go to Oakland to look at the cars, and leave their customs at home. If your car's not in the arena, you have to leave it in the parking lot where no one gets to admire it; you might as well leave it home. It's nothing like driving your baby to Paso.

The three day event in Paso Robles is another great custom car show. Paso is a little town about 3.5 hours north of Los Angeles, mostly famous for being the place James Dean died when he crashed his speeding Porche Spyder on the dark highway outside of town. What the show in Paso Robles offers is a chance for custom guys to cruise, legally (cities in states from Delaware to California now enforce anti-cruising laws). It's also a place where participants can just sit and admire the work of their friends and to steal a few ideas.

As at the Oakland Roadster Show, there are plenty of trophies to pick up in Paso. They pick the best custom car, the best under construction that's not finished, best paint job, best flames, you name it. On Friday night they block the whole street off in Paso and cars cruise from six to ten; there's an all day show on Saturday and on Sunday people leave. Paso Robles is getting big right now; all the customizers know about it. They have three Paso Robles shows; one in May, one on Labor Day weekend, and the James Dean Run. "Paso's a beautiful town," says Jimmy. "You get in your car and go up there and get away from everything for the weekend. Everybody meets there; all the big guys in customizing and the little guys."

These car shows are important for yet another reason, it's where the old guys pass on their secrets and enthusiasm to the younger generation. The young guys are the ones who will keep some of the old ideas, work within current laws and EPA hoo-ha to create their visions of tomorrow. Eventually the Mercurys and the Fords are gonna be gone, and the youngsters will have to move to Chevys and, who knows, Toyotas and Hondas before the hobby dies out. But as long as they have backyards to work in, and ideas to express, they will continue to work with their fathers and share the interest of generations.

## BLESSING OF THE CARS—ANSWERING THE PRAYERS OF CAR LOVERS IN SoCAL

Since 1991, Stephanie and Gabriel Baltierra have provided a Southern Californian showcase for the elements of outlawouthful vigor. The husband and wife team expertly chopped and channeled an existing Mexican-Catholic tradition, then stripped and primered a bureaucratically-fucked up mess. The BOTC, as the Baltierras refer to it, is a recent addition to the parade of car shows that has grown and waned since their inception in the 1950s. But explaining the BOTC as a car show is like describing a hot rod as a fast car. Its beauty lies in the combination of enthusiasm and varied interests that each participant brings to the display under the trees in a Southern California park.

The highly dramatic Father Charles Lueras. (Elena Ray photo)

BOTC could be described as having a circus-like atmosphere—there's something for everybody. It is first and foremost, a display of automobiles. The qualifications for showing a vehicle are broad, it must simply be a pre-1968. What ends up sprawled on the lawn is a grocery list of early 1960s Cadillacs, Nashs, Mercurys and various permutations of the old stand-by—Ford Model Ts or As. The Baltierras designed the BOTC in this way so car clubs like the long term Road Kings would amiably rub shoulders with the young purple hairs of the hearse club who are parked near the East LA Chopmasters who chat with classic car owners. Sometimes the car clubs have specialties, whether it's customizing or painting, or classics. It's all in good spirits, and as Gabriel says, "the old timers have to deal with all these kids, talking to some who don't know anything." By lending an ear, the older guys learn that some of the young car enthusiasts do, in fact, know what they're talking about and it becomes a common area of interest. The old guy gets listened to, and the young kid learns something.

These conversations and mutual admiring are encircled by sounds from the stage. Sometimes it's rockabilly, sometimes it's surf and sometimes it's straight on punk. But one thing for sure, it's always there. Finding friends to play the BOTC is a happy task for the Baltierras. They find the inclusion of music makes everything mellow and comfortable. And it's expected. As long as people have been parking their cars to show them off, there's been a musical soundtrack to entertain the crowd. The look that Stephanie craves for the show is slightly retro, resembling the car shows her father and uncles took her to as a young child, where cars sat in displays of colored gravel with matching ribbons. Musically, the Baltierras book contemporary sounds. Says Stephanie, "we aren't trying to copy something that happened a long time ago." Looking at the stage, it's hard to believe that statement. Trophy girls, attired in 1950s style sun-suits, depart the stage and are replaced by a trio sporting greased DAs, cuffed blue jeans, and white t-shirts, with one member who thumps an upright bass to the rockabilly beat. Fashion choices aside, the bands—El Vez, the Bomboras, the Ghastly Ones, Whistle Bait, Doorslammer—are all young and often hot rod enthusiasts.

BOTC organizers, Stephanie and Gabriel Baltierra. (Andy Takakjian photo)

A smorgasbord of color dances from the cars' paint jobs, to the hair colors of the viewers, to the art gallery containing work from people who paint on hot rods to painters who work on canvas. The artist's touch is evident in the expertly flamed or pinstriped cars that are admired by owners and wannabe owners. So much so that there are awards for Best Flames and Best Paint Job, which are voted on by each person who enters a car into the show. The trends in color become noticeable—kandy kolors, metalflakes and suedes. Even the suedes—a form of matte finished primer paint—have variations such as flames in suede

The Blessing of the Cars offers tunes from the Ghastly Ones' deadly surf...
(Author photo)

...to Doorslammer's drag-punk.
(Melanie Bruck photo)

or gloss over the suede. The idea started the way many do, someone realized that primer is cheap. For the artists who may have never painted a car of their own, there is always a wreck of a paint-it-yourself car on the premises for anybody to try their hand.

The BOTC presented by the Baltierras is vastly different from the event that Gabriel first witnessed as a child in Mexico. There he saw people in flowered covered cars pull up to the church and a priest came out to bless them. Aiming for multicultural diversity, the city of Los Angeles decided to continue the Catholic tradition. However, the city organizers ran smack into the Constitution of the United States. The city's office of Cultural Affairs fashioned a separation of church and state that resulted in a Blessing of the Cars, with no actual blessing. When Stephanie and Gabriel discovered the fractured city event, it had turned into a badly attended mini-truck show. They did some research and in 1991 presented their own BOTC. Although neither is religious, the BOTC takes on a spiritual significance. As Stephanie says, "If you put the action out there, then maybe something is gonna hold that extra bolt on your engine. I believe that everyone convenes in one place and there's a certain amount of energy created and something happens with that."

Prayers against "tickets, dings, scrapes and random vandalism" are imparted by either the Elvis look-alike, Father Charles Lueras, or the bearded, long-haired, skateboarding Father Glen Sequiera. Father Charles was the first priest the Baltierras enlisted to bless the car show. Finding him was like a miracle following the grumpy reception that other area priests had offered them. "Father Charles is so into this event," says Stephanie. "He was in a band in the '60s. He had an awakening in the early '70s that made him become a priest. He makes religion very approachable. When we met him, he grabbed our hands, joined them together and said a blessing. He got really excited when we told him what we wanted to do. He pulled out this huge book of blessings that are sanctioned by the church. There are blessings for strip malls, blessings for freeway overpasses, there's blessing for everything. So he showed us the blessing for the cars, which is really cool." Father Charles performs the church sanctioned blessing trailing smoking incense, sprinkling holy water and wearing gold flamed vestments made by Gabriel's mom. Stephanie adds, "It's not just for the cars, it's for friends and family who enter the car, or ride in the car." The crowd, even those who describe themselves as atheists, love it. The extra protection could be the difference between a near miss and a new paint job. And the priests have fun as well. "I think there's a certain sense of competition among priests, a certain sense of politics," says Stephanie. "I think that Father Charles, given his background, really loves the press and an audience and the attention. He loves performing and getting into it."

The dribbling of holy water is fascinating to more than the crowd that gathers in the park to watch first hand. Australian newspapers, *Spin Magazine,* MTV, and the local press are all over the BOTC like the exciting event that it is. Drawing a crowd as diverse as car lover and *Tonight Show* host Jay Leno and psychobilly performers Ivy Rorschach and Lux Interior of the Cramps fame, the car show is press ready. The Baltierras are proud of their baby, warts and all and bristle at the inanities they have to deal with. "There's a magazine that wanted us to put this spin on the show that it's a white show. My husband's Latin, I'm white and part black, and I was like, what are they talking about? The whole deal is that there's something that happens when people come together around things like cars and art and music. A lot of different types of people can come together and we have this neutral object they can start to talk about." That goal of mixing is deftly accomplished—the most recent BOTC drew nearly 1,000 cars and 2,000 spectators. And cleared a profit for the first time in it's seven year infancy, which was a pleasant surprise for the Baltierras, "We take in money from registrants and advertising, but it really doesn't cover the expenses of the show. We usually end up eating the expenses. It doesn't fall into peoples' categories. It's either too funky for traditional car people or not funky enough for other people. Then we have the art gallery and that throws things off. The event encompasses a huge group of people — everyone from little kids with their families, to really old people, to guys with shaved heads and tattoos, to people with mohawks, to the old traditional hot rodders."

Father Glen Sequiera steps off his skateboard to bless cars in the park. (Author photo)

"We're really into old cars and always have been. Gabriel fell in love with cars when he was little and in my early memories my dad was taking apart a '57 Chevy. All of my uncles raced. I grew up in the white trash community and cars are a big deal there. You've got your trailer, you've got your car." The BOTC reflects their personal history in the mix of music and art. In college Gabriel fell into a group of poets. He produced a cable TV show with music, poetry and spoken word, then later began to present poetry readings in unusual settings—LA's downtown subway and local laundromats. Stephanie's early presentation experience took the form of punk rock shows. They were illegal, because they lacked permits, but what do you expect from a group of 13, 14 and 15 year olds? Stephanie remembers, "I don't think we ever had a show that somebody didn't get carried out of. But it was more exciting that way."

Now their excitement is in the year-round wrangling of a car show that threatens to bust its britches in a very short time. Immediately following the show in July, the Baltierras find themselves heavy into preparation for the next show. Finding sponsors, obtaining insurance, contacting car clubs, commissioning trophies from various artists, tracking press and printing t-shirts and programs begins as soon as the last car drives away from the park. It's time consuming, but the Baltierras think it's worth it because of the huge resurgence taking place in hot rodding and racing.

Whether people choose to restore cars to their original state, or add new facets, it's still an art form. Stephanie describes the work a friend's doing on an old Eastern European beauty, "He was a real purist. Everything he has was done exactly the way it used to be. He can't go to the store and pull something off of the shelf, he hand crafts everything. So, in that sense, there's a true art form and individuality to it." Then in what seems to be a direct opposite, she describes the work of another artist, "One of the great things with Coop's Ford is he's painted the eyeball and the flames. He's added his own artistic style into it. To me that's two totally different aspects of the same thing. Cars are the last American folk art. That's what's happening. We're not painters or sculptors, but we are when it comes to our car." Gabriel adds, "Whether or not you do the work yourself, you're putting a part of yourself into each car, especially when you're talking about hot rods and customizing.

The Baltierra's enjoying the BOTC. (Author photo)

So that's how they shape and highlight their customized event. The Blessing of the Cars is a big show because it has to present all of its elements. As Stephanie says, "we feel that the music, the cars, the art, the people—it's all part of a subculture. They all influence one another and exist because the others exist."

## LOWRIDERS—WHAT ME HURRY?

Using automobiles as expression breaks down to Hot Rods as Mean, Customs as Cool, and Lowriders…? Well, lowriders, like these other automotive expressions, have a mixed bag going on. Like the Eskimo word for snow, "lowrider" is a complex term. It can refer to the magazine, the bikes, or the female models. Lowrider is a cultural style and a person who drives the car. It's indicative of a style of custom heavy in chrome and sporting sensational paint jobs. But most specifically it refers to huge, impeccably decorated 1960s Impalas nearly scraping the asphalt as they leisurely cruise the boulevard leaving admiring onlookers in their wake.

Zoot suits at the lowrider show.
(Andy Takakjian photo)

The guys who later created the distinctive lowrider style began attracting attention to themselves in the 1930s. That's when groups of young Chicano "Pachucos" in Chicago, El Paso and East LA took to wearing zoot suits. Black kids dressed in bright colors and wore huge fedoras, while Chicanos tended toward long chains and big pompadours. They were bold, and they were in your face, so when street racers raked their cars to the front to go fast, Pachuco's raked theirs to the back just to be assholes.

The availability of cheap, old cars following World War II kick-started the lowrider movement, in the same way it did for hot rodders. Mexican American veterans returned home and thanks to the GI bill, had more money than they had traditionally made before they went to war. And just as the car of choice for racers was the Ford, lowriders snagged all the Chevys. They were less expensive and they could haul around a larger family. Impalas are the lowrider canvas of choice, it has long sleek lines, and jaunty fins. Often it was some well-off white family's car handed down to the Mexican family maid.

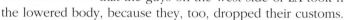

Belly-rubbing lowrider at a car show. (Amy Hobby photo)

For a lot of these guys it was the first time they owned their own car. It was a source of pride and respect. For a group of people who struggled to earn money in a newly affluent society, earning respect was important. The image of a clean, beautifully painted car helped achieve that status. Part of this new independence was doing whatever you wanted, and these guys wanted to drop their cars. It's obvious that the guys on the west side of LA took note of the cool attitude of the lowered body, because they, too, dropped their customs.

The lower the cars got, the harder it was to maneuver them. The cars cornered like anchored boats. Cops hassled drivers, concocting tests that required lowriders to clear at least four inches. A young Mexican American lowrider from San Bernardino, Ron Aguirre, figured an innovative way around these problems. He installed hydraulics from the wing flaps of B52s, modified the cylinders to run on twelve volts and installed a hand pump which he operated from the driver's seat. Whenever he was stopped for riding too low, the cop would walk over to the car, measure it, and it'd check out. As the cop walked away, Aguirre would pump it down again and baffle the cop. He wowed everyone with his innovative hydraulics at a show at the Long Beach Auditorium in 1959. Soon black kids in South Central and Chicanos in East LA were rushing out to hydraulically modify their cars.

Lowrider, the car style, as well as the magazine, have enjoyed periods of popularity and times of neglect. Custom car building among Chicanos is again on the raise, as evidenced by the fact that *Lowrider* magazine is the nation's highest selling newsstand publication. As Mexican Americans moved outside of the Southwestern states, lowriding clubs surfaced in Indiana, Tennessee and even Hawaii. What began as a measure of ethnic pride, now includes anyone with the desire to win admirers with a flashy vehicle. Car clubs in Japan, obsessed with American culture, buy imported Impalas to cruise with their own lowriding clubs.

These slow and low cars have money dumped into them for modifications, but performance isn't what the owners are interested in. They desire opulence. Reflecting traditional Chicano art's extensive use of murals, lowriders are often covered in scenes based in fantasy or real life. Gleaming multicoats of metal flake and showroom shiny finishes are lovingly buffed at shows. Chromed everything has given way to 24K gold plated everything—engines, chassis, rims—anything made of metal is apt to be given the Midas touch. Symbolic of the owner achieving a higher status in life, the interiors are packed with every creature comfort. Thick velvet upholstery, overstuffed reclining and swiveling seats, plush carpeting, TVs, bars and eardrum busting sound systems are fit into car that may offer more comforts than home. To hot rodders from the "take it off" school, this is gaudy and excessive, but to a lowrider's keen eye, it says that the owner has arrived, that they can afford the finer things in life. It commands respect.

Another reflection of the finer things in life are the well-endowed, bikini wearing models that often pose alongside of the cars. These women are all over the pages of the *Lowrider* magazines, at every car show and riding in the passenger seat when the cars cruise the neighborhoods. To other women who've fought hard to earn respect with their clothes on, this may seem to be a step back. Having once been an exotic dancer, *Lowrider* writer Paige Penland understands the freedom these non-professional models are experiencing. They've taken possession of their bodies and their images, and can display themselves if they want and no one can tell them not to. They too, earn respect at car shows and make appearances in magazines.

Much of the lowrider involvement has a political edge to it. The magazine, with its distribution of 230,000 offers the only nationwide forum for concerns of young Chicanos. "El Larry" Gonzales and David Nunez started *Lowrider* magazine in the 1970s, with the intention of informing Atzlan (as many Chicanos call the Southwestern United States). One reporter, Roberto Rodriguez was beaten by cops for offering complete coverage of lowrider cruises. A large number of lowrider enthusiasts enjoy their hobby from behind bars in prisons across the country. The political aspect of the magazine and movement allow them to voice an opinion when they may feel shut out. The name itself may come from a more political time, when following Los Angeles' Watts riots in 1965, black men often took out the seats of their cars to keep their heads low and possibly avoid any stray activist and/or police bullets.

While looking a world apart, hot rods, lowriders and customs still share many of today's problems. They all cherish American early model cars that are getting near impossible to find. Misunderstood by local law enforcement agents, showing off your car by cruising around is out and out illegal. While so many people build their fast cars or slow cars to use as everyday drivers, more car shows are being dominated by "trailer queens." Owners who baby their cars, moving them from garage to trailer to show and back again, are unwanted pests at many car shows. Lowrider events attempt to flush out these undesirables by requiring that the car be able to drive in and out of the show. Many years ago, hot rodders were seen as hooligans when in fact, they were mostly over-enthusiastic young kids. Lowriders today face those same unfounded fears. Young men from outside neighborhoods could just as easily be called clubs instead of the connotation-heavy term "gang."

You'd never catch a lowered Merc or a fast rod dancing; that's strictly lowriding "hopper" territory. Cars and trucks with heavy duty hydraulics are designed to "dance" as the operator stands outside of the car and makes the car hop and skip using a hand pump. Because these cars have a much more rugged lifestyle, they have a minimal showing of gloss, and a trunk full of batteries to provide them power. During competition, the front end may bounce to almost two feet high, or the entire car could dance in a circle, alternately lifting each of its tires off the ground. Another unusual and growing division is the "bed dancer" sect. These are usually mini-trucks chopped and fitted with scissor lifts so that the bed may raise up and spin, as does the cab or doors. Watching the operator put these vehicles through the motions, you might think you're watching a ride at the amusement park.

The hobby continues to attract new players. And like anybody working with available cars, they're turning to import cars. Mazdas and Hondas are much easier to get than Impalas or 1960s Cadillacs. *Lowrider* continues to be a needed forum for the people.

Chrome—hot rodders shave it off and lowriders slather it on. (Andy Takakjian photo)

Models at shows get as many looks as the cars. (Paige Penland photos)

A trunk full of batteries and heavy duty hydraulics allow this "hopper" to dance. (Paige Penland photos)

Recognizing its responsibility to the community, *Lowrider* stresses education and offers annual scholarships. A growing aspect of lowriding is lowrider bikes. They are heavily gold plated, chopped, painted and often feature plush upholstery like the grown up versions, but usually they're built by kids, honing their skills for when they can earn respect and continue the tradition of going low and slow in a lowrider of their own.

## HOT ROD GIRLS—MAKING THE OLD STYLE THEIR OWN

Breaking out in the 1950s as a youthful force to be reckoned with, kids, newly christened as "teenagers," found ways to identify themselves. Like souped up cars, clothes became an identifying mark of free thinkers. The look for guys—cuffed blue jeans, white t-shirts, engineer boots, greased pompadours—has survived the decades and is readily seen at car shows and tracks today. Track women often sport that white bread mall look—overdone makeup, blow dried bleached blonde coifs, tight fitting jeans and gaudy tee shirts. Then like a breath of recycled air you might spot a vixen in pedal pushers, blood red lipstick and heavily sprayed pincurls. These stylish women are the living embodiment of the hot rod/racing/custom credo—beautiful, efficient, no holds barred and in your face. A random survey of these fashion throwbacks/trend setters revealed strong personal style and a need for fun.

Hidden away in an Southern Californian animation studio, Mary Pagone makes herself known when she steps out on the street. She finds the "sensitive line" of post WWII clothing flattering to the female form. All those darts, pleats and cuts in dresses,

Mary Pagone and Rochelle Bassarer. (Sam Painter photo)

suits and pants accentuate the natural figure eight shape and is, as Mary says, a great icebreaker in meeting men. Unlike today's factory made, planned obsolescent components, earlier designers offered an abundance of eye pleasing, well made fashions. Mary's background as a graphic designer and character animator naturally lead her to appreciate the design elements in everything she surrounds herself with—1930s to 1960s clothing, 1950s furniture and her love for 1950s cars.

Stepping out of her friend's flamed Studebaker truck, or her own '64 Falcon, Rochelle Bassarer also turns heads with her mixed era beatnik look. She understands the reliability of a new car, but can't see herself in one. Neither can Josie Kruezer who pilots a '62 Valiant. She says she doesn't race, but the highway patrolman who clocked Josie at over 100 mph would disagree. Josie's CD, *Hot Rod Girl* explains how she sees herself, as do the 1940s and 1950s style clothes she wears.

Just as hot rods appeal to some women, customs are the way that Treetie Hampton likes to go. Only she likes to go in the custom Riviera that she's building herself. Even putting in shop time doesn't keep her out of her self-described "five oh slash nineties" style. While other women hedge on pinpointing their style, Kina Stewart names it head on—vintage with a 1950s Grease influence. All of these Hot Rod Girls get their influences from those wild and glamorous years, but where they take the look is stunningly individual.

Their look is their lifestyle. Vintage gems have to be searched out. Mary makes a point of visiting little thrift and vintage stores wherever she travels. *I Love Lucy* and the polished look of 1940s and 1950s starlets made deep impressions on all of these women. Mary can remember watching *The Donna Reed Show* for fashion tips and Lucy, not for plot lines, but to see what she was wearing. Lucille Ball was also an inspiration to Treetie. Having fun is utmost, says Kina, the more cheesy the look, the better. She complains that too many people take the clothes, cars and scene way too seriously—consequently striving to look and act cool makes them somewhat petty.

Developing a love of these styles is one thing, but recreating them takes a lot of experimentation. Old magazines and even etiquette books give hints on how to achieve the 1950s smartness with 1990s tools. As a make up artist, Treetie's got a foot up on technique. Kina asks her grandma for tips. Even then, it takes time. Kina has refined her curling and pinning operation from it's original hour plus to less than ten minutes. Rochelle, taken by Marlene Detrich's brows, discovered that shaving hers then drawing on the famous arch worked just fine.

Being this glamorous doesn't come easily, it's very high maintenance. But like the work put into a fine custom car, making a statement takes time. Sometimes what these fashion denizens are saying is confused by the man on the street. As Treetie says, people think they can come up and touch her at will. Or Kina says in her small town, they don't know what to think, but they've gotten used to seeing her all dolled up in the grocery store. Older women approach Mary to tell her she looks so cute in her doo rag. It reminds them of what they wore when they worked in the airport hangars supporting the war effort. But perhaps the best attention it brings is from the Hot Rod Boys.

Josie Kruezer.
(Josie Kruezer collection)

Guys look good on the arm of women with style, "Especially ones that you don't have to help. They're already done," explains Mary. "There's something sexy and admirable and cool about that whole delinquent look that came from another time." Her purist sense is attracted to the few manly details—a cool bowling shirt or a white t-shirt with some nice old Levis. But anyone who pays lots of attention to the way they look, may not have as much going on under the surface. Kina recognizes it's great to be around these good-looking hot rod boys, but they're usually more fun to look at than to keep.

Aside from their flair for style, there's another similarity between these women; in their previous fashion lives they all dressed in extreme punk rock clothes. As their musical tastes widened, so did their taste in clothes. The rigors of dressing in ripped clothes and drawing looks for sporting dyed ink-black hair was perfect preparation for a switch to pedal pushers and pushup bras. Their newer sleeker look doesn't necessarily translate to tamer musical tastes. They all fessed up to a love of psychobilly—bands like the Cramps and Reverend Horton Heat. And like their love of mixing of eras, these gals mix their music as well. Harry Balafonte, Portishead, blues, Motown, jazz and even some rockabilly are on their turntables and CD players. In an obvious ode to her love of rockabilly, Josie's new CD is entitled *My Way Or The Highway—Rockabilly or Bust*.

It is plainly obvious that cars are a common interest between these women. The look of them, the scene around them, the guys who drive them and the feel of that metal has seduced these women since they were kids. Treetie tracks her interest to her first car ride ever, coming home from the hospital in a late '60s GTO. Mary used to hang in the garage with her dad as he restored cars, and later they bought her first dream car, a '66 Mustang. Back in Iowa, Rochelle's grandpa took her along to the track, and instilled in her an early love of racing. Songs about highways and cars show up in Josie's music, because that's what motivates her.

Kina Stewart.
(Jack C. Stewart photo)

And while they adore most of the trappings of the 1950s deal, returning to the past attitudes just wouldn't fly. Don't be mistaken, these are 1990s women in retro drag.

Women musicians didn't start to achieve respect until the 1960s or 1970s and you couldn't pay Josie to return to the days when the clothes she wears were contemporary. Maybe revisiting chivalry is worth a try, because as Rochelle points out, she's already done the 1990s thing of supporting a man, so it's nice to see the reverse again. Maybe finding a hot daddy who's got the money so you can stay home, redecorate and choose new fabrics for the house sounds attractive, but Mary prefers somebody with their mind firmly in today. She's self-reliant and independent and doesn't want anybody to tell her she's got to perfect her pot roast.

Guys too, like Michael Farr and Dan Collins, have updated the '50s hot rod style. (Andy Takakjian photo)

Treetie Hampton. (Sam Painter photo)

## WAGONS OF STEEL—GROCERY GETTERS GO RACING

Drag racing generally shouts youth and virility. Station wagons do not. Except to a choice few. And for that few there's a 'zine—*Wagons of Steel.* In probably the same sort of twist of taste that makes someone crave latex as erotic, Chris Barnes has decided that Mopar station wagons are his racing vehicle of choice.

Gaffo F. Jones, Barnes' alter ego, got his drag race cherry popped on his 29th birthday. Like the rest of us, he was hooked. "I thought 'that's what I want to do when I grow up'. It brought so many aspects of the car hobby together. I've always been drawing pictures of station wagons and writing about shoestring, seat of the pants kind of culture and it seemed to dovetail with the drag racing thing."

The promise of autonomy in sportsman racing appeals to Gaffo. He has no qualms about building, racing and paying for his own speeding bulk. Racing is an expensive hobby. It drains the pocket, whether you are turning low 4s or dial in your handicap in the low 13s. He sells his designs on t-shirts through the 'zine and also while he's at the track. But he also figured the most realistic way to deal with the costs was to find a sponsor, and in order to keep his wagon zipping down the drag strip, that's what Gaffo did. The local Mopar dealer helps him with parts, the guy who built his motor gives him advice and his local auto parts store paid for his paint job. Like other low buck guys, Gaffo's found a way to keep his '64 Valiant wagon competitive. Now, the performance he's achieved may be his biggest enemy. "Things kept breaking. I'm going faster and faster. I finally realized that putting a 4,700 pound car in the 13s is like putting a Dodge Dart into the 11s. You start breaking things when you cross certain barriers."

These same realizations were dealt with by other racers in the 1960s. Dan Dvorak got his '62 and '63 Dart wagons into the 12s in Florida in the late sixties. His wagons were the Lawman I and II, which even had the opportunity to run against each other. *WOS* has also heard from a group of Chrysler engineers that raced from 1959 through 1967 as the Plymouth Golden Commandos. They were a factory-sponsored team who were excited to read *WOS* and know that folks were still up to the challenge of getting these monsters down the track, fast.

The 'zine didn't used to be about racing, Gaffo started it in 1991 after laying out $200 for the Plymouth Valiant station wagon that he

- Tool Substitution Guide
- Magazine Reviews
- Stinky Trees
- Big T-Shirt

WAGONS OF STEEL MAGAZINE

HIGHWAY 10 MPG WHO CARES?

#10

IT'S SO BIG!

(Artist, Chris Barnes)

ultimately fell in love with. Love of racing followed the love of the cars. This unusual affection is, perhaps, not so unusual if the letters *WOS* gets are any indication. "All different kinds of people respond to it. It's the most exciting part about it and it keeps me doing it." The stands often empty out when the slower sportsman classes run at the national races, but I must be overlooking those people who can identify with the slower cars barreling down the track. "People always call them grocery getters and mom mobiles

Chris Barnes powering his WOS bulk down the drag strip. (Mike Bumbeck photo)

and things that aren't really meant in a positive way. It's not totally negative, it's not like calling it a piece of shit, but they don't look at it as a performance victory." That old idea of getting this hulking piece of machinery to perform better than another person's hulk is appealing to a growing number, even if the speeds are less than stellar. Gaffo finds that lots of people are running wagons. He doesn't meet them under the tree, however—they're all faster than him. "There's a Nova wagon running in the 10s. The Chevy wagons also come out of the box so much lighter than mine that they're all running in the 13s."

Racing wagons? Why not? There are more built every year, soon all these sport utility vehicles will be pacing themselves alongside. WOS may be riding the wave of popularity. Like any other baby boomer fascination, enthusiasts are reminded of a kinder, gentler period in their lives. "Everyone's got these crazy stories about station wagons," says Gaffo. "They say 'My mom had one just like that. It used to dust the neighbors Camaro.' They generate so many cool stories. Which is kind of the reason I got into the magazine." Talking about wagons is a comforting turn from the self-proclaimed "red flag waving liberal freakazoid" politics that Chris Barnes used to spout. Now, instead of relating nasty stories about Reagan and other low lifes, he gets "nice stories" about wagons. Lots of them. "I think that in all aspects of car hobbies, station wagons are becoming more and more popular. The same way that shoeboxy Chevys are popular because they don't make them anymore. You see wagons less and less, which makes them more interesting." So interesting that each issue of his small photocopied 'zine is sold and distributed to 500 people hot off the presses. There is also a high demand for back issues, requiring Gaffo and wife, Natalie, to reissue most of the 12 volumes.

Chris Barnes gets cozy with a race sponsor. (Mike Bumbeck photo)

Having drawn stations wagons for so long, Gaffo's illustrations in WOS punch out on the page. Like his racing, the 'zine is low budget, but the graphics don't suffer for it. "There's something about black and white paper. It's even stronger than color." Sure he'd like to go to full size color, but for now he considers working in black and white to be a not too distant second best. Barnes also knows that not everybody is into the racing side of wagons so WOS tries not to drive the non-car people crazy. "I always try to do stuff that other car magazines don't to make fun of car magazines. I'm gonna put recipes back in, you don't see those in other car magazines. Real ones and fake ones." Neither do you see horoscopes in other car magazines with their—"Aquarius: You finally figure out what that irritating rattling noise is. Celebrate by taking your friends out for a good sunset opportunity in your biggest wagon." And "Gemini: Get prepared, your guardian angel is about to take a vacation. Check tires, oil, coolant levels—pack a spare and pay off the insurance man. You won't regret it." WOS still has this stuff, because the editor is exploring all aspects of station wagon culture. And he is still in touch with the real world. "I'm personally exploring the high performance thing right now. But it's a joke that's funny no matter how many times you tell it. Draggin' Wagons."

(Artist, Chris Barnes)

SoCal style—fast cars, palm trees and Mooneyes.
(Andy Takakjian photo)

Jack Logan at Liquor Cabinet show.
(Jack Logan collection)

## IT'S A LIFESTYLE JACK

The hot rod and racing bug goes deep, whether completely immersed, like artist Von Franco, or lurking beneath the surface as with Jack Logan or Mark Foster. Kids in the 1950s and 1960s grew up immersed in Hot Wheels, Hot Rod magazine, muscle cars and generalized car love. Some were raised around mechanics, others watched dad changing the oil or perform other manly fiddling with the family car. That imagery runs deep, leaving grown men with hot rods in their blood. Whether they choose to work it out on the track or not, it shows up in their work, and their lives. The sounds of the engine won't quiet for them.

## JACK LOGAN

Jack's a musician now. But he doesn't sing about cars. He respects that his audience would rather hear about love, sex, death and tortured horrible lives than about the beauty of fleeing down a quarter mile track, leaving your troubles behind. Jack keeps it that way because he likes having the racing stuff stay pure, apolitical and free. As he says, "it's just guys tuning their cars, looking cool and chrome." Even with that respect, the love of cars is so much a part of his life that he slips a reference into his songs every now and then.

A songwriter that draws from real life experience, it's near impossible for Logan to omit such a large part of his life. As a child, Logan's dad took him and his brother to a eighth mile strip in the middle of a cow field. He built models, read *Car Craft* and *Hot Rod* magazines like other automotively obsessed young boys. And he drew them. All his favorite stockers like he saw in the fields in Southern Illinois. Boyhood drawings of Arnie Beswick and the Ramchargers and Dick Landy present the aura of detail obscured by memory. His style has changed over the years, Logan no longer draws cars in a U shape, where you see the taillights and the grill in one shot.

While planning a show of his car drawings and cartoons in Athens, Georgia, Logan's only regret about music is that it was the point where he lost interest in cars. He found he was more interested in getting stoned and playing guitar than going out into the garage and getting greasy. Today the extent of Logan's car stuff is driving a somewhat modified '67 Dart, drawing his childhood favorite front engines and doorslammers, and slipping a couple of benign references into the songs he sings about real life.

Tim Woods and Doug Cook
(Artist, Jack Logan)

Dick Landy
(Artist, Jack Logan)

# MARK FOSTER

The tedious and consuming work of building a '27 Ford hardly seems like a hobby, but it is for Mark Foster. A leisurely day at the bone yard or a swap meet is how he spends his down time between directing commercials. Restoring cars and selling them for a loss has been a way of life for Foster since he first got hooked in high school. It started with late model Mustangs, then moved back in time to where we find Foster now—searching for parts for a '29 Model A.

Owning and driving a seventy year old car is a form of collecting. You're in a sort of "club" where people pass around parts and information about an old hull in a neighbor's field that might have a bushing or whatever you need. The time spent searching for required parts, or perhaps fabricating it yourself, is a large part of the hobby. This work is fine with Foster and other enthusiasts, because they love everything about cars. In the same way that men undress women with their minds, Foster will sex up new cars. "I'll look at a brand new Mercedes and I think 'all you have to do is lose those wheels, primer the lower third and lose the back window'," Foster explains of his obsession. "I'm always cropping and shortening and stretching in my mind." And just like being either a breast or leg man, Foster is only vaguely interested in performance, but design is what gets his nut. Like an anthropologist, he crawls through wrecks at the junkyard deciphering the changes people effected to craft factory spawn into their dream car. The abandoned cars become time machines as he imagines the new shiny car driving out of the showroom, the dealer happily waving at the leaving customer.

*Mark Foster cruising in his '27 Ford.*
*(Mark Foster photo)*

'57 CHEVY BELAIR 2dr H.T. p/s
Sharpest one in town with 18k
miles, loaded!+ custom chrm
$15.8K (2fwa465)310/923-0587

'49 FORD. Driven less than 20
mi per yr by lady for shop-
ping. 63mpg! Immaculate cond
$4400 (boopsy) 714-722-0492pp

*(Artist, Mark Foster)*

*The Race (Artist, Mark Foster)*

Foster's created a loving photographic record of his hobby. Grainy photos of nostalgia events, street racing and a junkyard series show the ratty old side, as well as the enthusiasm for the hobby. His travel pictures of Europe are heavy with shots of vintage 1970s boxy autos. In a dark ghostly series of photos, Foster documented the street racing scene in his Long Island hometown. He and his buddy would take a '69 Chevelle on a flatbed to an airport exit where 100-200 people were ready to watch a race. The only illumination in the photographs is from the headlights of the traffic waiting for the high school hooligans to finish their illegal business and unblock the highway.

## VON FRANCO

Von Franco (Author photo)

Self-portrait. (Artist, Von Franco)

Pinstripe people. (Artist, Von Franco)

The hot rod trend has risen and receded in typical popular culture fashion. The cars have always been there, and so have true fans. For some people, the automotive lifestyle is a choice, for others, there's no escaping. The full-on hot rod lovin' style fits not like a prison sentence, but a well worn pair of jeans on Von Franco. Sure, he could have escaped, but he wouldn't have it any other way. The culture, cars and celebrity are his life.

Car culture popularity has been a roller coaster ride from its initial rise in the 1950s, through its stronghold in the 1960s, eventual near demise in the 1970s and now the 1980s resurgence that now most likely will close the century. Through the entire scary, dark and joyful ride, Von Franco, held his ground, never swaying from his initial grasp on what's right and cool and essential about the culture he calls home.

Von Franco explains that he's the only one in his family to turn out the way he did, a sunglassed, pompadoured, tattooed artist, living the beatnik life. They couldn't have been surprised, the attraction started while he was still in elementary school. He was the first in his San Jose neighborhood to get out the markers and decorate the other kids' t-shirts. His mom would catch hell from the other mothers saying that he'd destroyed their son's brand new sweatshirts. During one of his car show appearances, the burgeoning icon Ed "Big Daddy" Roth swiped one of Von Franco's (surely he had a different nom de plum as a 13 year old) hand painted t-shirts. Roth offered an exchange of information on what kind of airbrush to replace the primitive markers the kid had been using. Von Franco left the show feeling honored and ripped off, not quite realizing that Roth spoke the truth in saying that the Pache airbrush would be the key to his future. Years later the two worked together, airbrushing t-shirts on the car show circuit. Because Roth's name went onto everything the artists he employed did, lots of your favorite Rat Fink stuff out there is uncredited Von Franco work.

Von Franco absorbed technique from magazines and watching the guys around him. His airbrushing and pinstriping was influenced by Larry Watson, Dean Jeffries and the king—Von Dutch. He spent lots of time watching, because no one would show kids how to do stuff back then. His technique was taught by Roth, but Von Franco's love of the lifestyle is directly traceable to Von Dutch's free and easy existence. Franco loved the wine, women and wild nights, and emulated it well.

A diligent student, Von Franco honed his craft and spent time airbrushing t-shirts, race cars, pinstriping and living the beatnik life. But things changed and slowly the work dried up. 1960s hippies were into Volkswagens that, if they had decoration, it sure wasn't the hot rod style. In the 1970s, dual attacks by the new European chic and the gas crunch, made imports the fuel saving car of choice. As people's tastes changed, they bought identical Audis, Toyotas or Datsuns and stayed away from individual touches, which cut into Von Franco's customizing market. He starved, not working for a year. Rather than do the psychedelic, floral pattern stuff that people leaned toward, he waited for people to return to their senses. Franco tried going back to art school to see if he had missed something, but the teacher looked at his healthy portfolio and admitted that he didn't need to take the class, he could teach it.

It was the van work that kept him alive. Franco calls them an airbrush artist's dream. He traveled the car shows with artists Roth and Dennis Ronero and painted vans all day long. Apparently those 1970s vans were traveling motels on wheels. Franco describes them as pimp motels, complete with disco lights, mirrors, velvet, bars and TVs. They'd play movies, drink and chase women all night long. As he did the shows and painted murals on these traveling parties he got in on the action, because as Franco says, "if you're painting them, you're inside of them."

While this was a slow time in car culture, it was the speediest period of Franco's life. In the choice between customs and hot rods, he tended toward the meaner, quicker of the two. His short-lived racing career featured a '32 Ford pickup, a '59 Corvette with a 427 and a couple of motorcycles. In a grand step from street racing, one year a friend broke his leg and Franco did a stint in a nitro burning Funny Car without the benefit of a license or racing experience. As if riding behind a 6,000 hp engine underneath a fiberglass body isn't exciting enough, Franco and his friend added to the intrigue by hiding Franco's identity from the sponsors. They simply displayed his unnamed friend, a fire suit hiding his cast, in the pre-race parade, then Von Franco surreptitiously piloted the car down the track. He did well, making it to the semi finals where he blew a piston and drove through an engine fire at almost 200 mph. Although his heart was beating 100 mph when he pulled the chute, he was glad to escape the entire escapade with light burns on his forehead. You can tell he misses the track and the nitro, he speeds up as he tells the story, "I go to drag strips now and just inhale. I'm like a kid in a candy store. You guys can have all your drugs, just give me nitro."

In its ongoing ebb and flow, the hot rod scene resurfaced concurrent with yuppie identity crises of the 1980s. All the baby boomers who'd earned some dough and wanted to be cool rediscovered a way to play with life sized Hot Wheels. They even get a bad boy image to boot. Some guys would take the time to put their love and life into building a personalized project. Many others were, as Franco calls them, "check writers" who simply paid for someone else's image of what they should drive. The trend was also revived by older men who'd been there since the beginning, had raised their families, and now had time to devote to their project cars. When the work on cars increased, so did the awareness of the art.

Like other "lowbrow" artists who made the leap to galleries, Von Franco found himself a sought after commodity in the art scene. Going into the gallery world was a natural transition for Von Franco, he's always felt that cars and art are connected. Any time you draw an idea, it's art, therefore a designer putting his concept of a car on paper is an art form. Actually Franco's definition of an art form is wide and includes all sorts of expression. The art of sex, the art of manipulation, the art of conversation—any way that one person attempts to communicate with another is valid art. He is equally accepting of car culture's common practice of copying another artist's work. Like anything straddling creativity and commercialism, there's room for abuse, but in its purest form, Franco sees copying art as evolution. He points out that since day one, everybody's emulated the work they like, adding their own touches. Von Dutch imbedded faces in his intricate pinstriping. Franco likes to do the same. And as he says, sometimes you can tell the difference between their work, and sometimes not. He's doing lots of varied work now, pinstriping, gallery shows, cover art, like the cover for Heart's new CD, he flamed the chair on the front of Southern Culture on the Skids CD. He likes the competition from the young guys.

Being friends with Jackie Wilson and going to James Brown and Martha and the Vandellas road shows as a kid, shaped Von Franco's love of music. He of course had music in his car, a record player. He says the bitch was leaving the albums in the sun. Now that love of music is played out as a guitarist in the garage band the Bomboras and more recently playing vibes with a psychobilly group, the Hyperions. He appreciates the link between music and cars, particularly surf and rock and roll.

When he was a kid, he also started the drawing thing. He drew the image in the TV Guide so well, that the president of the art school came to his house to offer him a scholarship. His dad offered him a choice between a minibike and the scholarship, Von Franco made the kid choice. Knowing what kids choose to do is important, Franco tries to turn them onto stuff that's cool.

Early images. (Artist, Von Franco)

Hell On Wheels (1999)
(Artist, Von Franco)

(Rescue photo)

# On the Radio
# Hot Rod Music

Cruising down the highway with the sun in your face and the wind in your hair offers the feeling of unlimited freedom, the power of possibility and fun, fun, fun. It makes you feel like singing. People have sung about cars since we first became entranced with the power of the automobile's world-opening views. Fast cars simply meant more power and more freedom.

Blues musicians, in their double entrende way, used fast cars as a metaphor for sex since the beginnings of recorded blues. In 1941 when Memphis Minnie sang "I wants him to drive me downtown" in "Me And My Chauffeur," she sure wasn't talking about an automobile ride. By the time Jackie Brenston and Ike Turner's recording of "Rocket 88" hit the charts, the blues sound was more industrial, faster and more machine like. Far removed from the slap of the acoustic guitar that had been practiced on front porches for a couple of decades.

*Hot Rods & Custom Classics—a big block box set. (1999, Rhino Records)*

The first recorded instance of an ode to a hot rod was "Hot Rod Boogie" performed by Connie Jordan and the Jordanaires in 1946 where the exuberant swing of a typical piano instrumental approximates the thrill of a fast car ride. For every genre of popular music, there was a car song recorded. Mary Healy sang the novelty tune "I Wish I Were A Car" to grab her boyfriend's attention; Sonny Cole did a hillbilly rendition of sporting around in your car and trying to outrun cops in "Curfew Cops," and a country and western rendering of "Hot Rod Rag" was recorded by Paul Westmoreland. Painter Robert Williams along with Mark Deaver and Anthony D'Amico put together a particularly hard to find double picture disc of all sorts of hot rod rarities for Blast First Records in 1987, *Chrome, Smoke and Fire*. What they compiled were boogies, country and western, rockabilly, R&B and novelty ramblings about the sins and pleasures of cruising in a souped up car.

Until the 1950s, there was no term for those lost years between grade school and marriage. Indeed, there were no lost years. As parents who had endured the Depression and a couple of World Wars made life better for their young 'uns, they created a leisure class. As this group of energetic youngsters wandered around with pockets full of allowance, merchants found ways to relieve them of it. It was already obvious that these kids were expressing their newfound freedom by buying their own cars and hopping them up. They were also dressing the way they wanted and started buying their own music. Bored with the do-wop and concert music of their parents, these kids dug Rock and Roll.

*The only surfer in the Beach Boys, Dennis Wilson, as The Mechanic in "Two Lane Blacktop" (1971, Universal Pictures)*

Just like hot rodding was the DIY of the automotive world, rock and roll had the potential of letting down its hair and letting the kids be themselves. But not at the beginning. First they had to be told what they wanted. Kids had been buying records by Doris Day singing about her boyfriends and other sappy stuff. The songwriters were young, but they were just trying to make a buck. At its best, rock and roll is the lively child of the unlikely union of African American rhythm and blues and white redneck music. At its worst— like early 1950s pop—it was neither, simply rice pudding that was pushed on kids. It was their parents' music prancing around with a face lift. It was a balding old guy riding around in a convertible trying to pretend he was still young. It was missing something.

The problem was that it was pop music, it wasn't rock and roll. Like Joe Carducci says in his book *Rock and the Pop Narcotic*, rock and roll is about the "construction and the stoking of a runaway train." It's not about control. And that's what scared the old folks. When they first started singing, the Wilson boys, their cousin Mike Love and friend Al Jardine, were a bunch of young kids. Growing up in California had taught them the meaning of fun, fun, fun. So when they started singing about it, you knew they meant it. Those Beach Boys even had a resident surfer/hot rodder, Dennis, so when their first single, "Surfer Safari" backed with "409" hit the world, it sounded just right. Purity of tone. The hot rod scene screamed "kids" so much that the 1957 premiere issue of *Teen* magazine boasted a cover pictorial of hot rods and even included an article on car clubs.

## THE 1960s HOT ROD HOOTENANNY

In 1962 a 19 year-old Brian Wilson met the 24 year-old Gary Usher, who had recorded a few independent singles. They had a common enjoyment of music and love for cars. That combination turned out to be a huge commercial hit. Their anthem, "409," was about a guy in love—with his car. It was born during a conversation between the two while cruising in Usher's street rod, about what they would buy if they'd "save up their pennies and dimes." They wrote about the car as a she and knew proudly that no other car in town would turn in a faster time (giddy up, giddy up 409). Chevrolet had built the 409 (the cubic inch size of the motor) so that drivers could "do a better job at racing." They were tired of getting their asses whipped by Ford flatheads. This was what struck a chord with Usher and Wilson, they were singing their true feelings. Usher even took four passes in front of the Wilson household to record his Chevy's tire squeal for the sounds at the beginning of the recording.

The song "409" began as added material to a Beach Boys demo for Capitol. Once the band was signed it was issued as the B side to "Surfin' Safari." By October of 1962, "Safari" was at number 14 on the Billboard chart and "409" went to 76. The guys at Capitol could hardly contain themselves. Here, in one neat package, was the stuff teens were doing and they were sure would buy. The Beach Boys followed with chart successes of "Shut Down," "Little Deuce Coupe" and "I Get Around," all odes to the car lifestyle of California teens. The Beach Boys released the album *Little Deuce Coupe* followed in October of 1963 with 12 car tunes and not a single one mentioned surfing.

While surfing music told the story of young, carefree kids on the West Coast exclusively, hot rod music traveled better. Even the Surf King, Dick Dale, released an album with a car theme entitled *Checkered Flag*. Kids in the Midwest never got a chance to "catch a wave and sit on top of the world," but they were all hopping up the family car and cruising. Songs like "Fun, Fun, Fun" and the Ripchords' "Hey Little Cobra" were their soundtracks to life, making hot rod music actually sell better outside of California. Soon bands from Colorado (Astronauts), Michigan (Mitch Ryder and the Detroit Wheels), Tennessee (Ronny & the Daytonas), and Minnesota (Trashmen) released songs that evoked fast cars and good times. Hell, even Cajun accordionist Clifton Chenier recorded songs entitled "Hot Rod" and "Grand Prix."

It's no wonder that this music did well in the heartland. Guitarists like Dick Dale were employing the guitar in the country/hillbilly style of the past, as a vocal instrument. This "talking" guitar had been heard in the music of cowboys, Mexicans, rural blacks and Hawaiians. Its universal sound wailed and sang and made you get off your seat and on your feet. It was perfect for dances and times

*(1963, Capitol Records)*
*(1964, Capitol Records)*

The Deuce Coupes
*(1963, Del-Fi Records)*
The Darts
*(1964, Del-Fi Records)*

when kids were getting away from home and finding a way to get a little closer to each other. Instrumentals hopped up with reverb and the introduction of the hot rod fuzz had girls wiggling out of their jeans all over the country.

If you didn't hear the sounds of cars, or there were no lyrics, there wasn't much to distinguish the hot rod sound from surfing music. Both genres featured twangy guitars, reverb, stripped down beat and often raunchy sax and piano or organ. Exploitation films had been around since the 1950's to give teenagers another place to spend their dough. Surfing and hot rod sounds were youth-themed soundtracks looking for visuals. The myth of "Golden West Coast" was sold through the highly provocative film market. Beach party, surfing and California movies were highly successful on this platform of revved-up music. What better way to sell records to a captive audience?

In a search for more of the hot rod dollar, Capitol released two novelty albums, *Hot Rod Hootenanny* and *Rods 'N Rat Finks* by Mr. Gasser and the Weirdos. Mr. Gasser was none other than Ed "Big Daddy" Roth backed by a group of studio musicians put together by Gary Usher. By stocking his "wrecking crew" with musicians including Leon Russell and Glen Campbell, Usher was creating a Phil Spector-like persona of his own. He was a songwriter, vocalist, arranger, and he produced multitudes of bands. The work that Usher produced between 1963-65 became the standard that hot rod music was (and still is) measured against. His projects included songs like "Custom City," "Draggin' USA" and albums with the Four Speeds, Hondells, Revells, Road Runners, Super Stocks, Wheelmen and others.

Another addition to the burgeoning hot rod music scene was a car lover from way back. At fourteen Roger Christian hitchhiked from New York to LA to make money to buy a deuce. He diligently washed dishes until he had enough pennies and dimes, bought his '32 and drove it home to New York. A little older and back in LA working as a radio station DJ, Christian had given up on the hot rod lifestyle. But he was a great lyricist, and he sure knew how to write about what a teenager wants. He scoured the car mags and picked up terms that he used in his songs. It was his words that revved "Little Deuce Coupe," "The Little Old Lady (From Pasadena)" and "My Mighty G.T.O."

The first hot rod song recorded by Jan and Dean was written by the experts, Roger Christian, Gary Usher and Brian Wilson. "Drag City" was Jan and Dean's entrée into the car scene. Following the single's rise up the charts, Jan Berry hooked up with these guys and they were responsible for the bulk of true hot rod material. They wrote and sang about what they loved; cars, girls and fun. But in 1966, perhaps foreshadowed by their popular song "Dead Man's Curve," Jan Berry was in a near-fatal crash putting J&D's already slowing careers on a multiyear hold.

Brian Wilson, also emulating Phil Spector, spread his producing talents around town. His touch (and sometimes vocals) was all over recordings by the Honeys, Jan and Dean, Glen Campbell, Annette Funnicello and Dino, Desi & Billy. Capitol wasn't happy with this arrangement, but they couldn't do a thing about it. Wilson had brokered a deal where he had not only the artistic freedom to roam, but also complete creative control over the Beach Boys' product. The Wilson family had also retained rights to the multi-million dollar music publishing company, Sea of Tunes. Both of these actions had been unheard of prior to the Beach Boys' contract, but it reflected the growth and evolution of the music scene. Surf and hot rod production and the records' resulting sales shifted the center of pop industry from New York's Brill Building, to the glass edifice resembling a stack records at Hollywood and Vine in Los Angeles. Rock and roll music experienced a revolution and the ideas of the kids had taken over.

*In 1966, Brian Wilson, Dennis Wilson, Mike Love, Carl Wilson and Al Jardine (on top) hang on their Capitol Records–paid, Barris–made Mini Surfer. (Barris collection)*

*1995 Del-Fi Records compilation featuring Deuce Coupes, De-Fenders and the Darts.*

*The De-Fenders (1964, Del-Fi Records)*

About the car on the cover: Owned by Jim Treadway of Burbank, California, it has a Model T body on a homemade chassis. The engine is a Corvette with a six carburetor fuel system which drives this little rod in excess of 130 miles per hour.

**DRAG-RACING GLOSSARY...**

**Drop The Hammer; Put Your Foot In It**
*Full throttle, wide open acceleration*

**A Tube Steak**
*A Hot Dog sandwich. Standard fare at Drag track*

**Stuffer; Puffer; Blower; Pump; Windmill**
*Supercharger*

**Ratchet Jaw**
*A constant talker*

**Bench Racing**
*After-race quarterbacking or theorizing on wins or losses*

**Jack-The-Bear**
*A car ran "Like Jack The Bear," etc.*

**Run a Typewriter**
*A Dodge pushbutton automatic transmission*

**Tack**
*Tachometer*

**Box**
*Type of transmission*

**Juice; Punch**
*Fuel mixture of Nitro, Methane, Alcohol, Crystal T.N.T. used in hot cars*

**Put The Can In**
*Use of complete fuel mixture*

Plaques courtesy of Stylized Company, Hollywood

DEL·FI RECORDS, INC. HOLLYWOOD, CALIF., U.S.A.

The back of Del-Fi's hot rod records provided a semi-serious glossary of popular terms. (Del-Fi Records)

"500 Miles to Glory" compilation featuring the Drags, Supersuckers and Teengenerate among others. (1997, Man's Ruin Records)

New sounds were being released at a breakneck pace and previous boundaries were disregarded. Everybody "slept around," meaning they played, often unaccredited, on each others' recordings. Session musicians played under numerous names wherever they were paid to show up. There was work for everyone and various combinations of Brian Wilson, Jan Berry, Roger Christian and Gary Usher were found on most of the car-related material. The trend was so hot, that labels like Corvette and Drag Race appeared out of nowhere to release one-off singles.

Having been dealt a bum hand or two, producer Bob Keane jumped into the fray. His label, Del-Fi Records, had earlier success with Richie Valens ("La Bamba") and Bobby Fuller ("I Fought The Law"). But true fame was snatched out of his hands by the untimely deaths of both of these stars. Keane had already dipped into the surf trend, so as soon as he realized that kids were gonna go for the new hot rod music, he tossed some musicians into the studio and got three albums out, pronto. Deke Dickerson's liner notes to a Del-Fi's 1995 compilation, *Hell Bound Hot Rods!*, point out that Keane's hot rod vision "evoked the visual imagery of flashy cars rumbling at breakneck speed through the set of Gidget."

Keane's marketing ideas were genius. To catch eyes, he put pictures of cool hot rods and a '32 with chute wide open on the covers. The back of all three albums were the same—a glossary of hot rod terms so you could sound sufficiently knowledgeable when you claimed that your gasser is a haulin' mother no matter what that ratchet jaw fink says while bench racing. Del-Fi's platters were also the loudest around. Rife with overdubbed 120 decibel sound effects of dragsters roaring off the starting line, his 45s blew away the competition on the jukebox. These same insane decibels were sure to infuriate any teenagers' parents when popped onto the home hi-fi. Cool!

Drawing from Phil Spector's "Wrecking Crew" of studio musicians, Keane put together his own studio combos. The De-Fenders relied on the talents of Tommy Tedesco, a session guitarist who played with the other hot rod top eliminators—Beach Boys and Jan & Dean. David Gates, in his pre-Bread years, was also included on the De-Fender's sessions for their Drag Beat album. Glen Campbell's guitar went head-to-head against the dragster burnouts on the Darts recordings, and the pre-Redbone Pat and Lally Vasquez brothers fronted the Deuce Coupes.

During these years, the musicians, street rodders and strip racers were all riding high, but an off shore phenomena stopped them all dead in their tracks. With a shake of their mop tops, everything Continental became cool—sports cars, long hair, pallid skin, skinny unhealthy looks, accents and slowly—political statements. No one had time for fast cars and hanging out. There was a new implied elitism that no longer had tolerance for doting on "grease monkeys" or "beach bunnies."

In what's been a really strange twist, the more popular hot rod music has faded, while surfing music has continued to live a long happy life. One of its proponents from the get go is been John Blair. Riding out the waves of surf revival, first in the 1980s, and now again with the recent reissues, Blair's band, Jon and the Nightriders are active players in the Southern California club scene. With a handful of albums and singles under their baggies, they continue to keep the sound they love alive. Blair found time to chronicle the sound of the 1960s in two books, *The Illustrated Discography of Hot Rod Music, 1961-1965* and *The Illustrated Discography of Surf Music*. All of the obscure, one-offs and hugely popular hits are documented in their flaming glory.

*Hot Rod Magazine*, along with Tom Cartwright are keeping that Sixties hot rod feeling alive for listeners today with a series of CDs. Rather than just call them oldies, like so many people are wont to do, they market them as they are, hot rod songs. Composed of songs dead on about driving (The Surfaris "Burnin' Rubber") or sounds that are just right for cruising (Link Wray's "Rumble"), the Hot Rod Rock series puts all these past songs in one place for easy access.

## LOW RIDING IN THE '70s

The 1970s were definitely a low point in the automotive world. Hot rodders were assaulted at every front. Designers' lack of imagination created sloppy, boring autos from Detroit's Big Three. Lack of fossil fuels brought on the onslaught of fuel-miser Japanese cars. Bad cars and no fuel had lots of folks spending time dreaming they were recording cowboys or traipsing off to the discos to do the hustle. The power of hot rod music was still out there—Brit bands, cowboy rock, the folkie movement and disco years obscured it, but it survived. Hot rod disciples—ZZ Top, Bruce, Motorhead—kept it going.

---

### TOP TEN SONGS OF THE 1970s

1 - Bridge Over Troubled Water–Simon & Garfunkel
2 - Night Fever–Bee Gees
3 - Tonight's the Night–Rod Stewart
4 - Shadow Dancing–Andy Gibb
5 - Le Freak–Chic

6 - My Sharona–The Knack
7 - The First Time…–Roberta Flack
8 - Alone Again (Naturally)–Gilbert O'Sullivan
9 - Joy to the world–Three Dog Night
10 - You Light Up My Life–Debby Boone

---

This is not road music. It's not cruising music. It's not parking music. It's not music for anything that displays power or will or heritage. The 1970s were also a period of genre. If it had a label, it found a crowd. Disco, Folk Rock, Pop, R&B, Country, Blues, Rock; splinters occurred everywhere. Some aimed higher and wimpier like Country-Rock or corporate rock' of Kansas, Journey and Boston. Thankfully, there were still some free thinkers that took us on the road.

The 1960s image of hot rods and surfing degenerated to the 1970s pedestrian image as portrayed by Joni Mitchell, Jackson Browne, the Eagles, and (turncoats) Loggins and Messina. Here was a much mellower "Tequila Sunrise," or "Takin It Easy," where they "paved paradise and put up a parking lot."

Oh, there was the stray car reference—the Eagles crooned "put me on the highway, and show me the way, and take it to the limit one more time." Foghat took a "Slow Ride"—it wasn't really a song about cars, but that's how it often is with car songs. Meatloaf was looking at "Paradise By the Dashboard Lights," the Doobie Brothers claimed "It Keeps Me Runnin,'" and Bachman-Turner were in perpetual Overdrive, but it wasn't the same. The sprit of rebellion and freedom was missing. Right smack in this middle of 1970s sap, Springsteen rocked with his E Street band and the 1975 release, *Born To Run*. Here the previously popular images of hitting the road to find yourself resurfaced in the Boss' odes to American youth. The title song spoke of kids in their "chrome wheeled, fuel injected suicide machines steppin' over the line." Bruce recalled "hemi-powered drones screaming down the boulevard and the highway jammed with broken heroes on a last chance power drive." With wails and almost under control screeching saxes, Springsteen and the E Street Band unleashed rock and roll the way it was supposed to sound—like a runaway train.

The New Jersey native had grown up with plenty of street racing and the strength of its images fueled his songs. A '69 Chevy with a 396, going from town to town to shut 'em up and shut 'em down. Cars roaring past to carry adventures out of town leaving burnt out Chevrolets and a trail of dust in their wake got folks singing in their hopped up Camaros once again. "Tramps like us, baby we were born to run."

(1995, Artist, Coop)

Owner of the 200+ mph guitar, ZZ Top's Billy Gibbons hangs with Gearhead editor Mike LaVella. (David Perry photo)

Top: Compilation featuring The Demonics, Man or Astroman, Nomads and Quadrajets. (1998 Lookout Records)
Bottom: Gearhead shows insure the drag-punk gospel gets heard. (Artist, Frank Kozik)

Springsteen was not left alone to recall where the automobile had gotten us, tres hombres from Texas also had gas in their blood and it seeped out into their songs. ZZ Top's early efforts, like "Arrested for Driving While Blind" and "Move Me On Down the Line" were blues-heavy bottom lines that celebrated cars, guitars and pretty girls. Continuing the well established trend of cars as a metaphor for sex, Top thumped out a steamy boogie that encouraged a pretty girl to "ride my Chevrolet" and it was more than an invitation to cruise.

Their songs are autobiographical and the need for metal is more than just a front for Billy Gibbons of the band. When the first record money hit his pocket, he satisfied his desire with musclecars. Upon checking out a California Roadster show, Gibbons embarked on a project that led to the public vision of their hot rod leanings. The red '33 Ford Eliminator Coupe took five years from concept to street worthiness and showed up in three videos in 1983: "Gimme All Your Lovin'," "Sharp Dressed Man" and "Legs." With the recent invention of MTV, and ZZ living all over it, the vision of the bearded ones and customs rode hand-in-hand. They built momentum from there, contracting a stretched '48 Cadillac, CadZZila, then the Leapin' Limo '48 Pontiac Silver Streak stretch and even a Pearl Necklace VW.

In their free time, bassist Dusty Hill favors chopped, lowered Mercs, drummer Frank Beard (the one without a foot-long beard) sometimes races at Daytona, and guitarist Billy Gibbons follows the tour bus in one or another of his customs rides. The sound of speed is also added to their music courtesy of the world's fastest guitar—a six string that Gibbons had taped into a '32 Ford for a 200+ mph run on Bonneville's Salt Flats.

The rockin' blues sound of ZZ Top was joined by other bands who shunned the disco beat for something heavier that often praised the power of metal. AC/DC was on a "Highway to Hell." Golden Earring had a "Radar Love" that had them "speedin' into a new sunrise." And Deep Purple's "Highway Star" described a girl/car killing machine—"I'm gonna race it to the ground, it's gonna break the speed of sound"—and crescendoed with "Now that I'm on the road again, Oooh I'm in heaven and I've got everything. I love it I need it. I seed it, eight cylinders all mine."

The world of funk and soul also sang odes to their autos—Rose Royce's "Car Wash" slipped its way to the top five in 1977. The go-slow street culture of Long Beach and Compton, California was immortalized by some local kids. WAR—with its rockin' funky Latin-spiced blues released "Low Rider" and driving a little slower and takin' a little trip sounded like the right thing to do.

### 1980s PUNKMOBILE

Despite getting together in Detroit in 1965, the Motor City 5 (or the MC5 as they were much better known), had nothing to do with the local big three and everything to do with the energy, radical notions and fuck you-ness that punk picked up on by the mid-1970s. A few years earlier screaming guitar solos popularized by Jimi Hendrix frequented the bass-heavy driven songs of bands that spread the gospel of the automobile. By the 1980s, this had changed again. Do-It-Yourself came on strong, and young, snotty misfits were screeching lyrics that were barely intelligible and hardly heard above the ear-splitting feedback of over-amped guitars.

Bands like the Ramones, Sex Pistols and Minutemen took the early raw elements of the MC5, Sonics and Stooges' garage sound and turned it way up. Punkers were generally urban dwellers, but they made sure that the automobile was a part of the youthful anthems to rebellion. While lyrically sticking it to the government, schools, established mores, preconceived ideas and outdated thoughts, punk rockers also had time to pay tribute to the things that rocked them—sex drugs rock and roll—and cars. To these bands that

The Demonic's "Formaldehyde Injection" (1998, Man's Ruin Records)

had little or nothing to do with the automotive world, cars still meant freedom and fast cars still meant sex.

The first real drag punk band was Illinois artists, the Didjits. In 1986 they released "Max Wedge" and "Stingray" on Touch and Go records, and also adopted the Dodge muscle car Super Bee logo as their mascot.

The Ramones, those milky white New York City boys, probably never drove a car and definitely never surfed—yet they sang about girls, cars, sun and fun like a regular Beach Boy. Their renditions of "California Sun," "Li'l Camaro" and "Rockaway Beach" don't let on that they know more about subways than freeways. Another New York City outfit, the Dictators, also sang odes to the alien West Coast. Their song "(I Live for) Cars and Girls" is the original punk rock hot rod credo.

Sounding like they may have actually owned automobiles, the Modern Lovers related the true anthem "Road Runner." Jonathan Richman's lyrics, "the highway is your girlfriend and you go by quick," knowingly praise driving past all that barely matters with your radio on.

Big Black sang about "Racer X" ("I need a little more speed") and Vom had a "Punkmobile" ("razor blades on my hubcaps"). Pussy Galore took a "Spin Out" and Teengenerate sang about "My G.T.O."

## 1990s JESUS BUILT MY HOT ROD MUSIC

By the end of the 1980s the Post Punk movement signaled what bands finally figured out—yes indeedy, anything goes. Rockabilly was cool again and punkers dragged up the old surfing and hot rod classics and let loose with a new power. Bands like Big Stick even resurrected racing sound effects.

Estrus Records put out *The Gearbox*, a three record box set that introduced the world at large to twelve bands at the forefront the "drag punk" scene. Drag punk came on surprisingly strong and it seemed every band had a car song in its set. One group, Ministry, even managed a "hit" of sorts—1991's "Jesus Built My Hot Rod." Featuring the satanic growl of guest vocalist Gibby Haynes rolling on about sex and guns and yes, the fact that "Jesus built my car."

Across the waters, Brits, who's sole transportation is the Tube, chimed in with their praise of cars. A band that sounds like a drunken motorist, Swervedriver, hails from London and sings songs entitled "Son of Mustang Ford," "Jaguar XE" and "Expressway." Lead singer Adam Franklin relates the common childhood love of cars, playing with Hot Wheels and naming autos coming down the wrong side of the street. Of course they don't own vehicles, but they still manage to spin images of driving from trouble, toward wanton relationships.

The only thing that never made a come back is the clear delineation between this and that. Psychobilly, rockabilly, death rock, surf rock, garage, lounge, ei, ei, ei, my head is swimming.

(1991, Sire Records)

(1997, Geffen Records)

Compilation featuring the
Bomboras, Boss Martians,
Satan's Pilgrims and others.
(1996, Blood Red Records)

What is clear is that a punk outfit like Big Drill Car is just as likely to release a car song ("Mag Wheel" on their *Small Block* ep) as the English band Eddie and the Hot Rods. There are a few that make surf, beer, cars and girls their priority: Witness Los Angeles' Muff's "Brand New Chevy," San Francisco's Demonics "Jesus Chrysler Super Stock" and Sweden's Nomads' "Let's Go To The Dragstrip." The mostly girl band, L7 paid homage to Ms. Cha-Cha Muldowney with "Shirley"—"feel so real clutching the steering wheel." South Eastern Michigan offered up the Hentchmen, sounding like they came from 1965 with songs like "Hot Rod Millie" and "Red Hot Car."

Many bands take their name from the automotive world—The Drags, Cheater Slicks, Dragstrip Riot, the Superchargers. Sometimes genres pop up like rockabilly and all that's white trash—trailers, tattoos, big hair, customs cars and rust bucket hot rods. The Cramps have visited this scary arena with "I'm Customized." You can find the Amazing Royal Crowns (who are named after their favorite hair grease) mixing devils and drunken frenzies on "1965 G.T.O." And nobody seems to look more like they grew up in a trailer park than Southern Culture on the Skids. Guitarist Rick Miller cites his youth spent near dirt tracks as a prime grimy influence on the tunes he writes today. The release, *Dirt Track Date* made it obvious that the fast car life has influenced theirs.

## WILDGIRL—ROCKING RACING RADIO

All these permutations are great, and need not be preached to the converted. But without sending the tunes out to the world, the whole form would die. Thanks to the magic of radio and the whims of a DJ, the true sounds of racing had nine years of burning rubber and rocking sounds at WFMU. Ericka Peterson Dana, better known around Newark, New Jersey as Wildgirl, made getting folks to the track her main priority.

Her young girl crush on cars started early, with televised figure 8 races. Then she built her automotive expertise on drives with her Grandma where she gave animal attributes to the fabulously finned, generously grilled, highly ornamented hoods. Fords became foxes, Studebakers sharks, Buicks bunnies. The design stylings of 1950s automobiles caught her young artistic eye about the same time music charmed her ears. A collector early on, Wildgirl still owns the Status Quo's 1968 single of "Pictures of Matchstick Men" she bought for 67 cents after calling a radio station and finding out the name.

That love of cars and knack for art lead Wildgirl to studying at the Art Institute in Chicago. Her 3D artist bent was obvious in her cars. Although primer black was her favorite paint job color, they had other wild additions. She flamed Karmann Ghias, added tiger stripes, jack-o-lanterns, skeletons and palm trees to her Volkswagen, and mounted roof racks and extra truck lights. Sometimes she invited artist friends to help hand paint her transportation.

Wildgirl's love of cars and racing was so apparent, that it became part of her courtship. Before he married her, husband Rich Dana, presented Wildgirl with a childhood drawing of "Cool Bear on His Mean Chopper" left over from being eight years old. Dana, like his wife, took to the car thing as a child.

*Ericka Peterson, a/k/a Wildgirl, spread her Rocking Racing Radio over New Jersey's airwaves. (John McCartney photo)*

Wildgirl's Rocking Racing show started with what she loved most. As quickly as she could the program grew around tunes by recording heroes like Mitch Ryder, Duane Eddy and Marc Bolan. "I taped live sound at Raceway Park and I edited sound bites and revving engines and track noise into my show." Then it all snowballed. She dedicated songs to her personal racing heroes like Animal Jim and played motorcycle songs and tunes from his movies for Evel Knievel. She reported track schedules on Rocking Racing which resulted in a press pass. With unlimited access to the racers, Wildgirl started taping interviews to air during the weekly show. This rock and roll coverage of the racing scene started getting national coverage by photographers and reporters.

Wildgirl at the track.
(John McCartney photo)

Hot rod celebrities like the Big Daddies—Ed Roth and Don Garlits—did station IDs for the show that pointed out its "live weather, black leather, fast cars, loud guitars." Her interviews in *Hot Rod* magazine and *Bracket Racing USA* attracted performance sponsors who donated bumper stickers, t-shirts and tickets to see monster trucks at Englishtown to aid in her fundraising efforts for WFMU.

Listeners, intrigued by the phoned in racing reports and the sounds of the track, gave the old drag strip a try. In her bid to turn more rockers onto the world of drag racing, Wildgirl succeeded. "I'd try to get people to the track. That was my whole MO. Once people went, they got hooked. Then they'd be forever grateful and really into this connection between myself and the track. They'd call in requests for songs for a car they liked."

Part of her attraction to climbing into a car is the fact that it's a great equalizer. "I like the fact that I'm a girl with a birth defect—with one leg shorter than the other, that never was good at sports or had much athletic ability, but a highly competitive nature and not much money—can get in a car. By the fact of bracket racing and the way it works, I can win against a totally physically capable, big strong man with a lot of money driving a fancy 'Vette with all the tricks." And she's got a trophy to prove the strength of her competitive nature. When she won that one media race, the defeated male in the losing lane jumped out of his car and threw his helmet on the ground in disgust. Wildgirl felt, "just like Cha Cha."

She loves both racing and music and her choices show no delineation. After all, asks the DJ, what is the sound of hot rod music exactly? "Link Wray? Stray Cats? The retro '50s stuff?," asks Wildgirl. "I don't separate it. My feeling is if it's a good song and it rocks me, I'll play it. I don't care if it's heavy metal, rockabilly or pop or punk or whatever." She understands how the whole motion/music connection came about. "You didn't have a car without a radio and you didn't have a sock hop or some sort of band playing without some cool cars parked out front. AND, "People that like loud rock and roll music and its beat tend to think speed is beauty—the roar of the engines and the smoke. To me, when I'm standing at the starting line and top fuel cars are running, it does something to your heart beat. It changes your body from the inside. Good garage bands do the same thing. It's this total physical sensational experience."

Up until the decision to leave the city behind, and provide fresh eggs and vegetables to folks in Iowa, Wildgirl supercharged the airways with the sound of fury. Radio in Newark will never be the same.

## BIG STICK

Across the river, but reached by the pounding airwaves of WFMU, were other noisemakers that could not live without the combined sounds of popping nitro and heavy bass. John Gill and Yanna Trance make their own big noise as Big Stick.

When they sprung onto the scene in 1986, their initial release was about crack life in the city called "Drag Racing." The repetitive sample of Yanna's seductive "in the summer I wear my tube top and Eddie takes me to the drags" mixed with roaring track sounds,

Big Stick's "Crack 'n' Drag".
(1988, Blast First Records)

Yanna Trance and John Gill in Big Stick drag. (Big Stick collection)

probably reminded more than one kid of their own summers at the strip. Or, if you hadn't been to the track, the incessant bottom end mixed with the sound of 3,000 hp motors certainly made you want to get there soon. Their aim was to mimic the drag racing radio commercials. Big Stick snagged racing sound effects with a Walkman and Gill fell back on his announcing abilities to put the track together. Maybe because they're both alumni of the Newark School of Fine and Industrial Art, it didn't turn out so straight. The result was what Gill calls "eclectic little punk pop."

It's ironic that Big Stick's portrayal of urban "Americana"—drag strips, Puerto Rican crack addicts, shooting the president and bowling alleys with liquor licenses—earn more air play in England then in their motherland. To understand what was going on over in the new land, London's cutting edge journal, *New Music Express*, sent reporters to chat with Gill and Trance. To show, rather than tell, the band took the *NME* crew to their local track, Raceway Park in Englishtown and blew their ears off. "I don't know if they were bored or what they really thought. I guess they thought we were just being Americans." Since then, Big Stick has seen some racing in Santa Pod, England. And recorded it. And sold the videotape—*From England to Englishtown.*

Because that's what they do—get a regular dose of drag racing by working at the strip. Gill and Yanna alternately use the name Drag Racing Underground for their band or their videotaping/mail order company. And because he sees it as very conservative at the track, it's fine with Gill that the racers he talks with every day don't know he's records punk rock music at home. One of the perks is that at the end of the day, the Big Stickers can drive their truck down the strip to retrieve equipment. But they don't race. Rock and roll is expensive enough, Gill explains, "I'm hesitant to [race cars] because this bug has bitten me enough without starting that." And it's not just Gill—he describes Yanna as "as much as a pain in the ass to go to the races as I am any day."

Live, the band sports big wigs and pleather, practically hiding their identities. While they've rarely toured the US, they have been seen at Wildgirl's Go-Go-Rama. Big Stick took their "pain in the ass" enthusiasm on the road with My Life With The Thrill Kill Kult and got into some trouble with their label for including a dancer that play-whipped male audience members during the show. But they did manage to spread the drag racing theme. Perhaps, they played a major part in reviving the thrill of loud guitars and louder cars. Robert Williams must have thought so too, because he included Big Stick's "Drag Racing" on his *Chrome, Smoke and Fire* picture disc hot rod compilation.

## DOORSLAMMER

Smashed between a car-fan dad and a musical family, Todd Westover had no other choice but to combine the influences and it all spills out into his punk band, Doorslammer. But drag racing is not the ultimate game for this punk and drag guy. His dad also drug him to see stock cars, Indy cars, midget races—the Westovers figured a race car is a race car is a race car.

The attraction doesn't stop in the stands for this car fan, however. Whenever he can wrangle it, Westover maneuvers his body into the cockpit of a race car and gives it a go. If circumstances ever permit, he'd give up the band and his great job as art director of *Hot Rod* magazine and just race. According to Westover, driving a road course is a lot like drumming. All your limbs are going in a rhythm of downshifting, braking, upshifting, braking, downshifting. Between that physical work, the hum of your engine, concentrating on track surfaces and turns and thinking about what the other cars are doing—you fall into a meditative state similar to drumming and driving a band.

Driving the band from the drummer's seat was too far from the spotlight for Westover, so he found a way to get to the front and bob his head. His first excursion was as a one man band—billed as Westover Todd—which featured just the man and

The brains and bass behind Doorslammer, Todd Westover. (Todd Westover photo)

his keyboard and a lamp. It was a kind of screaming folk punk kind of thing (before Beck) and the lamp was more famous than the singer. Nowadays, the front man urge is satiated by a bass playing, lead-singing Westover in Doorslammer. His newest band, Toothpick Elbow, features Westover on keyboards, and a return appearance of the lamp.

And cars are just one of the things he's on about. Doorslammer's song, "Drag Strip Sweetheart"—written about his wife and drag strip denizen—features car noises a la 1960s hot rod bands. The band's name, which eludes to street cars that get hopped up and make it down the drag strip, replaces the previous band name, Buster Couch. The recently retired Couch was NHRA's head starter seemingly forever and an easily recognizable figure on the racing scene. A great name for a guy, but it didn't work for the band. People seem to like Doorslammer better, even if they do think the name refers to an irate husband. Whatever, they can feel the racing power.

(1997, 1+2 Records)

## RADIO RUMPUS ROOM

Since Wildgirl left the airways, radio's been a cold barren place for lovers of drag-punk tunes. Unless, of course, you're within the transmitting range of KFAI-FM in the twin city area. Tune in on Friday nites and get the pre-party set up from Radio Rumpus Room, featuring "radio that caters to your sick musical needs." The man doing the catering is Ron Thums, the same DJ who's been catering to the Minneapolis/St. Paul listenership since the summer of 1994.

There are plenty of hot rod tunes for your listening pleasure, supplemented by a wide range of lo-fi/hi-octane sounds. For RRR, that means rockabilly, surf, '60s Garage, and also back-to-roots country can be heard during the show.

His love of the magic of radio came from Thum's childhood, in a time, pre-marriage, pre-army, pre-Vietnam, when he was a kid on the family farm in Wisconsin. Thums sang cool radio songs to himself out riding the tractor through the fields (actually, he remembers singing "It's my party and I'll cry if I want to" as he cruised in the tractor, but with puberty came embarrassment about all that). Lucky for Thums, when his dad wasn't hauling cars—like teeny ole' Nash Metropolitans—he was takin' the kids to the oval tracks. Sure, from early on he frequented the roundy rounds, but they didn't touch him in that special place like the drags did. On his first venture seven miles away to the Great Lakes Dragaway, Thums was treated to the mythic vision of Jet Car Bob struggling for his life as his Untouchable 2 jetted off the end of the track and into a field. That was just the beginning for Thums; thereafter he spent entire days at the track watching guardrail banging fuel altereds and grooving to the drag strip sounds. "At the end of the day I was heavily sunburned on half my face and covered by powdered resin and rubber dust," recalls Thums. And "I was happy." On the nights he couldn't make the race, he'd sit out on his folks' lawn and listen to the 2,000 hp big blown hemis, "pounding the air from seven miles away."

The host of Radio Rumpus Room revels in the fact that—thanks to the release of "ungodly numbers of one-and two-off hot rod and drag related bands' songs"—there has been more hot rod music released in the last several years than during the entire hot rod heyday of the mid-sixties. And he finds new ways to showcase it. Some sets are structured around a sound—like an instrumental set featuring the Ventures and the Halibuts—or other sets play out a theme such as Deuces ("Little Deuce Coupe," "Fire Breathin' '32," "Three-Window Coupe" and "Draggin' Deuce"). There's always room for his rock and roll hero, Gary Usher, and one of "THE most important songs of all time," Minneapolis' Trashmen's classic, "Surfin' Bird."

The 5th (or 6th, whatever) anniversary edition of Radio Rumpus Room was a raucous mix of the whole range of Thums' favorites including 1960's Jan and Dean to more recent Untamed Youth. Whatever the time period, it all rocks (and rolls) and the party carries from KFAI's sound booth to the car stereos of hot rod fans all over the twin city area.

Hot benefit compilation to replace the masters, equipment and art destroyed in Estrus Records' warehouse fire. Features the Cheater Slicks, Fleshtones, Makers, Mono Men, Nomads, Quadrajets, and more. (1997, Man's Ruin Records)

**the Untamed Youth**
**Untamed Melodies**

*(1996, Norton Records)*

Place SPEED in SKULL.
Place, DO NOT CEMENT.
SKULL CAP on SKULL.

SPEED
KILLS

## UNTAMED YOUTH

The sounds of these wild beer drinking fools grew out of every place that had a garage. Influenced by the MC5, Gene Vincent and way too much beer, Untamed Youth was born in a garage in Columbia, Missouri. Actually, founder Derek "Deke" Dickerson describes the band's sound as "'60s/surf/hot rod mixed frat rock and garage punk" and there's no question about their allegiance—cars and girls. Or maybe as the Dictator's song they cover says, "cars, girls, surfing, beer—nothing else matters here."

They've always numbered four, with Dickerson always in attendance and Steve "Mace" Mace usually. Otherwise the organ/guitar/bass/drums line-up has varied over the band's on and off gatherings. Whoever filled the roster remained true to the sound that grew out of the Astronauts and the Trashmen and countless bands before them—the raucous, unbound, lo-fi stomp. Their second album, *More Gone Gassers*, featured devotional hot rod ditties like "Santa's Gonna Shut 'em Down," "Drag Race Tragedy" and "Supercharged Steamroller."

Untamed Youth offer a stage show full of dancing and beer drinking and a tradition of garage rocking. Although they come from the garage tradition of primitive music where musicians barely knew how to deal with their instruments, the Youth's have learned a trick or two over the ten years plus since their formation. Whatever tuneful abilities they acquired, Dickerson thinks they still appeal to what he calls the "universal motorcycle club"—or the drivers of the beat up hot rods you find at the Untamed Youth shows.

Geography works against the band, with members scattered across the U.S. Dickerson moved to California, joined another outfit and sold his '60 Cadillac Coupe Deville and '59 hearse that the band used to tour with, to stick with more traditional band vehicles—vans. That is if you can call the Go-Nuts van traditional. The Go-Nuts are a superhero, snack rock, gorilla entertainment review that look like they've arrived fresh from Saturday morning cartoonland. Fellow band member, Captain Cornnut built the Nut Wagon and bestowed it with a fine tangerine, metal flake paint job complete with cartoons on the side.

Favoring yet another side of his personae, Dickerson recorded as the Dave and Deke combo playing country-hillbilly music with a tip of the hat to West Coast country swing. If you thought the parking lot was full of hot rods for the garage tunes, you should see them turn out for the rockabilly world. And that pleases Dickerson just fine. "I think unskilled laborers and your basic low life types will always be into it. But you know what, those are my people. Other people laugh at them, but those are the people that dig that kind of music. So they're my friends."

## SPEED KILLS

The jumble of hot rod music needs a road map. Luckily there are a couple that can drive you to the heart of the matter. One, in publication since 1992, is *Speed Kills*, a fan/magazine put out by Scott Rutherford. As the editor and sole force behind *SK*, Rutherford's decided it's his mission to provide what's noteworthy in a wide range of music and anything related to car culture.

Rutherford explains, "there's volume, there's a sense of rebellion and of doing something different. I don't know if there's a whole lot of difference between going out to the garage to practice with your band, or going out to the garage to work on your car. Either way you're getting out tensions of your daily life."

There are features on Evel Knievel, Carhenge, hot rod pulp fiction, and fuel altereds. Rutherford strives to put out a varied magazine. *SK's* visual style is built around old ads snagged out of hot rod mags from decades before. There are microscopic ads about products to improve your performance or clothing or super-8 nudie movies. "*Speed Kills* is not just about blown Hemis and quarter mile races and guitar bands that play two minute punk songs." That range of interest encourages readers to pick up *SK* for the Mopar stuff, but he also gets letters saying: "I enjoy your magazine, I think cars suck. I'm a bike messenger and hopefully some day cars will be outlawed."

So, a publication with a name that sounds like a drug reference (it really came from Ralph Nader's histrionic warnings about highway accidents) is on a search and display mission to find "car bands" and just good music and getting the info out to a receptive public. A component of that mission has *SK* issuing 7" or 10" records by bands hooked to that hot rod fence—or any other sounds Rutherford feels needs to get out there. So far Gaunt, Portastatic, Rocket From the Crypt and Superchunk are among those that made it to *SK's* qualifying sessions.

this is issue #6. inside are features on: beastie boys/slant 6/gravel/neu/slow loris gorecki/mr. norm's grand-spaulding dodge carhenge/evel knievel/reviews & much more plus bonus superchunk 45 rpm single/$4.00

speed kills

## GEARHEAD

Louder, faster and more out of control, *Gearhead* magazine puts the West Coast spin on the drag punk scene. This San Francisco based publication has been hitting the newsstands since 1993, championed by mega-talker, writer and burgeoning publisher Mike LaVella and his band of rockin' hot rod misfits. LaVella cites three types of readers attracted to the vintage looking, new music covering publication: punk rock people, car people and (thank god) people that totally get it. It's a hybrid that he loves.

Two steps up from a fanzine and not yet a full color slick mag, *Gearhead* can be found on newsstands, at record stores and in high performance stores three or four times a year—more or less. Car themed covers have been done by high profile artists Coop, Peter Bagge, pal Kozik and David Perry. And inside is a smorgasbord of quality a publisher can be proud of along with a split single.

When he arrived on the Western Shore from his Pennsylvania home, LaVella was impressed with how prevalent cars were. Granted, he frequented the local dirt track and was into cars as a kid, but by the time LaVella was 16, punk rock knocked automobiles to second place. Following five hard-core years with Half-Life, his Pittsburgh-based band, LaVella found himself in the land of milk and honey and hot rods and writing for fanzines *Maximum Rock and Roll* and *Thrasher*. He even wrote for *Speed Kills*, before realizing in 1991 that he had the connections and ability to do his own publication. Or so he thought. Two years of floundering and three issues of *Speed Kills* passed before Nick Rubenstein (now art directing at Epitaph Records) came to LaVella's rescue. He matched LaVella in enthusiasm and surpassed him in expertise and within five months *Gearhead* hit the streets.

From the first sale of the speed rag in 1993, *Gearhead* was conceived as an elaborately packaged record. Each of its issues comes with a split 7" single. Featured bands have been Gas Huffer, Supercharger, Southern Culture on the Skids, Untamed Youth, the Meices, and Girl Trouble. Doing business this way gets the 'zine distributed through record channels, which LaVella has found to be more effective than the established magazine routes.

GAS HUFFER / SUPERCHARGER SPLIT SINGLE INSI

Gearhead

DIDJITS INTERVI

RAT FINK REUN

FIRST BIG ISSU

WINTERNATIONALS

*The 1993 first issue.*

The singles, the bands reviewed in the magazine and even the articles are picked in the same way—"Whatever I like," says LaVella. "If I like it, it's in." So far he's liked, and published articles on Motown's history, beatnik movies, readers' rides, surf music guru Dick Dale, the San Francisco Illegal Soapbox Society, where and how to get drunk, LaVella's trip to Graceland and various tech notes by musician/mechanic Kevin Thomson. And the music reviews are just as varied—hardcore punk rock, '60s hot rod, rockabilly, power pop and biker soundtracks. Readers clamored for the Beach Boys and *Gearhead* gave them three issues worth. There's even a degree of rockabilly added— due to the influences of Mike's girlfriend, Cathy Bauer and photographer David Perry. "I met all these guys and they love *Gearhead*," says LaVella of the mostly custom car fans. "I guess they were into musclecars first, then went backwards. Or they used to be punk and they went to rockabilly."

*Artists Suzanne and Robert Williams embrace fellow car fan, Mike LaVella. (Mike LaVella Collection)*

(Artist, Frank Kozik)

Or whatever. LaVella likes mixing the genres together—it's more punk rock. He uses Detroit's vast musical output as an example. The same town that produced Motown and Funkadelic also was home to the MC5, Stooges and Alice Cooper. Like LaVella says, "If somebody told me I had to get rid of my Curtis Mayfield records because I like the Fastbacks, I'd be like 'fuck you'."

The automotive genre is a mixed bag of dragsters, customs and street cars. The casual reader may not catch it, but *Gearhead* also functions as the newsletter for LaVella's car club. "There are other Scat Packs, but we're Scat Pack—San Francisco. We're the world's only all punk rock Mopar club," says the man who sports a Super Bee emblem tattoo. As times (and LaVella's affections) change, the low-dollar, lowbrow, DIY, Billet Proof car show scene becomes more appealing. "It's what *Gearhead* is all about," proclaims LaVella.

(Artist, Frank Kozik)

---

### THE 5 MOST IMPORTANT BANDS OF THE DRAG PUNK UNDERGROUND
### BY MICHAEL LAVELLA EDITOR/PUBLISHER GEARHEAD MAGAZINE

*THE DIDJITS*

*The grandfathers of the whole movement. While most of us still had mohawks and were dancing around in a circle with our shirts off in a futile attempt to change the world, they were doing songs like "Max Wedge." It still boggles the mind how ahead of their time they were. Thank God, they released 6 amazing LP's so we'll never forget them.*

*GAS HUFFER*

*This Seattle quartet took everything to the next level. With individual personalities as large and distinct as the Beatles, they wave the greasy rag of Drag Punk like no one else. "King Of Hubcaps" indeed.*

*THE MONO MEN*

*The logical choice. Big block garage rock that never looks back at the smoke it leaves behind. Play "Warm Piston" the next time you take a long drive, your foot will be through the floorboards before you realize what hit you. The preferred soundtrack for drag racing everywhere.*

*THE UNTAMED YOUTH*

*The closest thing to "Frat Rock" all off us uneducated slobs will ever experience. Seriously, their commitment to the Gary Usher sound/way of life is obvious from the first spin. When they ain't singing about hot rods or racing, the subject is generally beer or girls, and that just suits me fine.*

*GIRL TROUBLE*

*Perhaps an odd choice, but anyone who has ever seen them perform "Spinout" live knows just how important this Tacoma band is. Basically, they embody everything that's great about rock and roll, and brother, that ain't easy.*

(Rescue photo)

(Rescue photo)

# At the Drive-In Hot Rod Movies

Hot Rod Movies

**CHAPTER 6**

Left: (1957, American International Pictures)
Right: (1956, American International Pictures)

A s in music, cars have been in movies as long as there have been pictures projected on a screen. The earliest images are of open wheeled, road racing speed demons in *Burn 'Em Up* (1921), *Burn 'Em Up Barnes* (1934) and *Burn 'Em Up O'Connor* (1939). With the inclusion of helmets, seat belts, and roll cages, speed got safer and racing images calmed down and then died out. Escapist cinema experienced a boom when veterans returned during the post-World War II years. Then, just as suddenly as theater seats had filled up, attendance again dropped off. By the mid-1950s, film production companies gauged 70% of their viewers as twelve to twenty year-olds, and they tailored movies just for them in an attempt to draw audiences back to the empty movie palaces. The post-WWII trend of hot rod fever showed up on the silver screen in movies targeted at a young audience.

Films of the 1930s and 1940s were aimed at an older audience. Adults laid their ticket money down to see crime movies, film noir and explorations of social themes. When 1950s teenagers became the target audience, movie fare evolved into exploitation movies. Movie studios had found the perfect vehicle to speak to kids. These B grade films insightfully tapped into kids' fears and offered escapism at the same time. Because they were of the period, and focused on such a specific group, these nationally-distributed films showed kids on the East Coast how those bad kids on the West Coast filled their idle hours—or at least how filmmakers thought they spent their time. The films about kids gone bad were the trendsetters and starmakers of their day. What had started out as moral examples on how to live life, got out of control with the successes of *The Wild One* (1954) and *Blackboard Jungle* (1955).

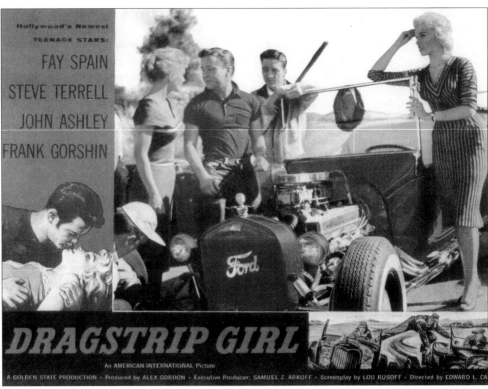

Hollywood's Newest
TEENAGE STARS:
FAY SPAIN
STEVE TERRELL
JOHN ASHLEY
FRANK GORSHIN

*DRAGSTRIP GIRL*

An AMERICAN-INTERNATIONAL Picture
A GOLDEN STATE PRODUCTION · Produced by ALEX GORDON · Executive Producer: SAMUEL Z. ARKOFF · Screenplay by LOU RUSOFF · Directed by EDWARD L. CA

*(1957, American International Pictures)*

Raucous loud rock and roll made this newly recognized group of individuals more noticeable. Teens had their own music, cars, clothing and trends. Markets took note and tried to sell them cameras, magazines and radios based on their youthful appeal. Recognizing their new found freedom, some kids went awry, and newspapers burst with stories of youth gone wrong. Television reports, radio shows, magazines articles, even Senate committees tried to figure out the problems of America's youth. Film production companies were just trying to figure out how to get their money from them. The posters were wild ad campaigns to draw youth in with lurid promises of sex, cars, and rock and roll. What they got were B grade films with repetitive plots, makeshift sets and ambiguous morals. And the kids loved it. In 1956 there were ten films released to this target audience. By 1957, there were forty.

Distributors of the 1958 films *Juvenile Jungle* ("A girl delinquent... a jet propelled gang... out for fast kicks!"), *Life Begins At 17* ("Today's 'shook-up' kids shaking loose!"), and *Live Fast, Die Young* ("they called her 'teenage tramp!'... the road she travels tonight is a one-way highway to hell!") made good return of their initial production budgets of $50,000-$100,000. Film titles were more dependent on what distributors thought would sell than the subject of the story. Titles could be changed just prior to release dependent on whatever recent social crisis—drugs, runaways, teenage prostitution, car theft—was currently making the daily news. The sexier, more violent and overblown the poster, the higher the box office guarantee. Movie goers were treated to JD movies, motorcycle films, teen pregnancy, problems in school, bad girl, teen horror, beach movies, drug movies, rebellion movies and, later, hippie films. Just one of the spokes in the cycle was hot rod films.

The industry was a group of big and little actors who worked together. Some became stars—Sal Mineo, John Saxon, Frank Gorshin, Jack Nicholson, Dean Stockwell, Robert Blake, Sally Kellerman, Connie Stevens—but most couldn't overcome their teen movie beginnings. This fast and dirty industry was a breeding ground for indie writers, directors and producers.

By 1959, some of the original rock and rollers were dead, in jail or in the army. The industry had been sullied with a payola scandal, and the young audience was ready for something cleaner. The number of exploitation films kept dropping as these changes occurred. From twenty-nine in 1959, to twenty in 1960, to only ten in each of 1961 and 1962. A direct result of the wholesome trend was the squeaky clean beach movies. In 1963 five of them surfaced. A sort of surf and turf packaging of hot rod films and beach movies kept teens in their movie seats.

This cycle came to an end when the outside world was too much to ignore. The Vietnam war, drugs, assassinations and racial unrest all forced teens to grow up a little quicker and come out of the cozy cinematic cocoon. Now drug addled epics (*Psych Out*, 1968), biker flicks, and anti-establishment movies (*Billy Jack*, 1971) were the Saturday afternoon fare, and carefree kids whooping it up on the beach with their surfboards and dragsters became a thing of the past.

## RON MAIN

One man who refuses to grow up is the savior for many of these forgotten treasures. Ron Main collects, refurbishes and distributes hot rod flicks, and is probably the largest provider of automobile-involved videos. Main is a fan who watched car movies as a kid and grew up to collect them as an "adult."

Main grew up with his twin brother/twin trouble-maker in Southern California at the height of hot rod mania. His memories from the late 1950s are stuffed with images of cars and girls—cruising for girls in his flathead Model A hot rod, racing their lakester at Bonneville Salt Flats and watching local favorite Shirley Shahan race at the local track. He, his brother and all their friends lusted after hot rods in popular culture—they'd see any film with a car in it—and waited anxiously for each episode of *'77 Sunset Strip* that featured the Kookie car. And if there was no car—they flicked the set off. Because, if you were stuck in the Midwest or too young to have a car of your own, these were the movies and TV shows that got you closer to the action.

The "who gives a shit," fast life of films like *Devil On Wheels* (1947) mirrored Main's teen years and as an adult he wanted to revisit those good times. Only problem was they weren't playing on TV or at the local cinema. To satiate the desire, he collected movies posters, press books and stills. The accessibility of the images gave Main hope that the movies themselves were out there. And he began to find them by working his way into circles of collectors. Sci-Fi, western or nudie buffs would start calling Main to offer up the automobile related movies they found in their searches. Once he opened his arms to them, they started flooding in. He eagerly received teen exploitation flicks, Perfect Circle Rings' 16 mm stock car movies and Hearst's drag racing films.

One timeless aspect of these old films is how they present an era. Conflicting images of thoughtless hot rodders evolve into safety-cautious dragstrip drivers while their cars got faster. Over time and film, early 1950s junkyard wrecks were replaced with late 1950s smooth customs often supplied by Hollywood customizer George Barris, who hired Mercs, Fords and dragsters as set dressing. Barris strove to add authenticity, correcting scripts whenever directors would listen to his advice. So, as Main points out, even if you don't like a particular film, you can at least treat yourself to a journey through time and enjoy the car show.

As his house got too small to project the movies and more folks wanted copies of their own, Main's collecting hobby spread to copying and distributing. Now he has a collection of thousands of films that he sends out worldwide through his video mail-order business. But some of the stuff he keeps to himself. Many of the documentaries look like they were shot through a hole in the fence and some of the corny movies are just plain unwatchable—but Main claims that Leonard Maltin rates most of his favorite films as "bombs." So, for a trip back in time to when hot rods cruised the streets unfettered, Main's your man.

*(1958, American International Pictures)*

# LET'S GO TO THE MOVIES

*(1950, Monogram Pictures)*

## DRIVER'S ED MOVIES

### The Cool Hot Rod (1953)
The new kid in school, Bill, gets shown the real way to race his '29 Ford roadster—safely on the strip following a complete tech check. *Hot Rod Magazine*, Mobile Oil, and California's Inglewood Police made this film with the help of local car clubs. The Bean Bandits' rear engine roadster makes an appearance in this cool film.

### The Devil on Wheels (1947)
A message movie, informing that Speed Kills.

### Hot Rod (1950)
Scenes of six cars dragging at once and eluding cops through fields look like keen fun until numbers like "37,000 dead" are cited. When one of the gang ends up in the morgue, it puts a damper on their thrills. Perhaps the ultimate fucked up moment is having to tell your mom that you hit and run her car, nearly killing her. Ow. When shown in schools nationwide, this movie thrilled the captive audiences of adolescents and gave them hot rod fever.

### Hot Rod (1979)
While the story is worth forgetting, the cars featured are worth a watch. Roadsters, early dragsters and mid-seventies muscle cars make this a car spotter's delight.

## JD FILMS

### The Choppers (1961)
Bad kids doing what they do best—running wild in a teen gang, stealing hot rods, altering them in "chop shops" and ending up with a little murder.

### Daddy-O (1959)
"Meet the 'beat'! daring to live... daring to love!" The poster screams jazz, but the music is actually written by *Star Wars* (1977) composer, John Williams.

*(1966, Russ Meyers)*

### Dragstrip Girl (1957)

When Fay Spain's boyfriend can't drive at the strip, Dragstrip Girl shoes for him. Hot rods, drag racing and a little murder tossed in for spice. The streets were never like this, or the strips for that matter.

### Dragstrip Riot (1958)

Faye Wray's last film features Corvette races on railroad tracks as a train comes barreling near, Connie Stevens and rock and roll.

### Faster, Pussycat! Kill! Kill! (1966)

A cool film about three female battling go-go dancers, barely concerned with keeping clothes on their enormous bosoms and shapely hips. Gang leader and man hater, Varla, (Tura Satana) karate chops her prey to a jazzy score. "Superwomen! Belted, buckled and booted!"—director Russ Meyers likes it sleazy. Very little to do with dragging outside of the frenetic racing of their foreign sports cars out on El Mirage dry lake—the birthplace of drag racing.

### Hot Rod Gang (1958)

"Crazy kids... Living to a wild rock 'n roll beat!" Or Gene Vincent and the Blue Caps' beat, anyway. Eddie Cochran shows up in an unbilled role. John Ashley joins Vincent's band to make money to enter a drag race. What results is hot rods, hip lingo, and robbery balanced with romance and a neatly wrapped happy ending.

### Hot Rod Girl (1956)

Lori Nelson, Chuck "the Rifleman" Conners and Frank Gorshin show up in this rush to shut down hot car racing. Good racing at the now gone San Fernando Raceway makes up for the lack of "Youth on the loose! Teen-age Terrorists burning up the streets!" and negligible story.

### Hot Rod Rumble (1957)

More JDs, more racing and more death. They were "revved up youth in a souped up jungle of crazy thrills!"

### Hot Rods to Hell (1967)

The ads claim they are "Hotter than Hell's Angels!," but this made for TV movie seemed much calmer in the theater. The hooligans use a Corvette and a Model A roadster to terrorize a law-abiding family with an impressionable teen-aged daughter.

### Joy Ride (1958)

"What'll we do tonight for kicks? The hot cars, the cool parties, the easy dames!!" Kicks looked like violence, robbery and terrorizing an innocent sports car driver.

### Running Wild (1955)

An undercover cop (nicknamed "Hot Rod") poses as a tough guy mechanic to infiltrate a car theft ring operated by Keenan Wynn. Plenty of rock and roll and shots of Mamie Van Doren showing off her tight sweater.

### The Wild Ride (1960)

A morally unbound hot rodder—Jack Nicholson—who would just as soon murder you as steal your girlfriend.

*(1958, American International Pictures)*

*(1956, American International Pictures)*

*(1964, American International Pictures)*

## KID FLICKS

### Bikini Beach (1964)

A beach pic at Big Drag's (Don Rickles) dragstrip. A love triangle where surfer (Frankie Avalon) must drag race a Brit rock star/dragster driver (Avalon again) for the hand of bikini girl (Annette Funicello). The story is sappy, but they do show dragsters on the Pomona 1/4 mile, "Little" Stevie Wonder, and surf music wonders— The Pyramids. Exotica master Les Baxter handled the score.

*(1959, American International Pictures)*

### The Ghost of Dragstrip Hollow (1959)

This goofy sequel to *Hot Rod Gang* (1958) didn't have Gene Vincent, but did have drag racers and a haunted house.

### Hot Rod Hullabaloo (1966)

"Speed's their creed," but this tale of hot rods, chicken races, demo derbies and death is prime kiddy fare.

### The Lively Set (1964)

This James Darin flick featured Darin quitting college to race, "dragster duels at 3 miles a minute," an experimental turbine car, the Surfaris' "Boss Barracuda" and a nice happy ending.

## DOCUMENTARIES

### American Nitro (1979)

Subtitled the Saga of the Funny Cars and with its footage from Fremont in the mid-1970s, you get plenty of flopper action. Even the original score by Eugene Revs gets you going. Lots of squirrely action and fire burnouts, wheel standers, the famous cheeks of Jungle Pam in her crotch length shorts and famous faces of "TV" Tommy Ivo, Tom "the Mongoose" McEwen and Don "the Snake" Prudhomme when he was funny car's winningest driver.

### Funny Car Summer (1973)
Jim Dunn tours the country in his rear engine Barracuda—and we are there to experience all the smoke and fire. It's an illuminating look into the life of a racer on the road, even if sometimes it's pitch black at the track and the only thing lit up are the header flames of the competitors.

### Hot Rod Action (1966)
Produced by *Hot Rod Magazine* and full of footage from 1966—the NHRA Winternationals, Bakersfield March Meet, U.S. Nationals and NHRA's World Finals—and all the accompanying racers and fans. Even some spectacular footage of Craig Breedlove atop his jet car, Spirit of America, as he finished a Bonneville Salt Flats run out in the wet lake bottom.

### Vrooom! (1974)
What Ron Main calls "almost a satanic devil worship film" is a vintage 1970s psychedelic look at drag racing. Amid crazy visual effects and a rock soundtrack, there are plenty of cars and interviews with Shirley Muldowney, Don Garlits, and Jungle Jim Liberman who proclaims "Drag racing is faaarrr out!" Basically it's racing on acid.

## CRASH AND BURN FILMS

Fans of drag racing and other motorsports are conflicted—we want action, but we don't want anyone to lose their lives. Well, in answer to that thirst for the spectacular, there's crash footage. Not only can you find straight track blow-overs and flashy oil fires, these companies offer Unlimited Hydroplane smashes, NASCAR pile-ups and World of Outlaws sprint cars whacking the walls. Motorcycles, monster trucks, swamp buggies—just about anything with an engine can be seen on fire and in peril. Companies like Diamond P, Duke Video and Simitar Entertainment keep this adrenaline flowing with the knowledge that most of these drivers walked away.

Of the same vein are films by Drag Racing Underground that feature bracket racing for fans of doorslammers. In their video, *From England to Englishtown*, John Gill and Diana Thomas have put together drag bikes, Chevys, Dusters and Fords in Englishtown, New Jersey with Chevys, Dusters, Fords, and Minis in Santa Pod, England for a look at what the average racer is doing on both continents. Heavy guitar, drum machines and announcing from the videographers add to the experience. No burning wrecks, but more a look at what the guy next door is doing for fun. As the fan at the beginning says, "this is what gets me through the winter."

(1979, Cannon Pictures)

(1966, Cinerama Releasing)

## DRAMAS

### Drag Racer (1971)

Shot at the big three of drag racing—Lions Drag Strip, Irwindale Raceway and Orange County International Raceway—Drag Racer features Mark Slade (of TV's *High Chaparral* fame) as a guy just trying to get a ride in a rail. Once he succeeds, the owners of the car find that he's got no experience and causes him to take a hard look at himself. We, meanwhile, get to check out on-car camera shots that add authenticity to this realistic track visit.

### Heart Like A Wheel (1983)

A movie with real heart documenting women's rise in social status and one particular woman's rise from street racer to winner's circle. The events that led to Shirley "Cha Cha" Muldowney's (Bonnie Bedalia) departure from her waitressing job, marriage and gas powered car to the status of winning top fuel dragster driver are show with a realism that makes you want to get to the track. The love/hate affair with Connie Kalitta (Beau Bridges) and stunt driving by Tommy Ivo help as well.

### Two Lane Blacktop (1971)

Just as extraneous weight is removed from a race car, director Monte Hellman made damn sure this flick didn't carry any gratuitous dialog. But he didn't short us on the atmosphere in this road story of the Driver (James Taylor), the Mechanic (Dennis Wilson) and the Girl (Laurie Bird) as they match their '55 primered Chevy against motor mouth GTO (Warren Oates) in a race for pink slips. The group drive aimlessly across the Southwest with little feel of competition, displaying the uselessness of freedom without aim.

*(1983, Twentieth Century Fox Film Corporation)*

*(1971, Universal Pictures)*

## DEFIES DESCRIPTION

### Kustom Kar Commando (1965)

In this classic underground film, director Kenneth Anger has his man in leather lovingly polish his roadster with a powder puff to the tune of "Dream Lover."

### Red & Rosy (1990)

Frank Grow grew up influenced by head monster maker Ed Roth and at the race track, which is how he came to create *Red & Rosy*. In Grow's 1990 budget-basement short, a drag racer, Big Red McKenzie, has a horrific crash, resulting in the loss of his adrenal gland. In order to survive, he must receive adrenaline injections. "Big Red" clones plague innocent citizens with their inexplicable need to get high on adrenaline. The entire story spins out of control as these adrenaline junkies kill children and other innocents, and Red and his lover Rosy turn into adrenaline craving monsters.

Where the hell did this story come from? Much of it comes from one particular night at the local dragstrip when Grow was at the tender age of seven.

Grow's dad, Mike of Burbank, raced Studebakers and Triumph motorcycles, so they were at Lions Drag Strip all the time. Two new funny cars were built for exhibition along the lines of the Snake and Mongoose team. They were to be billed as Snoopy and the Red Baron. Grow had chosen the Snoopy car as his favorite, befriended the crew, got to sit in the cockpit before the thing even had its official paint job. On the first night of running the Snoopy car, Grow was in the stands, down toward the finish line, on the shoulders of his 6'8" Uncle Dave with all his dad's drug addicted biker friends. So the Snoopy car, this young kid's favorite, crashed and tumbled off the strip into the safety area between the track and the fence. His Uncle Dave, who's totally drunk, charges down to the wreckage with young Frank still on his shoulders.

The kid is treated to seeing his first dead body close up. The driver was in his cocoon-like fire suit, so there was no gore hanging out, but he was long gone. Grow stared as the announcer reported the closing of the track to clean up body parts—meaning the car, not the driver as the kid assumed.

Now all these drunken fans were treated to an unscheduled break, and they all trooped off to the huge communal urinal in the men's room, Grow's Uncle Dave included. Once there, he was peeing into the huge trough-like urinal with all the other bladder-heavy drunks with young Frank still atop his perch. The piss, the cigarette smoke, and the recent carnage must have been too much for the kid—he spewed right down on his uncle and fell backward to the bathroom floor. And the vomit train started. Next it was Uncle Dave who lost it, then others standing around the urinal. Grow retreated to Ed "Big Daddy" Roth's nearby poster/pinstriping/tattoo shop—or the "full on bitchin demonic toy store" as Grow calls it. What ensued was a rush of grown men stumbling from the men's room puking their guts up.

That's the atmosphere that created *Red & Rosy*. That and Grow's need to display his animated, twisted metal sculpture. This underground film, that has 3,000-4,000 "official" copies in circulation, was written, directed, produced, shot and edited by Grow. He also built the featured car, its monsters, did the animation, optical prints AND wrote and performed the music with the Blood Pumpers Racing Club. And he even stood in for one of his three Big Red McKenzie's. While I'm amazed that such a film exists, Grow can't figure out why this fucked up, adrenaline injected, nitro fueled, monster driven, seven year-old's nightmare won't die. And we're damn glad it won't.

*(Rescue photo)*

# Garage Wall to Gallery Hall
## High Art in Lowbrow Society

## CHAPTER 7

**S**ince humans first understood how to utilize carving tools and pigments everyone decorated what was dear to them. Done out of respect for the object and to leave an individual mark, it was just a part of life. Hot rods and custom cars started as rough images of the imagination. That they showed their uneven seams, or had hand painted words on the side were part of the appeal. If you had a little money, you could get someone who had a steadier hand than yours to help complete your expression. With the addition of a pinstripe here, a flame there... these craftsmen became recognized as artists. On their journey from fenders to canvas they leave flying eyeballs, surrealist daydreams and skeptical critics in their wake.

### VON DUTCH—KUSTOM KULTURE KREATOR

Imagine Hitler's distress had he learned the seeds of lowbrow art came from a man entranced by German culture and engineering. Kenneth Howard, who later named himself Von Dutch (attributed to either Germany—Von Deutschland—or from his childhood manner of being "as stubborn as a Dutchman"), is unerringly recognized as the father of modern pinstriping. He is credited with not only teaching a technique of automobile decoration, but also of inspiring surfboard designers, poster artists and vaguely surrealist painters. Von Dutch's work was so fresh and "right" that he helped define the sport of hot rodding. Combined with his love of precision was his notion that pinstriping was a way to personalize a car, a motorcycle, a knife—whatever. He felt the work should not be so overpowering that it outshone the object it was beautifying. Pinstriping is a tool to accentuate the good elements in design. Pinstriping should fit the person who requested, and above all—do the best job you possibly can.

His drive for perfection may have come from being raised by a sign writer. His dad also worked as a graphic artist for the Western Exterminator company. It was Dutch's dad who created one of Los Angeles' landmarks, the clean and whimsical logo of a pencil nosed mortician warning a little mouse that soon the massive mallet behind his back will swing and annihilate him. In earlier days, a stream of neon mice would race up to the exterminator outside of the Western's building in the Silver Lake area.

Born in 1929, Von Dutch grew up near the Watts Towers—a dizzying spired structure of concrete, madly decorated with broken soda bottles, smashed china and marbles. Simon Rodia's hand-built monument to art for no reason inspired the young Von Dutch as he handed the determined Rodia broken tile pieces. Von Dutch had a natural ability to work with his hands and later attended a trade school. Working as an engraver and also cleaning up in a motorcycle shop gave the kid a chance to jump right into pinstriping. His developed his skill fixing the body and painting over mistakes by striping to hide flaws.

During World War I, airplanes were sometimes decorated with flames coming from their exhaust manifold. Von Dutch used that idea as a spring board, but soon owners wanted his novel flames in all sorts of places, leading to outrageously flamed cars cruising down Southern California roads.

Von Dutch's tastes were based in the classical, but his imagination took his designs to places no one had been before. (Artist, Coop)

Von Dutch at work. (Mike Salisbury photo)

Von Dutch specialized in elaborate designs. (Greg Sharp collection)

Von Dutch was the son of a graphic artist who created Western Exterminator's classic image. (Andy Takakjian photo)

Flaming a car often covers its flaws. Barris shop car worked over by Von Dutch. (George Barris collection)

Seemingly Von Dutch followed his whims—sticking with things that worked for him and dumping those that didn't. The Air Force was one of those things that didn't fit. He was discharged during the Korean War for "borrowing" a piano. Later in life, when marriage and fatherhood didn't seem to suit him, he left his wife and two daughters in Arizona and tried Australia.

Von Dutch's talent for pinstriping blossomed and in 1954 he worked at the Barris Brothers' shop—Competitive Motors. He was at the height of his creative wave and pinstriped or airbrushed anything—sweat shirts, surfboards, radios, and even cars. Moving whenever the whim hit him, Von Dutch became a transitory worker, finally spending quite a bit of time working for Jimmy Brucker's family collection, "Movieworld Cars of the Stars and Planes of Fame." He simply showed up one day and asked to park his bus behind the museum.

Von Dutch reveled in novelty; he always wanted to do what hadn't already been done. He hid characters—rabbits, aliens—in his designs, discreetly waiting for a curious observer. His trademark was the flying eyeball he first drew as a kid in 1947 and could never remember why. Von Dutch's intricate lines graced hot rods all over Southern California, most notably on the Barris' shop car. He did flames or stripes, whichever you wanted for "$6.00 an hour," in 1956. The designs he created, of images within images, became the standard for hot rods. As good as he was, he was also an eccentric. Von Dutch designs often looked different on opposite sides of a car—after all you can only see one side at a time.

Fellow artist and striper Ed Roth recognized Von Dutch's genius and values the time they spent together. "He would only tell you his conception of the world. His famous statement to me was always, "You don't own nothing until you give it away." Which was a ridiculous statement to me when I was 35, but the older I get, the more sense it makes." Another of Von Dutch's truisms was "there's nothing new in this world. It's all been done before and nobody owns it." He and Roth came from the same German background. "Germans have a different twist on things than normal people do," says Roth. "Von Dutch used to say, 'That Salvador Dali's okay. He likes my work, but I could never repay the compliment.'"

Unusual tools, like the exotic welding machine he used to cut his name out of a razor blade, were attractive to Von Dutch. His love of trying new things defined his striping style. As Roth says, there's no big secret to working a striping brush. A large portion of the art is your style, your philosophy. Von Dutch's philosophy about pinstriping was, "Make the car look better, not the pinstriper." "So when these guys put the curlicues on these cars, they used to kill him," recalls Roth. The master's thought was that straight lines and colors could be used to make the car look low in front and to make it look like it's going fast when it's standing still.

Kids and what they'll be producing in the future were a big deal to Von Dutch. When a kid would come up to him, he'd always answer his questions and give him a striping brush and show him how to pinstripe. Because Roth told Von Dutch that his art would be lost to the kids after his death, he made Roth get out his video camera and they spent two hours laying it out for kids to come.

Early on Dutch became a recluse and spent more and more time playing his flute and just drinking. He traveled the country in an old public transportation bus that he fixed up with a toilet and a place to sleep. With those comforts and his tools, he was free to move around and survive printing signs, fixing machines and making guns and knives. Shortly before his 1992 death—presumably from a life of hard living and drinking—Von Dutch got to see the fruits of his labor. His striping styles are emulated on hot rods and customs nationwide. Work from his younger years are collector's items. His personal trademark of the bloodshot flying eyeball is copied, manipulated and recalled by an entire generation of young artists.

For all of this, the cynic in Von Dutch would simply say that people would remember him as they may, and the actuality of his life had little to do with their romantic reminiscences. He was simply a man who took pleasure in beautifying objects by taking away their cold machine-like appearance. He said of his work, that he treated the striping brushes like a musical instrument and whatever he striped became a melody.

## ED ROTH—Big Daddy Rat Fink

A man most famous for a fat rat with flies buzzing around doesn't fill the typical image of an artist. Ed Roth doesn't care. He doesn't care if you think he's proper or if you even know his name. What he does care about is the future and what his part will be in it. Because the future is where we can make our mark and yesterday will just have to take care of itself.

Many yesterdays ago, Ed "Big Daddy" Roth inked out a sketch on a napkin that became the symbol of individuality for teenagers and adults for at least four decades. Roth drew Rat Fink as a take off on Mickey Mouse, but real-life like. Roth was sick of the "real" life he'd been lectured about in school. He knew that in real life some folks were ugly and things just plain stank. So that's what he portrayed when a friend asked him to draw the rat. A fink. Somehow that idea got turned around into art. Art, for chrissakes. Fifty years later you'll still find Rat Fink on t-shirts, posters, trash cans (how appropriate), even on canvasses hanging in galleries. Art galleries. Roth started his hot rodding career as a high schooler in Buena Vista, California around 1949. In spite of the inevitable cop hassle, kids restyled their cars however they wanted. During the war and directly following, you couldn't buy new cars. "There was plenty of money, but no metal," recalls Roth. "So we went to all the big junkyards in LA and at that time they were divided. Half of the junkyard had surplus airplanes and the other half had old cars from the '20s, '30s and '40s. We assembled hot rods from an early model frame and a late model engine, at that time it was a '36 to '41 Ford V-8."

Fly-infested Rat Fink, Roth's conception of Mickey Mouse's father.
(Copro/Nason collection)

"The first style trend was to take Harley Davidson motorcycle tires and put them on the front and use larger tires on the rear. And that came from the old west where the wagons and the Connestoga wagons all had smaller spoked wheels on the front so the horse could pull it and turn a sharper corner with the smaller wheel. Yeah, that was the first hot rod styling thing and taking the fenders off." This style of car also had it's own name. The "hot rod," Roth explains, was named after the rod in the main part of the engine that the piston connects onto. "Those things would always get hot because the engines would overheat and they'd break, so we used to call them hot rods. And the public did not like us."

Kids latched onto this new pastime that gave them equal doses of freedom and self expression. "There were all these clubs that turned into the customs. And there were the hot rods, the guys who like to go fast. I was sort of right in the middle. I didn't like to go fast because it always broke my engine and I had to fix it and that cost money. I learned at an early age to cruise except when it was really necessary and you had to prove yourself. When the stop signal turned green, you just floored it if there was some better car beside you. But I never raced in the illegal street races. I went to them to spectate, but I didn't take part."

The Roth family came from a practical German background. Big Daddy's dad must have thought his son was nuts. I also used to take the family car apart a lot and my dad would watch me out the window wondering, What's that kid doing to my generator? He's up in heaven now shaking his head over the stuff I do. He said, What are you doing now" when I had all that plaster out building my car. He said, "You're building a car out of plaster? It'll fall apart. When I had it all done, he'd go around to all the guys, 'My son built that out of plaster.'"

Early in his rodding career, Roth learned what was stylish and what was not. "I was cutting lawns and working the menial jobs just to feed my car and have a few dates. I was conscious of one thing, that when you did something and it was good, guys would copy you. But if you did something and it was bad, like a styling trend that came along, like put an antenna on your left-hand side, that wasn't good. Put it on the right-hand side and it was great and everybody accepted it, and they did it. It was like a monkey see, monkey do thing and then we felt like we wanted to be part of a gang or a fraternity."

Ed "Big Daddy" Roth's rolling sculptures show his vision of the future. (Artist, Dennis McPhail)

Roth with a recent creation. (Ed Roth collection)

His interest in cars continued, even while he was far away from sunny California pulling an Air Force stint in Africa. "I'd hang up pictures of cars. The other guys thought all of us California guys were crazy because we didn't have any pictures of girls hanging up." He passed time conjuring the cars he would build when he got back to civilian life. Once out of the service, Roth got a regular job at Sears. Von Dutch had already gotten a name as a pinstriper and Roth figured he could support his family doing the same. He pinstriped at home and took his talent on the road with the car shows. Then guys started coming to him with special requests. They wanted Roth to put their car club's names on shirts. So he got out the felt tip pens and gave them what they wanted.

He did so many shows—two days, or three days—and kids wanted so many shirts, he started airbrushing them to keep up with the demand. Soon he'd put caricatures of the drivers on the shirt.

The crowd's desire for product was physically overwhelming for one guy with an airbrush. "I was doing pretty good caricatures of these guys in the cars and after four or five hours of doing this stuff I'd get really tired. And I'd have more people wanting more stuff. So I just thought, Well, if I did a thing with big eyeballs and not make them look like the kids that are getting the things, they'd go away." And it didn't work. It worked the opposite way, they wanted more bug eyed, big fanged creations. "Hey, Big Daddy put his finger through his ear and have it come out his mouth." His work got wilder and crazier and more outside of the "real" world.

Cars had been the great do-it-yourself project. As old car bodies got more scarce and expensive, kids turned to weirdo shirts for individuality. The monstrous car club shirts sold so well that Roth decided he needed a character to call his own. That was Rat Fink's job. The fat rodent showed up on decals and an ever increasing number of shirts. Rat Fink showed up on just about anything that Roth could market. So much money rolled in that he moved to a warehouse and opened Roth Studios on Slauson Boulevard in Culver City, California. This is where he painted the shirts, created his ads and turned out a weird car a year for the car shows.

Taking advantage of his ability to fantasize, Roth created a piece of art called the Outlaw. It came in the shape of a car. It was mind blowing for 1959. It was the first and only of it's kind. His work was a sort of mobile sculpture and was unique for a number of reasons. Roth didn't redo Detroit's work. He started fresh, with plaster that was later used to mold fiberglass. A year later Roth presented the Beatnik Bandit, another fiberglass mind blower. The Bandit, considered Roth's masterpiece, featured pearl white paint made from ground fish scales, a clear plastic bubble top, and a "Unicontrol" that controlled acceleration, braking and hydraulic steering. Other transports from the future included the Road Agent, Mysterion and Rotar. In a genius marketing move, Revell approached Roth about producing 1/25th-scale models of his hot rods. Soon boys and girls all over the country were assembling, painting and flaming their own monster kits. A whole culture was building around Roth—it was full of possibilities and he could do anything. Roth had the foresight to realize that he needed some real artists in his shop. Shirts were selling like crazy and he couldn't keep up with the demand. To his shop of crazies, he added Dirty Doug, "Jake" Jacobs, and a young reprobate named Robert Williams.

Rat Fink head.
(Copro/Nason collection)

Williams had been sent to Roth's place by a State Unemployment Agency. The relaxed yet wildly creative environment was one where Williams, Roth and their ideas thrived. Roth would only hang out between car shows. His time was equally divided between designing his one of a kind vehicles, collecting money for the booming t-shirt business, calming down Williams' wild ad designs and joking around to entertain the girls in the front office. As Roth became more well known, assorted oddballs would drop in; musicians, movie stars and writers who wanted to be a part of the "scene."

It was a wild time, drugs and alcohol were around, but according to Williams, Roth wasn't interested. Outside of a few tokes on a joint or some experimentation with wine, Roth stuck to work more than partying. Williams also considered Roth to be tough on his kids. He has five sons and at varying times, they all worked at the studio after school—like it or not.

Roth started wearing his trademark tux to create a different image—really it was sort of a slam. A Fresno promoter didn't like Roth's slovenly appearance so he handed over 100 bucks for a suit. The smartass Roth zipped into a tuxedo shop and picked out duds that were more flamboyant AND cheaper than a suit. "Business jumped like 100% with that thing, so I just kept that up. In fact, now when I leave the house and travel, I just always wear a necktie and a suit."

A RF for four decades, Ed "Big Daddy" Roth still makes appearances at car shows for the fans. (Ed Roth collection)

In 1966 Big Daddy's likes turned to trikes and Revell dropped him like a hot potato. His new obsession with motorcycles just didn't fit their image. Neither did the two or three wheeled creations fit into the car shows. He became a man without a car club. Somewhere down the line, he also became a Mormon. His rough style had to change to fit his new beliefs. This meant "cleaning up" the shirts he was selling. "I don't try to degrade anybody and I try to stay away from gray areas of double meanings. I've only failed a couple of times in the past 30 years." Big Daddy looked over his repertory and realized there were a few designs that had to be dropped. "I had this one Wild Child design where I had a set of brass knucks dangling from the car. So I put an ice cream cone in his hand and it looked badder than when he had the brass knucks. And Lover Boy, same thing. I had a grill with the pins through it like a voodoo doll. I took that out of his hands and put an ice cream cone in there and it looked so much better."

From the start Roth rode tough on Robert Williams to make his ad creative but not too extreme. "I would say 'It takes more thought to put a G-rated ad out than it does an X-rated one.' I'm proud of those ads. In the end, when the ad angel asks me, I carried out my responsibilities. I believe we're accountable for all of these things."

That seems to be Roth's outlook—it all matters in the end. Being imaginative worked for him. He suggests everyone try it. "I got a letter from a girl. You can tell she's not past six or seven. It says on the top 'Dare to be different. It's okay, isn't it?' This is the kind of thing that I'd like to go down in history for, saying that it is okay to be different and to think and to goof around in class and to get on the Internet and to think for yourself. And to find out what perceivably is the truth for yourself."

Rat Fink can be seen from Maine to Mexico and surely cool kids in Japan and farther sport Mother's Worry t-shirts, but Roth still has to work hard. He still builds cars, tours with the car shows and signs lots of autographs. Most of his cars have disappeared. Some of them were sold to Ed Lauivee who in turn sold them to an automobile museum, thinking they were safe. But Harrah's bought them and they've been scattered to the wind to be repainted by any idiot who thinks they have an eye for design. His business too, ended up with someone else. Roth complains today that he sold it to Moon Eyes and they now make a bundle. What won't disappear is the feeling of genius that Roth infused into the hot rod and, ultimately, fine art culture.

He figures today, the poor man's hot rod is—the computer: "I was looking at this catalog the other day and it says 'Fast Macs, do a burnout.' These kids are getting it. They don't want to talk about car speed, they talk about megahertz. 'I got 185 megahertz machine, but if I put this motherboard in with this panel, I get up to 300 megahertz.' Today they're drag racing with virtual reality. It's the greatest thing that ever happened to our country. I used to think Pac Man was a total waste of time. Then the war in Iran came along and I saw the bombs being guided in with the Pac Man technology. I went out and bought my grandson every program he could have."

Now a Mormon, Roth finds a revised way to justify his work—his religion. "It teaches me that service in whatever forms it comes is the most important thing that there is. So I have resolved myself to go to these shows, and sign these autographs. I do it because I feel that's my service and my duty to the people that have made, and are making this a good thing, this hot rodding. It's a good clean thing."

## STANLEY MOUSE

Like Ed "Big Daddy" Roth, Stanley Mouse came up through the ranks as an airbrush artist, providing weirdo hot rod and monster t-shirts for kids at car shows. (Copro/Nason collection)

About the same time Ed Roth was poking around the junkyards looking for parts to hop up his rod, Stanley Miller spent school hours sketching monsters. Because his obsession was shared both by other kids in his classes and nationwide, he helped spread the weirdo hot rod look across the country. And because Miller's father was an illustrator for Disney Studios, the quiet sketcher was nicknamed "Mouse," and because it was unusual, he kept the name.

As a teenager in the 1950s, Mouse was a true son of Detroit. "There was Motown and '57 Chevys," explains Mouse. "That was life. Motown and hot rods." At least it was *his* life. Mouse spent his summers at the state fair painting "Eat My Dust" and other weirdo designs on t-shirts at a booth strategically located near the Motown Review stage. The background music to his youth was provided by Little Stevie Wonder and Martha and the Vandellas and the Temptations and the Four Tops and the Supremes and Smokey Robinson and the Miracles. It was so natural to him, that it wasn't until many years later, when Mouse left his mixed neighborhood and headed for California, that he even realized he was white. He had grown up listening to local black stations and at 16 he bought a car just to sit in and listen to the "devil music" as his grandmother called it.

By 1960 Mouse widened his horizons from flaming, lettering and pinstriping the line of cars in his driveway every Saturday, to touring the East Coast with the Autorama car show. It was at the show's Pittsburgh stop that Mouse met a man who wanted to change his life—Ed Roth. "He said 'can I paint here with you? I came a long way from California. Plus I can show you the difference between making $100 and $300 at a car show.'" The bare chested, fat bellied Roth set up next to Mouse and proceeded to crank out little black and white drawings of snakes and skulls, and made his promised $300. Mouse, meanwhile, drew faster and in color, and made $1,000. In a move that Mouse likens to the Walt Disney of the hot rod world, Roth took Mouse's catalog back to his artists in California, and had them copy Mouse's renderings—particularly his Fred Flypogger, who had a nose and ears added and got a new name—Rat Fink.

Left: The skull theme is ever present in Stanley Mouse's work, be it hot rods (8 Ball) or...
Right: Grateful Dead work (Skull Mandala).
(Artist, Stanley Mouse)

There began a love/hate relationship that brought both notoriety and sales. Setting up across from each other at car shows, Mouse and Roth would each display signs. "I Hate Roth" and "I Hate Mouse" was part of the rivalry that was mostly good natured, but also tinged with disgust—at least on Mouse's part. "When anybody sees my old stuff, they say 'oh, Rat Fink stuff'." Not exactly a legacy one would want to live with.

Fortunately for Stanley Mouse, he's recognized in wider circles for his work produced following that hot rod phase. He and partner Alton Kelley "borrowed" a drawing of Omar Khayyam's Rubaiyat and developed the world famous logo for the Grateful Dead. Their skull and roses, along with the multitudes of psychedelic, pseudo Art Nouveau posters helped to define the visuals for the San Francisco Haight-Ashbury Summer of Love. The team worked as a collaborative unit—Mouse drew right handed and Kelly left, so working on a single project, they became a four handed monster.

Screamin' 40
(Artist, Stanley Mouse)

Mouse's signature and running critter logo grace much of the Grateful Dead art work as well as posters for San Francisco's Fillmore Auditorium and Avalon Ballroom. The critter also scampers across posters and album cover art for musicians including Eric Clapton, Janis Joplin, Jimi Hendrix, Steve Miller, Journey and on and on. Talents honed in art school are displayed in Mouse's favorite medium, oil, but acrylic, watercolor, pen and ink, pencil and computer are all employed—whatever it takes to get the job done.

As promised by at least one Grateful Dead song lyric, Stanley Mouse's world has come full circle. After a transplant, he now finds himself with a new 19 year-old liver that has cravings for McDonalds and french fries and cokes. His new life also included a desire to shift motorcycle gears and led Mouse to create the Harley Davidson Love Ride poster for the last five years. In trade for his poster work, Mouse bartered for a black fatboy. Now he's a full fledged biker. Reminiscent of his youth, Mouse spent a recent summer at Sears Point Dragway outside of San Francisco watching fuelers, getting deaf and painting—hot rods. So the music's changed, but the same little line drawing of a mouse frolics among the flames and flying eyeballs portrayed by the sure-handed Stanley Mouse.

## ROBERT WILLIAMS

Often described as the leader of this new school, Robert Williams says, "if I'm the biggest turd in this line of turds, we're all in trouble." Prior to our meeting, I could only guess what the life of a breathing icon is all about. As I sat with Williams in his '32 Ford Coupe at the weekly hooha at Bob's Big Boy in Burbank, I realized that a description I read about him was eerily accurate. Jim Woodring interviewed Williams back in 1988 or so for a fanzine called *Chemical Imbalance*. He described Williams as, "a compound of opposites. He is friendly yet hostile; refined yet coarse; cheerful yet grumpy; sophisticated yet provincial; calm yet tense. He heats up and cools off with astonishing rapidity, giving the impression of being a man who controls the various aspects of his personality instead of being controlled by them." Yep, yep, double yep. Not the easiest interview, but well worth the time spent.

Just to disprove Robert Williams' assumption that women don't like hot rods, his wife, Suzanne, owns a chopped '34 of her own.
(Sam Painter photo)

137

While waiting to cash in on his "next big thing" status (hopefully in the form of a Whitney Museum Biennial), Williams makes his way doing what he does—painting, going to car shows, selling posters and being the father of "lowbrow art." Although his influence is strongly felt, Williams attributes the entire hot rod art thing to Von Dutch. Williams describes Dutch as a pivotal, seminal character that made hot rod art a thing in itself by developing it into a fine science.

For Williams, growing up in New Mexico was tough. He wasn't particularly interested in school. Got into trouble all the time. And finding a crowd outside of school was equally difficult. So Williams ended up with the outsiders, of course. He later worked as a truck driver, short order cook, a carney, fork lift operator, boxcar loader and it was all horrible. Williams figured being an artist would be less horrible, so that's what he aimed for. "That was all I was good for. I had a propensity for it at an early age. Drawing pictures." His messy past resulted in spicy data for his paintings. Fast cars, drug-induced hallucinations, senseless beatings. At an early age he discovered the Surrealists—Dali, De Chirico and Pierre Roy. He slurped up their images along with the cartoons of Carl Banks and EC comics. It was the baby years of the '60s and the right time for Williams' relocation to California. After a series of ill-fitting commercial art jobs, he miraculously plopped down in a tailor-made place: Roth Studios.

Ed "Big Daddy" Roth was well recognized by the kids and adults. Advertisers were just catching on when Roth got lots of help from Williams in honing his image. Roth's "otherworldly" car designs were being featured by Revell and his t-shirt sales were going through the roof. Williams came aboard as the head of the art department and advertisement guy, of sorts, and the whole operation creaked up to 6,000 rpm. Finally Williams had a place where he was encouraged to explore what all those lessons in life had taught him. "It was like a psychedelic think tank. It was just wonderful. Roth required the most extreme, wild imagination. And I could supply that. It's just impossible to find a job where they're looking for someone with a wild imagination. And that's what I found. It straightened my life up. It got me going in life just perfectly." Sometimes Roth had to restrain Williams' output. But mostly Williams was free to do

*A White-Knuckle Ride for Lucky St. Christopher, 1991. Scholastic Designation: The Crime of Pure Automotive Thrill Is Exacerbated by the Emotional Dependency on a Lucky Catholic Talisman Commemorating Baby Jesus Fording a River on the Back on an Unlucky Good Samaritan Who Was Later Tortured to Death. Remedial Title: Tearin' a New Ass Without the Blessing of the D.M.V. (Artist, Robert Williams)*

*Hot Rod Race, 1976 (Artist, Robert Williams)*

what he does so well—turn over the rocks of our culture and put a magnifying glass to all the squirmy, icky things we hide under there. They had a hell of a ride together while Williams slid into a surrealism that defined his distinctive style.

Co-founding *Zap Comics* was one of his things that'll be mentioned in Williams' obituary, eventually. Williams, Robert Crumb, Rick Griffin, Stanley Mouse, and the other depraved screwed with the minds of teenagers like nobody's business. The country was in the midst of evaluating its morals and mores, and Williams was busy dodging the draft and working at Roth's Studios. The crew were obvious scofflaws and the IRS and FBI were keeping an eye on their activities. Out of this chaos arose the infamous issue, *Zap #4*, which was intended to push the buttons of the righteous world. More than a dirty comic, it examined people's notions of obscenity and propriety. Shop owners who dared sell *Zap* comic smut were hauled into court and relied on the First Amendment for their defense. They lost. The bashing at the Supreme Court was probably the high point of conversation over ice cold beers, but it didn't stop the comic mill.

Cartoons are an vital medium for Williams. He sees them as pictographs—an extension of a language that started 30,000 years ago with cave drawings. Williams feels the art world has denied the viability of this visual imagery for the last 60 years. "These things that are called lowbrow are gonna keep evolving and they're not gonna go away. Some of the strongest emblems of our period are tattoos and the goofy stuff on the bottom of skateboards. The stuff has to be real emblematic and carry for a long way. The art world is just trying to push that aside for a while, but that's gonna come back. And once it comes back and once it's realized what it is, then conscious alteration can be made to abstract it into a more poetic language." Obviously, this pictorial communication became more sophisticated over the centuries. Williams notes the changes, saying "If you look at a cartoon done in the 1860s where motion might have lines or some little jump things, back then they'd say, 'what's that?' But you look at it now and you know that means that thing's hauling ass." Graphic art and cartoons are the medium that Williams employs for their immediate impact. And Williams likes to make an impact.

Many a Friday night has found Williams and his wife Suzanne—in either his Aces and Eights '32 roadster or her chopped '34 sedan—parked at Bob's Big Boy in Burbank mingling with cars and admiring drivers of the revived hot rod scene. He explains the phenomena like a lecturer, like a historian, but mostly like a person that's been there: "I was always like a hot rodder. It was an indulgence for me. It's akin to masturbation. But now it's become like another phenomena." The myth of the delinquent hot rodder

Snuff Fink, 1988. Museum Catalogue Title: The Exuberance of Youth Bordering on Self-Destruction Lends Romance to the Notion That Acne is Never Really Cured, It's Just Thrilled into Remission. Colloquial Title: Brodyin' on Feces (Artist, Robert Williams)

stands tall in American psyche in the same way that Williams thinks we romanticized cowboys. Dime novels of the 1880s, 1890s touted the exploits of the daring cowboy. It lapped over into the Spanish-American War where an entire army went off to fight the Spanish dressed like cowboys with Teddy Roosevelt as the number one cowboy. Frederick Remington was the cowboy illustrator. So this fed upon itself as the American man was the cowboy and the American woman was the cowgirl. By the time World War I came, it was really imbedded. The Doughboys went off in their little campaign, cowboy hats and so forth.

"By the '20s and '30s it's gone beyond a misunderstanding of cowboys to a surreal abstraction of dude ranches and things like this that are really ridiculous. This whole thing that had nothing to do with nothing. I came into the world in the '40s and '50s in my little cowboy suit, and it's just like this thing. It's like this traditional garb that means 'man of the past' like Robin Hood or something. There's like a whole revitalization of it in the '50s with what's called 'adult westerns.' So this thing went from a thing that men could relate to down to something that was left for children. And then older people wanted to be back into it and they started developing dramas."

To Williams, the "new" hot rod scene is American's getting romantic all over again. "You're witnessing the same thing happening at the beginning of the next century." Instead of playing cowboys, adult men are portraying the *Rebel Without A Cause*—James Dean or toughs out of *Blackboard Jungle*." Whichever, they're stuck in the 1950s.

It's a very specific 1950s, however. It's the 1950s of the California Myth, featuring American strength, male virility, and flashy metal. Problem is, it never existed that way. "This hot rod thing represents a freedom their imagination needs to feed on," comments Williams. "I was there in the '50s and the economy was really terrible. People were really bigoted. Girls didn't put out. Girls that did fuck, fucked everybody. So you had to deal with that. It was horrible. A couple of good things were the availability of car parts and uncrowded roads. But I was in trouble with the police all the time. I was confused and scared and alienated. I had bad motorcycle accidents. One problem after another. I was always broke, I had to be a jerk. I hated it. I developed a mistrust and dislike for women it took years to shed." But that was then, now he recognizes what's going on in galleries like La Luz de Jesus and in that parking lot at Bob's—"They're jointly exercising the fantasy. It's okay."

In the real world, the artist gets all the toys. Coop at home. (Author photo)

## COOP—HOT ROD TO HELL

"I'm trying to be a full service artist." That's all Coop is up to. And he's succeeding. At a poster a week, he's doing his job at supplying the lowbrow-art collector with unlimited material. He churns out posters, paintings, lighters, t-shirts, stickers and album covers. Most of these display his inner landscape which is chock full of naked women, nearly naked devil-girls and ol' Satan himself. The vision of a car nut raised on cartoons and punk rock—Coop is a white trash Okie turned loose on the burgeoning Kustom Kulture Art World.

The year 1958 enjoyed the dual arrival of Hot Wheels and Coop (only his mother calls him Chris Cooper). What happened from then on is what you see in his artwork. Raised with cars—he tools around Los Angeles in a purple and green "loose custom" '50 Ford Delux Club with a trick motor. Also witness his numerous posters with kids in fast cars displaying wicked speed. Beatles for breakfast evolved into an early appreciation for punk rock and works its way out of his psyche in album covers for numerous bands including the Mono Men, the Lords of Acid and the Ramones.

His life now isn't far from what he imagined it would be as a high schooler. If he had any inkling at all of what the future entailed, Coop envisioned that maybe he could draw album covers. Well, sure, that and more it turns out. Coop's personal discovery of

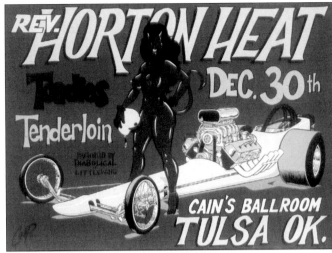

(Artist, Coop)

Loser. In Coop's world, the guy with
the cool car always gets the girl.
(Artist, Coop)

(Artist, Coop)

the Ramones turned him into a record collector. He took every opportunity available to search out and acquire music that was like theirs—full of energy and attitude. In the early 1980s the comic book and cartooning scene was just finding an growing audience, when Coop realized he wasn't too interested. Rather he became an adjunct to the "pathetic" punk rock scene in Tulsa by sketching fliers for bands. He didn't think it would go anywhere, but it was good for getting into shows for free and having somebody think he was cool. His work then was basically the same, but "just a little more primitive, retarded version" of what he produces now.

Like the Joads in "The Grapes of Wrath," Coop followed masses of dust bowl ravaged Oklahoma refugees from Tulsa to Southern California. "I was in Yucaipa, out by San Bernadino—another white trash central." Coop figures it's where multitudes of "scumbag, bottom of the barrel Okies" had set up housekeeping as far back as the 1920s. He picked up from there and started doing some album covers—like he fantasized as a kid—and pretty much ended up in the comfy world he lives in now.

Ultimately, providing affordable art to people who want to share in his vision, matters. "That's one thing that I like about what I'm doing. Somebody can buy one of my posters for $25 and get a limited edition, signed piece of art. It's fucking guaranteed to go up in value. Stuff I did a couple of years ago is selling for a couple hundred bucks now. I'm no commie or anything, but I like the fact of what I'm doing with the posters and stuff is art that is cheap and readily available for anyone. There's no snobbishness involved. You just have to have an appreciation for the image."

Often his images present difficulties for some people. A grinning, life-loving Lucifer who looks oddly like Coop often pilots hot rods or dallies with devil girls. Somehow Coop's read on his membership in the Church of Satan sounds mildly benign. Faith in the other side sometimes brings him a better parking space and his practice of the Seven Deadly Sins (pride, envy, anger, sloth, greed, gluttony and lust) simply leads to a hard-working, money-making work ethic.

His love of cars either hits you over the head, or makes itself felt in subtle ways. "A lot of the techniques I'm using are the same that pinstripers and sign painters use to do stuff on cars. So, in a vague way they're associated with that. I make strong pieces with simple images that are used as a decal for your car or you'd get as a tattoo or you'd see on a t-shirt." The strong color choices in his work are attributed to a semi-color blind artist's rendition of Hot Wheels' metal flake paint jobs. Many of those monster driven hot rods Coop's been putting out are slathered with pinstriper's One Shot enamel paint. "I'm not a terribly subtle person in my artwork. I like to have some kind of an obvious thing going on, but I also like to have a more subtle thing going on as well. You don't have to perceive it to enjoy what's going on. But if you do it's just one of the moments."

## ANTHONY AUSGANG—Cool Cats in Hot Rods

Anthony Ausgang. (Amy Darsa photo)

Seemingly worlds apart, yet in the same lowbrow neighborhood, is the work of Anthony Ausgang. Like Coop, Ausgang's work involves cars and a lack of "fine art appeal." And there's another similarity—it's all right with him that the fine art Mafia, as he calls them, aren't all that interested in him. Ausgang feels like he's getting to the people who need to know.

Ausgang's paintings are habituated by cartoonish cats—cats in hot rods, cats with guns, surrealist cats—a far cry from Coop's devil girls or Williams' twisting stories. But the same stories are being told—"give it up, humans don't learn by their mistakes and we're all fucked." The flip side of these tales of woe is, "since all is lost, have some fun while we're waiting to be wiped out." Ausgang isn't coming from some holier than thou pulpit, his tales are often autobiographical. He likes using the cats as an abstraction of the human form. Because the human figure has been used since cavemen first put charcoal to the cave wall, Ausgang wants to pass on his message about the human condition using fresher methods. His goofy cats find their way into found paintings from thrift stores. His pink or blue or green cats get run over or pay for blow jobs or get mugged just like any old stupid human.

While the stories are clear to others like him, who grew up playing with Hot Wheels and watching Saturday morning cartoons, Ausgang realizes that fine art galleries aren't particularly interested in his statement on humanity. Going from gallery to gallery, he wondered why these people would want his work. It was all cars and wild shit. Fortunately there is another success route for these "outsider" artists, because the car thing is in Ausgang's blood. "Ultimately, the hot rods are a big influence or starting point for me, more than anything. I don't really know what I would be doing right now if I hadn't recognized the beauty of cars."

That falling in love with the automobile happened when Ausgang was still a kid in Texas. He put together all those Roth models, played with Hot Wheels and constructed Odd Rods. What developed in him was a fetish for hot rods with a monster twist. "I could understand that these things were cool. And how they got tied into this whole thing about California—surfing and hot rods," recalls Ausgang. "I wanted to get the fuck over to California as soon as I could."

What Ausgang found on the West Coast was a group of loonies that shared his same fetish. To Ausgang this hot rod enthusiasm arises from the idea that cars freed up American culture, while making the country mobile. His love of cars gave him freedom to "get kicks" from things outside of the art world. It was legit for him to dig places like dirt tracks, car shows and junkyards. "I love to go to the junkyards and just look at these wrecks. You can see these cars that were in horrific accidents. Generally when you see these classic cars they're all beautifully restored, but you go to a junkyard and see these

*Freeze!* (Artist, Anthony Ausgang)

Anthony Ausgang adds his hot rod stories to thrift store found paintings. (Artist, Anthony Ausgang)

The Close Call.
(Artist, Anthony Ausgang)

things fucked up. That appeals to me. They can no longer run. They become strictly a sculptural object. It's just this gorgeous beast fucking thing."

The junkyard offers a peek into personal lives decades after the people are gone. Shells of cars offer family pictures, clothing, eyeglasses, all sorts of clues about the people who first drove these cars home, fresh off the showroom floor. Ausgang sees the whole history of a man in the rusted bodies of the most expensive thing a family could own. "It's this object of yearning until you get it. Then you've got it and you're so fucking proud of this thing. It's success and then it falls apart and eventually ends up in the junkyard." Stories like these and other fucked up realities are what Ausgang offers in his work. One gallery show featured a fatally crunched and artfully flamed '70 Cougar. To the artist, it concocted the story of a guy in the fast lane having phone sex and getting his comeuppance. A guy, like a speed freak, who's on the road all the time and at the whim of a woman who wants to have phone sex with somebody driving. Even when he included the phone and all the clues, Ausgang was surprised the viewers didn't get it.

What people do pick up on is what also attracts Ausgang to this lowbrow school. Camaraderie. Traditionally even competitors in the hot rod arena share secrets, tips and respect for each other's hard work. That feeling of community is often missing among artists. The creation of art necessitates a certain level of self-absorption. Creation in the car world is greeted with open praise—like right on, bitchin' car. Ausgang feels that same thing going on in lowbrow territory, particularly from the undisputed king—Robert Williams. "He's glad that everybody's out there working in the same school. He created this fucking art school. He created this style of art. He's a fucking saint."

The Great Catnip Drought.
(Artist, Anthony Ausgang)

Another of the lowbrow attributes carried over from hot rod standards is the lack of the ridiculous. "One thing about hot rods is you can't baffle somebody with bullshit. You can't write a 15 page theory about why your car should be going 150 mph. It has to go 150 mph. I try to find that kind of practicality in my art. I don't want to have to write a 15 page theory about what my paintings are all about. You look at them and you see it. Fuck it. This is it."

What's presented as straight ahead is just the beginning for Ausgang's search in his work. Sure eight balls and fuzzy dice have a proven attraction—but why? What is it about a custom Merc that embodies evil? Familiar with the empty feeling of walking away from art that functions as beautiful eye candy, Ausgang attempts to share more in his paintings. Including a message in the medium prevents him from doing what so many others in "homage" to Von Dutch and Ed Roth attempt to pass off as original art. An art enthusiast can only take in so many winged eyeballs or rats in souped up monster mobiles before craving a fresh thought. Or, as Ausgang says, "The amount of things you can choose to paint are infinite. So to repeat something that someone else has done blows my fucking mind." But he also admits that there's a difference between art and decoration, and if some guy wants the trillionth copy of Lady Luck on his car, well all right then.

Poster for the 1993 Kustom Kulture
Show at the Laguna Art Museum.
(Copro/Nason collection)

## COPRO/NASON—TAKING LOWBROW ART WHERE IT'S NEVER BEEN BEFORE

The rules of climbing the ranks in the "official" art world are strict. First of all, a "school," or a recognized style of art, or group of artists must have a name. Williams and his friends have called themselves "lowbrow" artists—an obvious snub to the accepted principles in snobby art circles. Greg Escalante and his partner Doug Nason are making it their business to establish lowbrow art's place in history. Escalante suggests this jolting new vision was actually "Newbrow"; brow suggests "just thinking." "So I thought we should call it Newbrow Art and maybe that would help get this whole thing going. It ended up getting published a few times, but it didn't really catch on. This school of art is a defined, definite, existing school of art. It's happening and it matters right now. And it's still pretty much unnamed. It's been called other things like Lowbrow Art, Cartoon Surrealism, a whole bunch of things." Most of these younger, hipper artists grew up with TV, cartoons, comic books—a barrage of commercial art. It defines how they see things, and how they present their vision.

For a period in the 1960s it appeared that Von Dutch, Ed Roth, Robert Williams and a group of San Francisco poster artists were gonna be the biggest names in art culture, and it turned out to be a fad. It died out. There was a real possibility that after 100 years, no one would even care about the contributions of these artists.

To prevent what would be a mistelling of history, Escalante reintroduced this art to the public. As a trustee at the Laguna Art Museum, he had a platform to suggest a show to present the work of these "outsiders." Through his constant prodding, the Kustom Kulture show was allowed to happen almost instantly. Although the exhibit was planned as a tribute that Von Dutch could enjoy, he died six months before the show he helped inspire opened.

Escalante's other major achievement was convincing Last Gasp to publish a book, which he then helped design. As a catalog, *Kustom Kulture* is a slim volume which thanks the grand daddies of the movement: Von Dutch, Ed "Big Daddy" Roth and Robert Williams. But it's as a tool to document the movement that *Kustom Kulture* does the most work.

Part of the payoff for his effort is bringing liveliness to the world of the previously art deprived. "The hardest group to get into a museum are younger boys or teenagers. What's interesting to them?," Escalante asks. "Girls, getting into trouble, drugs and gangs. But they like art too. They draw a lot. When they go to museums, you only have one chance to get their attention. Kustom Kulture was so cool, because you saw all these guys with dyed red hair spending a long time on each painting. We just knew that they deserved their chance to enjoy art too." *Juxtapose* magazine arose out of this need to display a youthful enjoyment of art. "Showing this kind of art—people smiling, like at a party—was a tremendously constructive thing, instead of having this whole thing that didn't make sense to them," says Escalante.

Some of those inspired, who possess more skill than ideas, "pay homage" to their heroes, freely decorating trash cans and canvas alike with borrowed images of flying eyeballs, or Rat Fink. They employ the color and excitement and the heart of the movement, but that's the end of the pavement for them. These tributes will be lost to time, but they may serve as links in the visual trail. Because these evident and traceable influences will get marked down in that big tally board of the "fine art" world pulling them hollering and fighting to the conclusion that this lowbrow/newbrow/kustom kulture discipline is one to be reckoned with.

# GALLERY LIFE

Pinstripers cum gallery denizens push the art envelope, and it's gonna bust. The art world's new shape looks more like a monster driven, flaming behemoth all the time. The dual automotive assaults on California museums signal that traditional art houses are hip to the cultural influence of hot rodders' eye for beauty. In 1993, the Laguna Art Museum tested the water with the *Kustom Kulture: Von Dutch, Ed "Big Daddy" Roth, Robert Williams & Others* exhibit, and the Oakland Museum of California dove right in by parking the outlaw beasts in the hallowed halls usually reserved for traditionally higher-minded exhibits.

*In 1960, nothing on the road resembled the Beatnik Bandit's out-of-this-world mobile sculpture. (Author photo)*

Curated by Michael Dobrin and Philip Linhares, the Oakland show, *Hot Rods and Customs: The Men and Machines of California's Car Culture,* detailed the history of the hot rod and explored the culture associated with customizing these cars. In its run from September 1996 to January 1997, a bunch of museum virgins dropped admission dollars to visit machines as comfortable on the gallery floor as they are on the asphalt byways.

On the floor was a selection of 30 hot rods, customs and lakesters chosen for their influence on Northern California's car culture. Some of the key players were there:

ED ROTH'S BEATNIK BANDIT—The story goes that Roth named this driveable sculpture after a newspaper headline, "Beatnik Bandit Robs Store." Instead of robbery, this was a gift of innovation. Shaped from a plaster mold, filled with fiberglass, the beauty and strangeness of the Beatnik Bandit encouraged other customizers to free their minds while expressing themselves with their cars.

CADZZILLA—A car nut who happens to be a rock and roller, Billy Gibbons, along with Larry Erickson, dreamed up this wild custom—brought to life by Boyd Coddington. The sleek, high tech design embodies generations of hot rodding: a 1948 Cadillac two-door body low and tough in the 1950s lead-sled manner, with the umph of a 1990s street rod motor. CadZZilla? What else could you name the lead sled owned by the lead guitarist of ZZ Top?

MYSTERY CAR—Probably called that because of the way Joe Bailon combined so many cars, and made a beauty that looks like no other. Bailon built this two door sedan in 1956 using all the custom tricks, flares, flanges, peaks, scoops, scallops and his trademark Candy Apple Red paint.

KOOKIE KAR I—The star of *77 Sunset Strip*, this '23 Ford T Roadster was the chase vehicle as Ed "Kookie" Byrnes hunted crooks on TV from 1958 to 1960. Norm Grabowski's flamed T-bucket drove hot rodding right into the homes of millions.

*The Pierson Brothers' Coupe was included in Oakland show for reasons beyond its classic styling. Dick and Bob Pierson had done such an unusual job of modifying the '34 chopped coupe, that the Russetta Timing Association created the D class for it to be included at El Mirage. (Steven DePinto/Walter Cotten, Rescue photo)*

Aside from pulling a crowd into the museum who'd probably never had reason to before, the Oakland show traced the influence of the hobby of a few on today's culture in general. These were the goals of the Laguna Art Museum's Kustom Kulture show as well. By far the most heavily attended exhibit at the Southern Californian museum, the Kustom Kulture exhibit had a great time making a spectacle of itself.

Work by the big three, Von Dutch, Ed Roth and Robert Williams, was featured, but again, influences outside the lowbrow area were highlighted. Art world sweethearts Judy Chicago, Mike Kelley and Jim Shaw, were shown alongside newer artists who borrow their high-gloss lacquers, pearlescent paints and other techniques from the car customizing arena. Not surprisingly, the show had mixed results. It was highly adored by hot rod enthusiasts and highly criticized by art critics.

### STEVE STANFORD—Automotive Artist

Like a worn out seat belt, the terms pinstriper, illustrator, designer, innovator are too restrictive for his work, so Steve Stanford simply prefers the tag Automotive Artist. That way he can happily continue drawing and writing for *Rodder's Journal*, as easily as applying the latest decorative details to a client's light truck. Which sits with Steve just fine. It's probably the reason why—although he's considered one of the hottest "car" guys out there—he's shunned the recruiting efforts of any of the automotive big three. High dollar paychecks equate to a golden pigeonhole—most likely finding Stanford designing single elements—a door handle, a headlight, a dash—as opposed to the freedom of complete automotive design that he now enjoys. The expanded title also covers all of the other activities he pursues—be it designing record covers, like the metal-flaked flames he created on the Cars retrospective for Rhino Records—or joining in an occasional art show or two. Stanford got to preview his drawings for the mildly customized Mustang used in the remake of *Gone in 60 Seconds* as the "special superstar guest of honor" at the sixth annual Blessing of the Cars.

Like every other "automotive artist," Stanford straddles the commercial/art fence. Sometimes he finds it uncomfortable. Sometimes it's simply unbelievable. When he started sketching, he would never have predicted that he'd become 1999's featured artist at the highly-cool car show, the Blessing of the Cars. As a child in a poor black section of St. Louis, Stanford practically lived at the library. His library card was his most treasured possession. It offered Stanford a view of worlds farther than he could reach from his city bus. He studied every automotive magazine that came through the doors— *Hot Rod, Motor Trend, Popular Mechanics,* even *Popular Science*. Articles on his heroes—Barris, Jefferies, Winfield—fueled dreams of becoming a customizer. "It would have been a different experience if I could have gotten the smell of the nitro and the rumbling and the thunder," explains Stanford. "All I had was pictures and images in magazines and newspapers and books."

The library was his school. Those images became his teachers. He took a class on flamboyant style from George Barris, the most prolific of his teachers. In the 1960s when Petersen Publications began printing their how-to annuals on painting, Stanford graduated to custom painting. The how-tos explained what striping brushes were, what lettering criles were, what kind of paint to use and how to employ masking tape and finger guides. All the tricks he needed were in that one article, and says Stanford, "It was like the clouds parted, the sun came out and the birds were chirping."

He practiced these new-found techniques on a piece of glass kept stashed in his school locker. Using a razor to scrape off the old paint produced a clean surface ready

*Top: Steve Stanford. (Marshall Spiegel photo)*
*Bottom: Steve Stanford at Blessing of the Cars. (Author photo)*

for any new ideas. While he copied the basics from the pictures in the magazines, Stanford added his own personality to the work—the only way that these arts flourish.

Practice sessions continued when Stanford joined the service. Despite his full time job, it bloomed. It was the crest of the 1970s van era and Stanford jumped from pinstriping to airbrushing murals in a matter of weeks. Weekends at the barracks usually found Stanford hard at work with a line of vans and mini-trucks as his canvasses. His commander took note of this artistic ability and even though Stanford was trained in munitions, his commander used him as a one-man graphic arts department. Signs, charts, maps and even touch-ups on small trucks became his detail. Wherever he was assigned—Georgia, Korea, and finally Utah—it was the same thing. In fact, Stanford's first ink was in the Stars and Stripes magazine about his rendering of a Bicentennial flag mural.

When the service released him in Utah, Stanford stuck. There was a growing custom scene and a local body shop that needed an artist. Being one of the few African Americans in the entire state of Utah didn't seem to bother Stanford. He'd left the "black baggage" behind long ago. While growing up in Missouri, folks in his community would tell him to leave the "white boy car thing" alone. Instead, Stanford realized the more varied the people he was around, the wider his life experience. Skin color is not the "be all and end all," so Stanford continued with the cars, he hung out with hippies, he did what he wanted.

In fact, if you ask Stanford about the color experience, he doesn't seem to notice any. "That's what's neat about the car world," he explains. "That's the common denominator. They don't care what color you are. They don't care what you do for a living. As long as you're cool as a person, that's all anybody asks." And he has no explanation as to why more blacks aren't involved in this common denominator. I suggest that blacks, like other minorities, have had to spend so much time just being able to survive, to struggle to get ahead, that cars were seen as a luxury. So, before there's a higher level of black participation, the community has to see it as something other than an unnecessary activity. As Stanford points out, the car world is comprised of self-starters—from shade-tree mechanics to the most prolific designers. "If you want one of these things, you have to get off your duff and find a way to do it." That's what he did to spread his name around.

His impromptu sketch of a dropped custom '58 Chevy, complete with scallops and custom tail lights, found its way from the exterior of an envelope of a letter to the editor. That drawing landed his first illustration assignment for *Street Rod*—six pages of black

and white pen and ink stuff in their October 1977 issue. (As a personal touch, he put Utah plates on all his drawings, making the guys at home proud.)

A flurry of magazine assignments with *Truckin' Magazine, Street Rodder,* and *Custom Rodder* followed his move to California. Stanford visited offices, scheduled lunches and dropped in on car shows; all activities that allowed editors to match his face to the beautiful images. And the assignments flowed. He did some work on a *Car Craft* magazine project car and got their star bio section—Hi Riser. And that brought him even more work.

Established painter, Bill Carter, saw Stanford as untried quantity worth taking a chance on. Carter encouraged patrons to get their annual winter dress-ups by the new guy. For the next twelve years Stanford painted art and lettering on race boats and cars for folks including Shirley Muldowney, Joe Paisano and Don "the Snake" Prudhomme. For many years, he found the track a great place to make a couple of bucks and hang out, at least until the introduction of corporate sponsorship, which led to painted ads on cars. He's left that world to workers who Stanford suspect use computers to make up for their lack of artistic vision. He (like me) misses the beauty of candy and pearl paint jobs that were lettered by hand.

Stanford's continual processing of outside influences led to the development of his mark in the field—the '80s dry brush look. That brushstroke appearing as a swirl of color that graced expensive paint jobs internationally was the result of Stanford's visual outputs from his experiential inputs including Japanese calligraphy, rock and jazz, and the world of surf wear colors. He's also credited as the innovator of splash graphics and splatter paint. Now that Stanford's a recognized entity in paint design, he feels free to continue to explore design and illustration.

This exploration has taken him back to his first love, customs. As a kid he first discovered a Petersen mag featuring the Gypsy Rose lowrider used on the TV show Chico and The Man—a '64 Chevy covered in roses—he fell in love. Hard. His favorite subjects are the lowered customs from the 1950s and 1960s, with a fetish for Cadillacs. "I think the fun begins with fins and chrome. That was the era where Detroit didn't even take itself seriously. If they wanted to slather on the chrome with a trowel, so be it. If they wanted to make the interior look like an F15 fighter, go for it." Following this

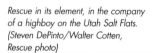

Rescue in its element, in the company of a highboy on the Utah Salt Flats. (Steven DePinto/Walter Cotten, Rescue photo)

wonderfully quirky period in automotive design, the low-maintenance, value-priced cars made by Datsun, Honda and Volkswagen, spurred consumers to reassess the role of private transportation in society. The 1970s reflected the desire to get good gas mileage, drive a car that was safe and environmentally clean—and keep these vehicles longer than a year. Two decades later, the result of these "innovations" are a fleet of internal combusting appliances. And as Stanford says, "I can't get worked up over a frost free refrigerator on four wheels. I like cars that talk back to you."

## RESCUE PHOTOGRAPHY—Walter Cotten and Steven DePinto

Walter Cotten and Steven DePinto's (collectively known as Rescue Photography) subjects of choice are the mph-seeking missiles built exclusively to demolish land speed records and their pilots and their fans. Rescue's arena is the severe expanse of the Bonneville Salt Flats. Racing has taken place there since 1898 when Count Gaston de Chasseloup-Laubat sped across the dry lake bed at 39 mph

Jocko Johnson designed flathead gas streamliner at Muroc. (Photo Walter Cotten/Steven DePinto, Rescue photo)

in 57 seconds. Electric cars, steam powered vehicles, internal combustion engines and now jets and rockets all have tested their know-how in Utah. But it's the hot rodders that have been dancing across the salt since 1949 that attract Rescue's attentions.

In August, temperatures of 100+ bounce off the salt flats' shiny surface and Cotten and DePinto think it's just fine. Cotten explains how he can get lost standing at the starting line and gazing ahead two or three miles. From there he can see the curvature of the earth. To the side is more salt and then the surrounding mountains. The incredible landscape provides its own photographic difficulties. There's a cruel learning curve that DePinto calls "photo juju." Until you learn to compensate for the brightness of the salt, everything gets overexposed and you go home with no images. Shooting 15 to 20 rolls before discovering the tricks is common.

In Southern California, dry lake tracks share real estate with motorbikes, paragliders, hang gliders, applied aircraft, two-wheelers, three-wheelers and four-wheelers and any other idiot that wants to spin wheels on the flat, hard surface. Not so at Bonneville. No one happens upon Bonneville and there's no recreation. Bonneville is for people dead serious about cars. Cotten describes the salt flat's sound as "pristine." "Because of the curvature of the earth you can hear the sound of a big car starting up five or six miles away. Then you see this rooster tail, this fountain of salt coming up from the back of the car like this apparition coming across the horizon."

This sounds all mysterious and new agey, but the Rescue crew refer to the scene as controlled chaos. There are few spectators, but the ones there, end up in their photographs. Some of their favorites are the Hellbillies—they're some kind of crazy rednecks from southern Idaho. "They're an old motorcycle club," explains Cotten. "I guess the men,

Rescue captured this Hinchliff brother taking a breather after piloting his '53 Studebaker on the salt. (Walter Cotten/Steven DePinto, Rescue photo)

who are now in their 50s, were fucking hellions. They settled down, got married, had kids, built cars and they qualify all of their kids in the cars." As their kids turn 16 and pick up their licenses for either 125, 150, or 175 mph, they have angel food cake and champagne. Says Cotten, "You want to talk family values? We've got family values here."

Another of their favorites are the Giovanne family, a father in his 80s and his son in his 60s, who have built a replica of the car the dad raced at Bonneville in 1949. The dad earned a record that year and has held it for decades. They brought out their replica with an updated 1925 Chevrolet engine in it and reset their own record. Don't be mistaken, this is not nostalgia. These guys are here to place their names in history. They strategize. They look at the class divisions and the records and figure if they put their engine in a car like whatever, they can go faster and set the record. And then they do it. And Cotten and DePinto shoot them at the other end. The end of the ten mile track is where the job begins for Rescue Photography. As drivers emerge from their lakesters or roadsters, fresh from their excitement-heavy three mile run, they're almost panicky with adrenaline. That's when the guys get their best shots, of the crystal sprayed car, chutes open on salt surface, of the sweaty, grinning driver of the team pulling up with news of setting a new record.

What Rescue does is outlaw. Not that it's illegal, but they grew up as did most of us middle class, suburban kids who thought that what was out "there" was "bad" and we shouldn't be doing it. "It's the spirit of being on the other side of the fence, on the other side of the wire, but in your head. You know you're being bad, and it's fun." For these desert rats, the other side of the fence is a place to make great art. They shoot salt encrusted belly tanks, shiny black Deuces, record-setting Studebakers and their greasy drivers in exquisite detail. You can see the motion in the salt resting on a car that's just worked its heart tearing across the flats. But that's the only motion you'll find in their work. They're more interested in what's going on behind the motion.

Although twelve years separate them, their boyhoods are almost identical. They read car magazines and frequented car races. They both even spent their early years camping in the Arizona deserts. Walter Cotten is a full time art professor at San Diego State University. It's where he met, and taught, Steven DePinto. Their influences were so similar, that in their combined work, they refuse to say who shot what. DePinto is a museum art preparator and transporter, where he deals with his share of art snobs. They had already begun working together when Cotten happened upon Bonneville in one of his regular desert adventures. He was amazed to find events were still run on the salt flats and he even recognized some of the cars from his studying the racing magazines decades earlier. By the next year, he had his partner out there with him.

The beginning of the project had them confused. Learning to deal with the scorching sun at Bonneville reduced their usable images. And they were having so much fun, they weren't sure it was art. Then they started talking to the racers. "The day before the races, these people love it when you talk to them. Any interest you show in the car and they're all over you. They'll tell you the whole history of the car. But when it's time to go in line and they're getting ready to go, it's like they've never seen you. But when they get to the end of the course, they're so revved up. We run over there, offer them a drink of water, see if they need any help, take pictures."

Part of Rescue's passion to continue is their love of Bonneville. The photographers, like the racers out there, don't have any sponsorship. Each group is spending their own money to continue the vision. For the racers, it's a quest for records. For Rescue, it's about documenting present day history. They are capturing cars today that are running with the same equipment as 50 years ago and going faster, even besting the occasional big money player who comes out to try. That's why the project's ongoing—"I think we have a job to do. I think more of that these days than I did ten years ago." Due to changes in environmental conditions, and human meddling, the salt at Bonneville gets thinner each year. If restoration efforts are not successful, racing there could be over within a few years. Capturing its last days is historically important. And to the Rescue Photography kids, it's the same as with the racers—"Being famous is not the issue. It is what it is. It's being out there."

*Bill Burke started the post-war trend of 300 gallon P-38 belly tanks being commonly used as bodies for lakesters. (Steven DePinto/Walter Cotten, Rescue photo)*

(Rescue photo)

# The Reinforcements

**J**ust like testing a new engine for the first time, the 1960s and 1970s introduction of women and minorities to pro racing had a rough start. Everyone found ways to work together, but except for Shirley Muldowney, the varied faces dropped out and corporate involvement encouraged the cookie cutter image of white male racers to the forefront. Once again African Americans were moved to the back of the bus and almost back to square one. What's different, or perhaps the very same, is despite the reverses, the racing "sickness" continues to grab outsiders. Grab them hard, so they have no other choice but to continue their quests. Whether it's against odds or competitors or their own limitations, they continue creating a legacy in racing that draws other outsiders like them to the track every goddamn week.

As the numbers of women and youngsters increase in drag racing, African Americans have been poorly represented in the "everyman's sport." At this writing, there are no black Top Fuel or Funny Car drivers. And only two NHRA Pro Stock contenders of color.

Disgusted with exclusion, in 1998 disgruntled African-American racers protested at racing venues.

This lack of inclusion has not gone unnoticed. Southern Californian racers Elliott Smith and Randy Thomas have shown up at events with placards held high—Boycott!, More Blacks Now!, Jobs Not Patronization! They've protested outside of NASCAR events and dragstrips alike. The only problem is that their concerns have not yet been answered. The problem isn't so overt that tracks have "whites only" laws, rather it's much more subtle. Whoever has the most dough is welcome to bring their car out on the track. Right now the big dollars come from corporate sponsorship. Unfortunately, the corporate powers make the decisions about whose wallet gets fatter with their sponsorship dollars and usually, they are young, white males, leaving women, minorities and elder statesmen out in the racing cold.

Again, this lack of vision isn't a direct result of racism, it's plain stupidity. Companies like Miller, Budweiser and Marlboro take the dollars of African American consumers, but neglect to spend their money on advertising by owning a winning black racing team. What transpires is a circle of no black faces to entice black consumer dollars to the track, resulting in no black teams in the winners' circle. Sport by sport, major corporations are being forced to reconsider the errors of their sponsorship ways. With the major black (and white) support of Tiger Woods in golf, Venus and Serena Williams in tennis and Dominique Dawes in gymnastics, it is finally recognized that where African Americans compete and do well in traditionally non-mixed venues, crowds follow. Look at the slew of urban kids flooding the golf courses, tennis courts and gyms.

## AFRICAN AMERICANS IN OTHER MOTORSPORTS

There was a time where you found many black competitors, granted it was on the roundy rounds and not at the straight strip, but for a time, African Americans ruled their own racing circuit. The Colored Speedway Association promoted events throughout the Midwest with their highlight being a 500 lap race—the annual Gold and Glory Sweepstakes. Each summer from 1924 to 1936 the Sweepstakes was hosted in Indianapolis, drew crowds of 10,000 and created its own heroes. Daredevil drivers— like Charlie Wiggins ("the Negro Speed King") and "Rojo" Jack DeSoto—flaunted their exploits on wet or dusty tracks that always thrilled fans and sometimes yielded spectacular accidents. As these stars faded and retired, so did their black fans.

Since that time, several African American participants have each been lauded as the "Jackie Robinson" of motorsports. Unfortunately, rather than bringing a feeling of renewal to the sport, each participant unceremoniously departed from the racing scene. First there was Joie Ray. Then Wendell Scott, an early Grand National (now known as NASCAR) driver who became had the longest stock car racing career of any African American. During the social eruptions of the Civil Rights period of 1961 to 1973, Scott faced opposition as an independent and as a black man in a white man's sport. Dogged diligence paid off in his sole major NASCAR win in Jacksonville, Florida in 1963. But even with that win he was disrespected. The laps were calculated "incorrectly" leading another driver to accept the winner's trophy. The "error" was later corrected and Scott quietly received his purse long after the reporters and photographers had gone home. He continued to compete, but his career was ended by injuries received in a race in 1973. There was not another major black player until the entrance of Willy T. Ribbs in the early 1980s.

*Willy T. Ribbs*
*(Andy Takakjian photo)*

## WILLY T. RIBBS—GREAT BLACK HOPE

Approaching the birth of the 21st century seems exceeding late to say "first black Formula 1 driver" or the "first black Indy winner." But that's the current position in which motorsports finds itself. We've yet to see black winners in many of these spots, hell, for the most part we don't even see African American participants! With Willy T. Ribbs' record of 46 Indy car starts and 17 SCCA wins, he seemed destined to become the "first" that everyone talked about. He had the support of the multi-million dollar entertainer, Bill Cosby, to hold an Indy 500 slot. Then, not even the promise of free TV ads from the high profile Cosby was enough to entice a sponsor and keep Willy T's butt in a car. Following a four year absence from racing, Ribbs competed in the NASCAR division of the 1998 Los Angeles Street Race. Engine problems caused him to qualify

low but Ribbs turned in a skilled performance, moving from 29th to 2nd place. Twice. With that level of faculty, and support from the African American community that he calls "phenomenal," Ribbs should receive major sponsorship and sit in a Formula 1 car—his "calling." Understandably, at $5 million for an IRL team, $10 million for CART or NASCAR and even higher over-the-moon costs of Formula 1, companies want assurance of returns on their advertising dollars before getting into bed with a team. Thus far they haven't allowed blacks to prove they can bring in the dough.

While Willy T. raced inside the Los Angeles Street Race, there were excluded African American racers protesting on the outside. It's tough for him to find a sponsor, but he'll continue, because he was born to. "The black/white thing is not why I race. I race because it's my right as an American citizen and that's what I want my career to be."

## FACES BEHIND THE SCENES

Willy T. Ribbs is one of the most visible African American faces in racing but there have always been others attempting to get their racing nut. These strivings are often lost to history due to "equality," magazines and papers didn't state the race of drivers, and their names are lost to history. On the West Coast, John Kimble, Jr., Charles Marquez, and many others struggled to make the big time. When Maurice Dupont drove the Hammertime car in the early 1990s, it appeared that a black presence was on the upswing. Unfortunately, that swing was short-ranged, as Hammer's team had no success and quickly dissolved.

## CLOY FITZGERALD—COLORBLIND OFFICIATING

As a Division 7 Technical Director, Cloy Fitzgerald spent 27 years studying the dragsters and doorslammers of weekend warriors determining who had the mechanical aspects down, and who had to go back to pits to try it again. And he did it because he couldn't get the time of day to race.

A young Fitzgerald frequented the Great Highway street races in San Francisco. He was the only black face in a group of young white racers because the brothers from Oakland would drop out when they learned how expensive and hard it is to keep a hot rod running. That left him as the sole African American kid racing up and down the

Cloy Fitzgerald
(Cloy Fitzgerald collection)

highway with his pals. When he took his '57 Chevy, "Wild Child," to the track, he was the only dark face there as well. The acceptance he had gained in the official venues faded away in the 1970s when he began racing at Lodi and Orrville. "They didn't want me winning," recalls Fitzgerald. "Every time I raced a guy, the clocks would break, or they would be set in a way that you couldn't tell who the winner was." In the end truth prevailed and the Wild Child left with a trophy, but no cash—the life blood of racing. It was a clear situation, says Fitzgerald: "Being black, you just couldn't win."

Following enough of those purse-less wins, Fitzgerald decided to call it a day, and moved onto the other side of the racing track—officiating. In his long stint, he was known as a stern and fair representative of NHRA. He was liked by racers and his opinions well-regarded by the sanctioning body—so much so that he was instrumental in refining the rules that birthed the Pro Stock class. Fitzgerald, racers and builders worked together to create a new group of cars that were raced safely and efficiently.

This hard work and level of respect didn't pay off at his part time NHRA job. Fitzgerald was never asked to climb the organizational ladder and instead watched as underlings were promoted over him. Folks at NHRA blamed this glass ceiling on his full time job, yet when he finally retired from that, rather than receive a well-deserved promotion, Fitzgerald was fired from his NHRA post.

This predominately white sport is so rife with ingrained racism that many people who explain "make-shift work" as having to "nigger rig" their equipment, never considered the origin of the term. Or would blindly assume that Fitzgerald or any other African American was in the know and could obtain drugs or hookers at the drop of a dime. Basically, the repeated defense "there's no racism here" comes from people who've never been counted as outsiders. Sure, if you don't feel it, you don't think it exists. And with not more than a handful of blacks, Asians, or Hispanics to show you the problems, you aren't stung by the wrong.

Francis Butler at the track.
(Steve Collison photo)

## FRANCIS BUTLER—BLACK AND WHITE IN COLOR

Sometimes being on the other side of the track is not a disadvantaged position. Veteran photojournalist Francis Butler wouldn't have it any other way. He gave up the ambitions of driving fast back in 1979, but still couldn't tear himself away from the track. So he made it a job. His work has filled the pages of *Super Stock* (a/k/a *Drag Racing Monthly*), *Popular Hot Rodding*, *Street Rodder*, *Super Chevy*, *Muscle Mustangs* and *Fast Fords*—if it has speedy vehicles in it, Butler's been there.

He's seen changes take place in the sport, but many of them are not fast enough to suit him. In his early days at the track, Butler was part of a scene were anybody with a little mechanical know-how could race. During this period there were independent black stars—"Machine Gun" Kelly, Malcolm Durham, the gassers run by Fred Stone and Tim Woods—who were hit with the need to find increased horsepower like each of their competitors. As Butler says, "now you have to go to someone else to get something." In ball and stick sports where individuality was the main component—where the drive for horsepower came from your muscles and equipment was no more expensive than a basketball or a mitt and a baseball—blacks excelled. When we needed to reach out to others for financial help, that's where the line between the haves and the have nots was drawn. "To say that racism didn't factor into it would be a lie," says Butler, who's visited the bottomless financial pit in racing. When he fell strictly into recording and documenting the sport, Butler was again affronted with racism and stupidity.

Francis Butler is not the only drag racing enthusiast to lack respect for the NHRA. The organization's obvious greed, commercialism and favoritism has created a gulf that sometimes cannot be crossed. While he heavily covered the sport and his work filled the pages of major racing magazines, Butler stayed away from NHRA's national events and remained a name without a face. When he did make those events, people couldn't fake their shock when introduced to the black professional. "They'd been talking to me on the phone for five or six years and they never knew Francis Butler was black."

Recognizing the entire sport is not filled with ineptitude and incompetence has kept Butler engaged. "I always got along with all the people that had brains—the great chassis builders, the great engine builders." He didn't come into the sport or business with any heroes or stars. "I came in and figured I was at least as smart as anyone I was talking to." Now that's teaching those racially challenged folks a lesson.

## TOM HAMMONDS AND LARRY NANCE—THE HIGH PROFILE GUYS

The fastest you can go in a car and still open a door to get out is the Pro Stock class. It's considered by many to be the most competitive. The difference between the top of the field and the bottom may vary by only 5 hundredths of a second. Gains are made slowly and require lots of funds. The heftiness of this sort of neck-and-neck action appeals to a select group and Tom Hammonds and Larry Nance are the sort of guys you'll find folding their NBA-sized frames into those doorslammers.

Ever since his dad took him racing in his Corvette or old '55 Chevys, Tom Hammonds has been a speed fiend. Street racing opened a world of power to the high-schooler. Competition thrilled him as much as the speeds he attained in his mom's car. Back in Florida, Hammonds recalls there were plenty of African Americans, both watching and racing. It wasn't until he reached the pro divisions that the color combinations changed.

Following in the footsteps of one hero, Kareem Abdul Jabar, Hammonds turned his love of competition into a college scholarship with his basketball abilities. Even then, he'd play ball at Georgia Tech during the week and make it to the drag strip on the weekend. As he's moved around the NBA, his teammates on the Washington Bullets, then the Minnesota Timberwolves knew basketball came first. As soon as the playoffs were finished, they could find the 6'9" power forward at the track. He pioneered the Pro Mod class, was one of the first (and fastest) Outlaw Street Racers—running the first ever side-by-side 7s—and was the first in the class to run 7.70, then 7.50.

Tom Hammonds (DRM files)

Also attracted to competition, Larry Nance turned his NBA earnings into a NHRA hobby. Following his stint as a power forward for the Phoenix Suns, then the Cleveland Cavaliers, Nance now splits the seasons between scouting for the Cavs and driving his Pro Stock Avenger. Even with this built-in media magnet, both men have difficulties get-ting sponsors to come on board. Since hitting the NHRA in 1996, both Hammonds and Nance have run limited seasons with limited success. Hammonds has carried the sponsorship of Winnebago Motorhomes, Mac Tools and Kendall on the side of his Camaro Z28, but chiefly runs out of his own pocket. The NBA's 1998 lockout surely affected the dollars Hammonds had to run his 1999 season.

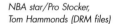

NBA star/Pro Stocker,
Tom Hammonds (DRM files)

Acutely aware of the lack of blacks in the pro ranks, Nance and Hammonds chalk it up to minimal opportunity. And racism. "There're a lot of politics involved with it," explains Hammonds. "I hate to say racism, but you have to look at a lot of situations

Larry Nance with author.
(Author's photo)

where guys who are capable enough to go out and do the same types of jobs just don't get the chance." He points out that as you climb the money hill from sportsman racing to the pro classes, you see fewer dark faces as you go.

But like Willy T. Ribbs, visit Nance's or Hammonds' pit area and you'll find plenty of blacks and racially diverse fans. They all come by the trailer to say they're doing a good job, and keep it up. "It makes me feel good," Hammonds says. "They're bringing their kids, they're bringing anybody they can get. And they're coming to the races just because of us." More of the traditional sponsors need to get in on this action, because it's also had a cross over effect. Many of these race fans find themselves opening their wallets for the NBA to check out what their favorite Pro Stock racer can do on the boards.

## RICKEY GADSON AND ANTRON BROWN—THE DRAG BIKE GUYS

Gripping a slab of vibrating metal between your legs while slipping down the drag strip at 190 mph with little more than 1/4" of leather to protect your hide should you slide off that ride seems like a less than enviable position. Some folks live for this thrill, and in a couple of divisions they allow it. Drag bikes race in NHRA, and even have their own world—American Motorcycle Association—Prostar. Bike competition, probably because it's cheaper to get a ride, has more independent black racers than you'll find in nitro burning classes. But again, that's only until you get to the motorcycle pro classes. In the Prostar series, where there are four classes with 16 bikes running in each, nine black racers is not a high percentage. NHRA doesn't chart any better with only five African Americans in professional bike drags.

Like Tom Hammonds and countless other African American kids, Rickey Gadson's dad introduced him to the world of speed quite early. Before he could walk, he was zipped into his dad's jacket for rides on the Harley. And like scores of others, he was hooked hard.

Gadson suspects many African Americans don't try to approach sponsors, anticipating a "no" before they even knock on the door. But Gadson didn't entertain any of those silly ideas. He and his late brother, Skip, were gonna race and that's all there was to it. They rented a van, took out the back seats and loaded up the bike. Begging, borrowing and bartering tools, tows, jump starts and parts, they managed to eke out a tour where Gadson came in third in the AMA's sportsman division. The environment was heaped with cooperation and covered with understanding. Every other racer knew how hard it was to get to every race to compete and they supported each other.

That support lasted as long as Gadson wasn't beating anyone. As he pulled ahead, support from others pulled out. "I don't know if it was just the fact that I was black, or the fact that I was black and doing so well."

Undaunted, he continued and now Gadson is the first factory sponsored rider in the sport. Kawasaki liked the way he raced on Sunday because it sold bikes on Monday. Capturing the Pro Superbike title for the second time in two years, along with setting a new E.T. record on his Kawasaki, and holding top speed, let the manufacturer know Gadson was their man. He also juggles bikes and rides in the Pro Stock and 600 Super Sport classes resulting in his making as many as 16 or 20 runs in a weekend.

The contract with Kawasaki persuaded Gadson to stick with the AMA and pass on his buddy Troy Vincent's offer to straddle a bike on the NHRA circuit. While Gadson wasn't available, his good friend Antron Brown was able to join the Vincent team.

Now riding high with his racing victories and new contract, Gadson's color doesn't seem to present problems. His success and contract spell money, and everybody wants to be associated with green.

Antron Brown (Nick Licata photo)

For Antron Brown, his celebrated arrival on NHRA's Pro Bike scene reads much like a Cinderella tale. Especially when contrasted with the low buck trek his close buddy Rickey Gadson followed. With his multi-million dollar NFL Philadelphia Eagles salary, Vincent was able to burst onto the pro scene with the best of everything—a top-of-the-line bike in a state-of-the-art trailer with a brand-new Kenworth rig towing it from track to track. It out-styles some of the top fuel rigs parked in the pits. But, says Brown, being a part of Troy Vincent's high-profile race team also has its pressures. With all this hooha, everyone says, "They look good, but can he ride?." His answer was a 7th place finish to his first season and winning at NHRA's Castrol Nationals in his second season and setting a top speed record, proving that the 23 year-old Brown lived well with those pressures. "I don't see any difference with my color." Says Brown, "If you race and do well and strive to be the best you can, they respect you as a racer."

## AFRICAN AMERICANS ON WHEELS

Clueing in sponsoring corporations that there really are blacks interested in racing falls hard on the shoulders of race participants, fans and the media. *African Americans on Wheels (AAOW)* is trying their darnedest to get across the message that we are in the stands and in the staging lanes, and, indeed, we've got our wallets with us. The shame, says *AAOW* editor Randi Payton, is not only are African Americans missing out on the fun of racing, they are also missing from the ranks of the entire automobile industry. Aside from the introduction of the Patterson-Greenfield Motor Car in 1915, blacks have not made a strong a presence in the design, manufacture and sales of an automotive product.

Rickey Gadson (Matt Polito photos)

AAOW continues the connection between blacks and cars. (Courtesy AAOW)

Recognizing that African Americans have the same love of cars and racing whites have, Payton has filled a thirst for inclusion by publishing the first auto enthusiast magazine written for black consumers. In its brief three year history, the quarterly *African Americans On Wheels* has doubled in volume and is also found online (www.automag.com) and inserted into 30 black newspapers nationwide, achieving a circulation of over 500,000.

Just like other automotive magazines, *AAOW* reviews new cars, gives technical advice and educates black consumers and the automotive industry alike. Unlike other popular magazines, *AAOW* has extensive coverage of blacks like historical automotive maker Patterson, high-achieving plant managers and designers, an RV rally in Ohio and up and coming young racers. Payton is stunned that his target audience, who shell out $33 billion annually for cars but have been routinely disregarded by automotive companies, marketers and advertisers.

## DIERDRA GIRARDEAU—DISNEY'S LOOK TO THE FUTURE

*Dierdra Girardeau (left) suited up to race. (Dierdra Girardeau collection)*

At 5'2" she may not look like a powerhouse, but if you want to take your motorsports game to Disney, Dierdra Girardeau is the woman you deal with. From her outpost as Sports Programming Manager for Walt Disney World, Girardeau has a front seat to the future. What she foresees in the coming millennium is a time when African Americans in motorsports will join together under a banner and finally get some notice. Already racers of African descent are gaining training in other countries, most notably Brazil, and will soon be strong contenders in Formula 1, CART, and at the heart of the good ole boy network—NASCAR where you still find confederate flags flying every five feet at southern tracks. Except for the occasional appearance of Willy T. Ribbs, or team owners Julius Erving and Walter Washington, the American pro circuits doesn't feature any black faces. Unless you check the stands.

In her work, Girardeau spends time at NASCAR, CART and IRL races and sees the African American fans out there. Right now the sponsors are missing the boat, but she predicts that soon a large traditionally white company will break the barrier. "Not because they care about blacks or about the black cause," explains Girardeau. Many corporations are considering the move because they could be first. In an environment where there is 70% fan loyalty (just ask American Express how many new African American customers they picked up after making Tiger Woods' name synonymous with their own), being the first sponsor to break the color barrier is gonna be a pretty position to be in.

The Quartermasters promote drag racing and possibilities in local schools. (Paul Rosner photo)

## QUARTERMASTERS AND UBDRA—KIDS, THE NEW HOPE OF TOMORROW

Based in the metropolitan DC-Maryland area, the Quartermasters have created a group that races for fun, and shows kids the fun of racing. In St. Louis, the United Black Drag Racers Association (UBDRA) is doing the same thing, but they also sponsor an annual event, Black Sunday, that joins communities from across the country to celebrate drag racing.

These enthusiastic sportsmen racers aren't fooling anyone. The Quartermasters' love of the sport is evident. Even their motives of accompanying kids to national meets and taking their pro mods, quick rods and hot rods to the local schools is glaringly transparent. These men are out to recruit youngsters into the sport. And more power to them. For kids in some urban areas, knowledge of race cars is as common as UFOs sightings. Community groups now realize that getting kids young is a way to get them interested when they can still make decisions about what to do with their lives. The Quartermasters also recognize that racing can be a great option for local kids to find their career paths. When they attend career days the Quartermasters wear their team uniforms, take their cars and speak to as many as 10 classes a day. In each, they explain the virtue of staying in school and off drugs.

Beyond talk, these racers know what speaks to kids—going to the track. For two NHRA national events a year—Englishtown, New Jersey and Maple Grove, Pennsylvania— the Quartermasters escort 50 kids to experience the roar of engines and the smell of nitro. The excitement felt there, along with the opportunity to talk to their favorite pro drivers gives these urban kids a look at what can be offered by racing at a national level.

Back at their home tracks of Maryland International Raceway, Potapsko and Capitol Raceway, the Quartermasters tear up the tracks themselves, and sponsor their families and other youth in Jr. Dragsters. Their efforts ensure that a new generation of African Americans will enjoy the pleasures and payoffs of straight-track racing. Excitement is what club president Ron Waters wants to introduce to these kids. Excitement and an introduction to a new world.

The Quartermasters and their cars. (Paul Rosner photo)

Black Sunday, United Black Drag Racing Association's annual celebration of a community in racing. (Author's photo)

UBDRA's assault includes kids, but they want to snag entire families as well. They remind newcomers and old racers alike what's to love about drag racing. UBDRA suggests it's the equal parts of cooperation and competition and hefty doses of pride that make it a lasting sport. The Quartermasters were reminded of those feelings as they rallied 30 members and 17 cars down to St. Louis for Black Sunday. They felt a connection cruising down the highway with their caravan of trailers and cars as people stopped them or just waved proudly.

Black Sunday evolved in the early 1990s when a group of local St. Louis racers relocated from the streets to Madison, Illinois' Gateway International Raceway to make good on their brags of high performance. Some guys bracket racing to "put up or shut up" grew into an event that draws contestants from all over the country, even Mexico, along with 10,000 fans to root for them.

Racers from UBDRA's Wisconsin division. (Arthor photo)

Because everyone involved with the UBDRA looks at drag racing as more than a fast time, Black Sunday was concocted as a fund-raiser. This sport that teaches physics, social responsibility and patience is one that fathers want to pass onto their sons, and neighbors. UBDRA members join as families and not individuals. Anyone over 18 is granted full voting privileges in the organization. Club members don't feel like they have to be at the top of the game to draw these benefits. These guys know their Mustangs, Corvettes and Monzas are not the fastest cars to trail down this world class track, but they know the gains they make are just as lofty as anyone else's.

The program features Super Pro, Pro, a trophy class and junior dragsters. And lots of bikes. There are Quick 8 events for cars and motorcycles. And the purse is nothing to shirk at. $2,000 for first and $1,000 for runner up, with payments down to the fourth place sitter.

Crowd enjoying the racing at Black Sunday. (Paul Rosner photo)

UBDRA president, Darrell Williams, sometimes wonders why he goes through the headache of wrangling volunteers and funds in a year-long planning frenzy for such a large event. But Williams once saw a 75 year-old man cry at the track who had attended races back when blacks got ejected from the drag strip if they actually beat their white competitors. The sight of black and white racers together brought him to tears. Between that heartfelt response and the ability to give local charities upwards of $20,000, Williams gets constant reminders of the worth of Black Sunday.

UBDRA also attends schools, participates in anti-drug events and gives generously to charities to reach kids. Williams never wants another youngster to assume he runs his '66 Nova on drug money. "If that's all a kid can look forward to in life is selling drugs to have a nice house, then we, as a country, are doing something wrong."

## A WOMAN'S TOUCH

Wives, mothers and girlfriends have always helped with tours, making food, and supporting their husbands, fathers and beaus. It took the talents of Alison Lee and Etta Glidden to show the world women had the know how to tear these machines down, then build them up and make them perform as well. Lee was the first woman to wrench a top fueler. She began by watching her husband when they first got interested in racing, then she started tuning, and liked it. She even decided she like tuning better than driving and never got a racing license. Their top fuel entry was the first on the east coast to record a 6 second E.T. in NHRA, making the Lee tuned vehicle a history maker in 1967. Then she made history again in 1971 by becoming the first woman recognized as the *Car Craft* magazine All-Star Crew Chief of the Year. This is an outstanding achievement because the award is voted on by all-male crews.

Alison Lee in car. (DRM files)

The next woman to take the *Car Craft* title—five times for the pro stock division—was Etta Glidden who, along with her husband Bob, spent the 1970s winning 43 national races and five World Championships in pro stock. As soon as Bob started driving the car in 1972, Etta began crewing. The Glidden family lived at the track, and sons Rusty and Billy continued the driving tradition.

Kim LaHaie's impressive work won her the honor as the *Car Craft* magazine Top Fuel Crew Chief of the Year in 1988. Her racing career began in 1982 when Kim sold team t-shirts for her dad, the legendary top fuel pilot and crew chief Dick LaHaie. Soon LaHaie realized his daughter was interested, a quick learner, and better than any crew person he had. Within two years Kim would fire up the top fueler, guide her dad back from the burn-out, then drive down the track and tow him back following the run. Once in the pits, she would dismantle the rear end and pull the motor apart; whatever it took to keep them on the track. As so often happens, proximity breeds marriage, and Kim found a wrencher to call her own. She married Tim Richards—or "The General" as he is called for his demanding crew chief style. Now Kim and Tim Richards are co-crew chiefs for Chuck Etchells, who pilots one of the quickest top fuel funny cars in the NHRA.

With the door opened regardless of gender, the next step was to break the age barrier. In the 1970s and 1980s men were owning cars and setting records in their late teens, but women had to wait until later in life to taste the fun.

Etta Glidden (Sky Wallace photo)

Crew chief Kim LaHaie and her driver dad, Dick LaHaie. (DRM files)

Alison Lee and Shirley Muldowney discuss track stuff. (DRM Files)

## WARRIOR PRINCESSES AND TOP FUEL TEENAGERS

Shirley Muldowney is probably the best known drag racer, male or female, but the women who had to push their way onto the track are numerous. Barbara Hamilton, Peggy Hart, Paula Murphy, Della Woods—they all had their firsts. Like blacks in motorsports, there are plenty of first time records for women to conquer.

### Danielle DePorter

At age 17, Danielle DePorter took up the youth baton becoming 1992's "top fuel teenager" when she shifted from running Super Comp to become the youngest in Top Fuel driver ever licensed.

### Rhonda Hartman

Rhonda Hartman's father and brother were both machinists on race cars, and she found herself as an active member of the family's funny car early on. At 18 she began driving top fuel, beating the old timers, setting records, winning meets and racking up points. And in 1994 she was named IHRA's Top Fuel Rookie of the Year.

### Cristen Powell

The next woman to run with that "top fuel teenager" crown was Portland, Oregon native, Cristen Powell. Her winning combination sets her up to be the second most famous drag racer, following in Ms. Muldowney's tire tracks in more than one sense. Her father, who'd packed away racing with his youth, took Cristen to her first drag race at 12, and she was underwhelmed—in fact, she hated it. Let's just say Disneyland made more of an impression. Things changed, like she got a car at 15 1/2 and was ready to race it. For a gift, her eager-to-return-to-the-track dad gave her a trip to Frank Hawley's Drag Racing School, where the speed and the speed lovers hooked her. When Powell got her top fuel license, she was the only driver eligible to also race in NHRA's Jr. Dragster division, which features kids from 8-17 years old in cars that run on 5 hp lawn mower engines.

She's well into more than 10 passes at over 300 mph and proclaims nitro as the "best smell in the world." Previous to this desire for horsepower, Powell was "into horses." So much so that she won 1992 U.S. National Championship in dressage at 13, beating foes that were twice her age. When horses no longer held a challenge for her, she quit. If something isn't fun, Powell figures, why bother?

Danielle DePorter
(Dave DeAngelis photo)

Rhonda Hartman
(Dave DeAngelis photo)

Watchers wonder if the young Powell let her father push her into the sport, but rest assured she's taking on the drags of her own accord. Juggling high school studies and a rookie season in Top Fuel, Powell succeeded at both. Old timers had qualms about sharing the two lane track with a young novice, knowing that piloting a 30 foot, 6,000 hp mechanical marvel is even difficult for the experienced. Powell had to prove herself quickly. She started by recording the quickest first run ever for a rookie in a NHRA national event competition by rolling her dragster down the track in 4.74 seconds and at 271 mph.

Motivated by her wild desire to win, Powell skipped her senior prom in May 1997. Instead her date that weekend was with destiny as she won a national event, making her the second youngest winner in history to pull off that feat. Only Jeb Allen, a 17 year old who'd lied about his age in 1972 had won big previous to the 18 year old Powell. She didn't regret the choice she'd made, telling the press "I'd rather be in a dragster than on a joyride with my friends." Hopefully she'll enjoy the ride in a Funny Car as well, because as of the summer of 1999, Powell found herself getting her license to pilot one.

Now in college, Powell wisely recognizes that due to the strife of her precursors, particularly Shirley Muldowney, being a woman in drag racing is not so tough for her today. Other "elder stateswomen" like Shelly Anderson and Rhonda Hartman have also helped her. She calls these women her heroes. But just as surely she'll pass them by and leave them smelling her exhaust if she gets the chance.

Cristen Powell
(Nick Licata photo)

## ANGELLE SEELING—Biker Babe

To weigh in at the required 600 pounds necessary to race in Pro Stock Bike, at least one competitor adds 75 pounds of lead to meet the challenge. But as far as taking on the riders twice her size and racking up speeds of 188.73 and E.T.s of 7.2, the 5'1", 100 pound Angelle Seeling has what it takes to measure up. Seeling just started racing in 1991 and first staged at the tree as a pro in 1996, but she's wrangled motorized two wheelers since she was 6 years old. Like others, she feels drag racing is a mental sport and not a physical one, so she can get out there and tangle with her competitors and have just as much chance as they do.

Seeling is a highly visible babe on a bike, but she's not the only woman rider. In NHRA's bike class, there are at least two other women who challenge Seeling on a bi-weekly basis. Unlike her competitors, males or female, Seeling is the only rider that's got a Hollywood screenwriter attempting to take her story to the screen. Her love of racing and diligence at the sport impress anyone who's watching. Daily practices with a timing tree might seem unnecessary, but they are probably the reason for her finishing the 1998 season in second place.

Shelly Anderson
(Ron Lewis photo)

Angelle Seeling
(Dave DeAngelis)

Angelle Seeling leads the competition at speeds exceeding 185 mph.
(Dave DeAngelis)

(Rescue photo)

# Tech Check

**GLOSSARY**

**alcohol/alky:** racing fuel, usually methanol sometimes mixed with nitromethane.

**ANRA/American Nostalgia Racing Association:** organization of racers and fans dedicated to races cars built in (or in the style of) 1974 and before, including front-motored dragsters.

**belly tank:** dry lakes race car made from a drop tank usually taken from a WWII P-38 fighter plane.

**big and littles:** hot rod style of larger, wide tires in back and small tires up front.

**billet:** smooth, sculpted auto components often made from solid blocks of aluminum or steel.

**bite:** tire traction on the asphalt track.

**blower:** supercharger.

**bump/bump spot:** the elapsed time of the last qualified driver in a closed field. For example, the 16th position in a field open to only the 16 quickest qualifiers.

**burndown:** psychological war between two competitors in which each refuse to fully pull up to the starting line, or "stage" for the race. The goal is to break an opponent's concentration, overheat their engine and/or cool down their tires.

**burnout:** spinning the rear tires in water at a high RPM to the point of smoking to improve traction by heating the tires; also warms the engine and excites spectators.

**candy apple:** 1950s paint application attributed to Joe Bailon where translucent paint is layered, simulating the coating on a candied apple.

**$CH_3NO_2$:** chemical formula for nitromethane.

**channel/channeled:** cutting and raising the floor of a vehicle to drop a car's body below the frame.

**cheater slicks:** racing tires made of specialized rubber compounds that have the appearance of street tread.

**chopped top:** lowering the top of a coupe by cutting and welding.

**Christmas Tree:** signal system between the lanes at the starting line that displays a calibrated "countdown" for each driver. Named for amber "staging" lights, green "go" light and red "foul" light.

**coupe:** a closed, two-door automobile.

**deuce:** a 1932 Ford; usually a roadster. Its V-8 made it the hot rodder's car of choice.

**digger:** a dragster.

**doorslammer:** full-bodied cars with working doors that race on gasoline.

**drag:** acceleration race between two cars over a quarter-mile distance.

**elapsed time/E.T.:** number of seconds required to cover the 1320 foot racing distance. Electronic timers are started by a racer's tires rolling through the beams, and stop when the same vehicle reaches the finish line.

**eliminations:** series of two-car style racing where the loser is "eliminated" from competition and the winner goes on to the next round of competition until only one remains.

**eyes:** light beams that start and stop the electronic timers.

**fire bottles:** car's fire extinguisher that driver activates by a push or pull control.

**fire suit:** completely body-covering fireproof safety suit drivers wear while drag racing.

**flathead:** 1932-1953 Ford or Mercury V-8 valve-in-block engine.

**foul:** disqualifying driver's actions including jumping a starting light or crossing the center line.

**french/frenched:** customizer's technique of creating seamless, smooth, aerodynamic look around taillights, headlights, door handles and other details.

**fuel altered:** highly modified vehicle on a radically shortened wheelbase, powered by blown nitromethane that ensures a curvy ride down the straight track.

**fueler:** racing car that runs on nitromethane as opposed to gasoline or alcohol.

**'glass:** lightweight fiberglass components (such as fenders, hoods, doors or bodies) used to lighten a car.

**gow job:** early term before "hot rod" to describe a car modified for high performance.

**Grand National Oakland Roadster Show:** operating since 1950 the Oakland Roadster Show is considered one of the top hot rod and custom shows.

**headers:** short pipes that move exhaust gases out and away from an engine.

**Hemi:** engine equipped with hemispherical combustion chambers in the heads, produced by Chrysler from 1951-1957 and 1964-1971.

**highboy:** fenderless hot rod mounted high on the frame, as opposed to a lowered, "channeled" car.

**holeshot:** reacting quicker to the Christmas Tree's starting lights than your opponent to win the race.

**hopped up:** slang for engine modified for performance.

**hydraulic:** extensive engine failure when a cylinder fills with too much fuel prohibiting compression and usually resulting in an explosive mechanical malfunction.

**IHRA/International Hot Rod Association:** organization of racers, officials and tracks that work to set rules and promote safe racing.

**lead sled:** a custom car; derived from the fact that lead was used for reshaping bodies.

**lowrider:** type of car that rides extremely low; often has elaborate paint jobs, upholstery and decorative details inside and out. Many lowriders feature hydraulic suspensions so they can be raised, lowered or bounced at will.

**make the show:** qualify for a race.

**match race:** pre-arranged, often paying race between two competitors; usually run best of two out of three races to determine the winner.

**mill:** engine

**NHRA/National Hot Rod Association:** founded in 1951 as an organization of racers, officials and tracks that set rules and promote safe racing.

**nitromethane/nitro/fuel:** racing fuel with legions of fans. Consumed in quick bursts by Top Fuel Dragster and Funny Cars, nitro produces bone-shaking sound waves, eye-watering fumes and otherworldly flames. In short, it is the shit.

**oildown:** when a drag car mechanically malfunctions and leaves oil on the racing surface that must be cleaned before racing can safely continue.

**parachute:** umbrella-shaped safety chute that slows and stops high speed cars at the end of a drag race.

**pinstripe:** painted accent lines applied by hand or with a fine-nozzle spray gun.

**rail:** dragster.

**rake:** car's stance where either the front end rides higher than the rear as in a lowrider, or the rear is higher due to bigger tires as in a hot rod.

**red-light:** leaving the starting line too soon and getting disqualified.

**SCTA/Southern California Timing Association:** sanctioning and record-keeping body for lakes and Bonneville racing.

**slicks:** wide, flat, no-tread tires especially designed to achieve maximum traction; used exclusively on drag racing vehicles.

**slingshot:** early dragster design where driver sits behind the rear wheels for maximum weight distribution and traction.

**souped up:** engine modified for high performance.

**street classes:** racing vehicles that still meet laws' requirements and can drive on public streets.

**street rod:** hot rod built for street and road use.

**suicide doors:** car doors hinged at the rear and opening forward into the car's direction of travel.

**supercharger/blower:** crank-driven pump-like machine which increases horsepower when placed on the engine to force the air-fuel mixture into the cylinders.

**top end/big end:** finish of quarter-mile racing distance where cars reach their top speeds.

**top fuel:** quickest and fastest classes, Top Fuel and Top Fuel Funny Car use blown nitro to get to top end in less than 5 seconds at faster than 320 mph.

**traps:** lights at the top end, or finish line, that measure car's top speed and stop elapsed time clocks.

**wheelie:** short for a wheelstand, when car's front tires rise up when launching from the starting line.

Leah M. Kerr...

...is old enough to remember the early days of punk rock and young enough to get out of the house and see live music regularly. Always on the prowl for free wine at 'edgy' art openings, spots on a band's guest list, and free film festival parties.

...worked in the motion picture entertainment arena for 12 jaded years before finally giving in to the writing muse. Like every "screenwriter" out there, she has a closet full of unproduced scripts – and one produced one. FOR HIRE, written with partner Karen Erbach and starring Rob Lowe and Joe Mantegna, is in video stores near you.

... is a freelance writer and photographer for magazines, including *African Americans on Wheels*, *Drag Racing Monthly*, *Full Throttle*, and *Gearhead*.

# BIBLIOGRAPHY RESOURCES

# Parts List

## BOOKS

Barris, George and David Fetherston. *Barris Kustoms of the 1950s*; Osceola, Wisconsin: Motorbooks International, 1994.
————. *Barris TV & Movie Cars*; Osceola, Wisconsin: Motorbooks International, 1996.

Batchelor, Dean. *The American Hot Rod*; Osceola, Wisconsin: Motorbooks International, 1995.

Betrock, Alan. *The I Was a Teenage Juvenile Delinquent Rock 'N' Roll Horror Beach Party Movie Book*; New York: St. Martin's Press, 1986.

Blair, John and Stephen McParland. *Illustrated Discography of Hot Rod Music 1961-1965*; Ann Arbor, Michigan: Popular Culture, 1990.

Burt, Rob. *Surf City, Drag City*; Blanford, 1986.

Force, John. *'I saw Elvis at a thousand feet'*; Glendora, California: National Hot Rod Association, 1995.

Garlits, Don. *'Big Daddy': The Autobiography of Don Garlits*; Ocala, Florida: Museum of Drag Racing, 1990.

Kusten, Howie. *Confessions of a Rat Fink: The Life and Times of Ed "Big Daddy" Roth*; Howie Kusten; Topper Books

Leaf, David. *The Beach Boys and the California Myth*; New York: Grosset & Dunlap, 1978.

Mann, Dave and Ron Main. *Races, Chases & Crashes: A Complete Guide to Car Movies and Biker Flicks*; Osceola, Wisconsin: Motorbooks International, 1994.

Martin, Chris. *The Top Fuel Handbook: Stories, Stats, and Stuff About Drag Racing's Most Powerful Class*; Wichita Eagle and Beacon Publishing Co. Inc., 1996.

Montgomery, Don. *Authentic Hot Rods: The Real 'Good Old Days'*; Don Montgomery, 1994.
————. *Supercharged Gas Coupes: Remembering the 'Sixties'*; Don Montgomery, 1992.
————. *Those Wide Fuel Altereds: Drag Racing in the Sixties*; Don Montgomery, 1997.

Oakland Museum of California. *Hot Rods and Customs: The Men & Machines of California's Car Culture*; Oakland, California: Oakland Museum of California, 1996.

Perry, David and Barry Gifford. *Hot Rod*; San Francisco, California: Chronicle Books, 1997.

Post, Robert C. *High Performance; The Culture and Technology of Drag Racing 1950-1990*; The John Hopkins University Press Baltimore, Maryland, 1994.

Turner, Ron (ed.). *Kustom Kulture: Von Dutch, Ed 'Big Daddy' Roth, Robert Williams and Others*; San Francisco, California: Last Gasp of San Francisco, 1993.

White, Timothy. *The Nearest Faraway Place: Brian Wilson the Beach Boys and the Southern California Experience;* New York: H. Holt, 1994.

## FILMS AND VIDEOS

Drag Racing Underground, 26-10 18th Street, Suite #1A, Astoria, New York 11102; www.dragracingunderground.com

Main Attractions, P.O. Box 4923, Chatsworth, California 91313

## MAGS

*African Americans On Wheels*, 529 14th Street, Suite 202, Washington, D.C. 20078-1216; www.automag.com

*Drag Racing USA*, McMullen Argus Publishing, 2400 E. Katella Avenue, 11th Floor, Anaheim, California 92806; www.dragracingusaweb.com

*Full Throttle News*, 1441 East 28th Street, Dept. HRE, Signal Hill, California 90806; http://hre.com/ftn/

*Gezarhead*, Gearhead Productions, P.O. Box 421219, San Francisco, California 94142-1219

*Juxtapoz Art & Culture*, 1303 Underwood Avenue, San Francisco, California 94124; www.juxtapoz.com

*Lowrider*, McMullen Argus Publishing, 2400 E. Katella, 11th Floor, Anaheim, California 92806; www.lowriderweb.com

*Rodders Journal*, P.O. Box 1880 Huntington Beach, California 92647; www.roddersjournal.com

*Wagons of Steel*, P.O. Box 1435, Vashon, Washington 98070; www.wagonsofsteel.com

## MUSIC

Del-Fi Records, 8271 Melrose Avenue, #103, Los Angeles, California 90046; www.del-fi.com

Estrus Records, P.O. Box 2125, Bellingham, Washington 98227-2125, www.estrus.com

Man's Ruin, 610 22nd Street # 302, San Francisco, California 94107, www.mansruin.com

Norton Records, P.O. Box 646 Cooper Station, New York, New York 10276-0646; http://members.aol.com/nortonrec/norton.html

## MUSEUMS

Don Garlits' Museum of Drag Racing, 13700 SW 16 Avenue, Ocala, Florida 34473

NHRA Motorsports Museum, Fairplex Gate 1, 1101 W. McKinley Avenue, Pomona, California

Petersen Automotive Museum, 6060 Wilshire Boulevard, Los Angeles. California

## RACING ASSOCIATIONS

American Nostalgia Racing Association, 7342 East Saddlehorn Way, Orange, California 92869; www.anra.com

Goodguys Rod & Custom Association, P.O. Box 424, Alamo, California 94507; www.goodguysgoodtimes.com

International Hot Rod Association, 9 1/2 East Main Street, Norwalk, OH 44857; www.ihra.com

National Hot Rod Association, 2035 Financial Way, Glendora, California 91741; www.nhra.com

Southern California Timing Association, 2517 Sycamore Drive #353, Simi Valley, California; http://www.scta-bni.org

United Black Drag Racers Association, 17 Santa Fe Drive, St. Louis, Missouri  63119

## SHOPPING

Aerobooks/Autobooks, 3524 West Magnolia Boulevard, Burbank, California 91505-2911

Hot Rod Nostalgia: Good Communications Inc., P.O. Box 249-WS, West Point, California 95255-0249; www.hotrodnostalgia.com

La Luz De Jesus, 4633 Hollywood Boulevard, Los Angeles, California 90027; www.laluzdejesus.com

Mooneyes USA, Inc., 10820 South Norwalk Boulevard, Santa Fe Springs, California  90670; www.mooneyesusa.com

*(Rescue photo)*

## RESCUE PHOTOGRAPHY—WALTER COTTEN/STEVEN DEPINTO

**INDEX**

# Finish Line

# New Titles!

## DEVIANT DESIRES
### Incredibly Strange Sex

By Katharine Gates

DEVIANT DESIRES is a lavishly illustrated guide to the most fascinating and obscure outposts of the erotic frontier. Self-described pervert Katharine Gates takes us on an expedition into the latest sexual communities bursting forth at the beginning of the new millennium. Gone are the pretentious black-clad S/M posers and humorless fetish fashion victims—you'll meet the refreshingly funny and irreverent heroes and heroines of a do-it-yourself porn revolution.

Spurred on by the internet explosion, these deviants defy all expectations as they actively participate in creating their own erotic entertainment, forging new art, original literature and fluid sexual identities. Come grab a first peek as they radically subvert mass culture for their own nefarious sexual purposes. Nothing is sacred and anything can be sexualized, from Disney™ characters and B-Movie monsters to baked beans, children's birthday balloons and Thanksgiving dinner. You'll never watch TV the same way again!

Katharine Gates has worked extensively with Annie Sprinkle and other sexual pioneers. Her collaborative efforts in the domain of the perverse include Joe Coleman's ORIGINAL SIN, and Maurice Vellekoop's ABC BOOK: A HOMOEROTIC PRIMER. She is the founder of Gates of Heck, an alternative culture press. Gates studied anthopology at Yale University and lives in New York City.

"Katharine Gates is the smartest / sexiest / bestest / freshest / coolest / funniest sex researcher in the universe. This book is brilliant, thoroughly entertaining, and super-outrageous. Finally someone has done something sexually-oriented that is truly original. I dare you to read it and not get turned on!"
—Annie Sprinkle, Queen of Kink, artist, author, and sex pioneer

"Fun book! Deep down, everyone wants to be / look / behave like some other creature. DEVIANT DESIRES gives us a startling new look at a few of these variations."
—Fakir Musafar, Father of the Modern Primitive movement

**www.JunoBooks.com**

**EROTICA/SELF HELP/GENDER STUDIES**
Paperback, 8.5 x 11 inches, 248 pages, lots of pictures
**ISBN 1-890451-03-7**
$24.99

# New Titles!

## BREAD & WINE
### An Erotic Tale of New York

Written by Samuel R. Delany
Drawn by Mia Wolff
Introduced by Alan Moore

BREAD & WINE is a beautifully drawn graphic novel about the beginning of a moving and lasting gay relationship, with all the complexities, fumblings, and excitement of two people coming together after a chance encounter. Award-winning African American author Samuel Delany and Dennis, a white homeless New Yorker selling books from a blanket, discover sexual joy and explode stereotypes while exploring the possibilities for compassion and acceptance—all the more touching because it's true.

"Samuel Delany is one of the finest living American writers....[His] brilliance shines. It's filthy and earthy and beautiful, like an orchid in a gutter."
— **Neil Gaiman** author of SANDMAN and NEVERWHERE

"Samuel Delany breaks all the taboos in BREAD & WINE....How Jean Genet would have loved it!"
—**Edmund White** author of THE FAREWELL SYMPHONY

**Samuel R. Delany** is a four-time Nebula Award winner, two-time Hugo award winner, and winner of the William Whitehead Memorial Award for Lifetime Contribution to Gay and Lesbian Literature. He is the author of DHALGREN (Bantam Books, 1975), ATLANTIS: THREE TALES (Wesleyan University Press, 1995), THE MAD MAN (Rhinoceros Books, 1996), and TIMES SQUARE RED, TIMES SQUARE BLUE (New York University Press, 1999) Delany is a professor of comparative literature at the University of Massachusetts, Amherst, and lives in New York City.

**Mia Wolff**, author of the children's book, CATCHER (Farrar, Straus & Giroux, 1994), is a former trapeze artist and martial arts instructor, and is now a painter living in upstate New York.

**Alan Moore** is one of the best known and respected writers in comix today, and is the author of THE WATCHMAN

www.JunoBooks.com

**AUTOBIOGRAPHY/EROTICA/GAY LETTERS**
Paperback, 8 x 10 inches, 80 pages, more than 50 pages of line art
ISBN 1-890451-02-9                                        $14.99

# New Reprints!

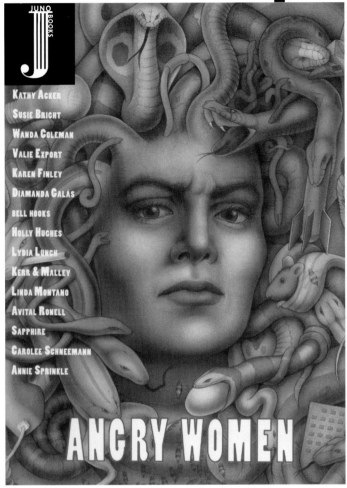

KATHY ACKER
SUSIE BRIGHT
WANDA COLEMAN
VALIE EXPORT
KAREN FINLEY
DIAMANDA GALAS
BELL HOOKS
HOLLY HUGHES
LYDIA LUNCH
KERR & MALLEY
LINDA MONTANO
AVITAL RONELL
SAPPHIRE
CAROLEE SCHNEEMANN
ANNIE SPRINKLE

ANGRY WOMEN

**"This book is a Bible...it hails the dawn of a new era—the era of an inclusive, fun, sexy feminism.... Every interview contains brilliant moments of wisdom."**
*—American Book Review*

## ANGRY WOMEN

by A. Juno

An enduring bestseller since its first printing in 1991, ANGRY WOMEN has been equipping a new generation of women with an expanded vision of what feminism could be, influencing Riot Grrrls, neo-feminists, lipstick lesbians, and suburban breeders alike. A classic textbook widespread in college curriculae, ANGRY WOMEN is the most influential book on women, culture, and radical ideology since THE SECOND SEX.

ANGRY WOMEN features: Diamanda Galas, Lydia Lunch, Sapphire, Karen Finley, Annie Sprinkle, Susie Bright, bell hooks, Kathy Acker, Avital Ronell, Holly Hughes, Carolee Schneeman, Valie Export, Linda Montano, and Wanda Coleman among others.

"This is hardly the nurturing, womanist vision espoused in the 1970s. The view here is largely pro-sex, pro-porn, and pro-choice. Separatism is out, community in. Art and activism are inseparable from life and being." *—The Village Voice*

"These women—potent agents for cultural destabilization—are definitely dangerous models of subversion!" *—MONDO 2000*

**WOMEN'S STUDIES/POP CULTURE/PERFORMING ARTS**
Paperback, 8.5 x 11 inches, 240 pages, illustrated
**ISBN 1-890451-05-3**                    **$18.99**

www.JunoBooks.com

JUNO CATALOG

# New Reprints!

## FREAKS
### We Who Are Not As Others
by Daniel P. Mannix

Originally printed in a small edition and withdrawn by the publisher Pocket Books after one month, FREAKS—out of print for nearly 20 years—was brought back to eye-popping life, with many new photos, by the renowned marginal culture press RE/Search, which became a dominant 80s publishing force. Juno Books, morphed from the now-defunct RE/Search, is bringing FREAKS back into print.

In FREAKS meet the strangest people who ever lived, and read about:
- the notorious love affairs of midgets;
- the strange sex lives of Siamese twins;
- the dwarf clown's wife whose feet grew directly from her body;
- the mule-faced woman whose son became her manager;
- the unusual amours of Jolly Daisy, the fat woman;
- the famous pinhead who inspired Verdi's *Rigoletto*;
- the tragedy of Betty Lou Williams and her parasitic twin;
- the 34-inch-tall midget happily married to his 264 lbs. wife;
- the human torso who could sew, crochet, and type;
- the other bizarre accounts of normal humans turned into freaks—either voluntarily or by evil design!

**Daniel P. Mannix**, now enjoying a cult revival, is the author of such enduring noir classics as MEMOIRS OF A SWORD SWALLOWER; THOSE ABOUT TO DIE; THE HELL-FIRE CLUB; THE HISTORY OF TORTURE; and many others. A former sword-swallower, fire-eater, fakir, and world traveller, Mannix still lives on the family farm with his falcon, miniature horses, and reptile collection.

www.JunoBooks.com

**CULTURAL STUDIES/MEDICAL CASE HISTORIES**
Paperback, 8.5 x 11 inches, 124 pages with illustrations
**ISBN 0-9651042-5-7**                    $15.99

# New Reprints!

## THE RE/SEARCH GUIDE TO BODILY FLUIDS

by Paul Spinrad

Now in its third printing, this provocative guide sparks a radical rethinking of our relationship with our bodies and nature, humorously (and seriously) spanning the gamut of everything you ever wanted to know about bodily functions and excreta. Each bodily function is discussed from a variety of viewpoints: scientific, anthropological, historical, mythological, sociological, and artistic.

Topics include constipation (such as its relationship to cornflakes and graham crackers!); the history and evolution of toilet paper; farting (spotlighting the famous Joseph Pujol, a turn-of-the-century Fartiste who was so well known internationally for his fart-singing and comedy routines that a street was named after him in Paris); urine (including little known facts about urinalysis); earwax, smegma, and many other engrossing topics!

## You think you know shit? How about: Scatological Lives of the Greats; Thomas Crapper, Closet

Genius; Excrement in Psychoanalysis; Holy & Unholy Shit; Filth Medicine; Excretal Customs Worldwide; Bodily Functions in Literature & Cinema; Historical Applications of Excrement; Excrement in Food and Drink; Sanitation and Excrement Through Western History.

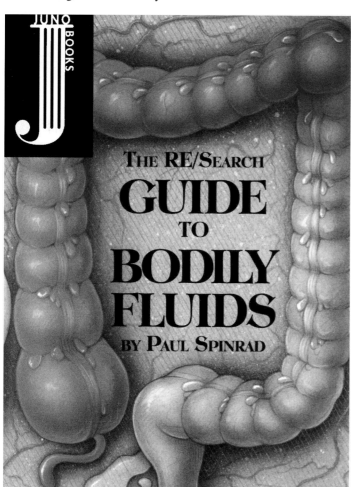

Spend a little time getting to know yourself! Read all about Feces, Flatus, Vomit, Urine, Mucus, Menstruation, Saliva, Sweat, and more!

"A stunning new release... THE RE/SEARCH GUIDE TO BODILY FLUIDS is a must buy..." —*Bikini*

"This is an important work that shouldn't be ignored, packed with fascinating tacts on excreta." —*Loaded*

JUNO CATALOG

# Classics!

## DANGEROUS DRAWINGS
### Interviews with Comix and Graphix Artists
by A. Juno

"A must for any modern-comix fan." —*Details*

"A bold collection of interviews with 14 of the world's most outstanding pop artists." —*Vibe*

"This often entertaining medium is revealed to contain many complex and provocative ideas, and the serious treatment it gets here makes this a worthwhile purchase." —*Library Journal*

"Based on the list of cartoonists and artists interviewed in the book, you know it's bound to be a great book. But as you pour through the discussions, you realize that it's far more than that." —*Amazon.com* "Pick of the Month"…unpaid!

"DANGEROUS DRAWINGS is required reading for anyone interested in comix. The impressive collection of interviews and art is a reliable and informative look at this increasingly popular field. It provides both an interesting look at well known artists and an exciting introduction into the field's rising stars." —*Spin*

**COMICS/ART/BIOGRAPHY**
Paperback, 8.5 x 11 inches, 224 pages with killer pics
**ISBN 0-9651042-8-1**                          **$24.95**

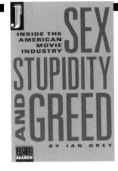

## SEX, STUPIDITY AND GREED
### Inside the American Movie Industry
by Ian Grey

"…Ian Grey's SEX, STUPIDITY AND GREED crankily explains what's wrong with American flickdom." —*Entertainment Weekly*

"Essential reading for anyone who wonders about the chilling downward-spiral of big budget films in the last decade." —*Spin*

"Grey's interviews are hard-won…porn-stars, gore film directors, Grey's own shrink….It's hard to disagree with him that Hollywood movies bite like dogs." —*The Village Voice*

"Several anecdotes about popular figures, such as Sylvester Stallone, are priceless, and an interview with the often maligned actress Sean Young reveals her to be intelligent and savvy." —*Time Out*

"SEX, STUPIDITY AND GREED gets straight to the rotten core. With intelligence and biting humor, Ian Grey peels under the glamorous veneer and shows us the guts of the American movie industry." —*Revolt In Style*

**FILM/POP CULTURE**
Paperback, 6 x 9 inches, 240 pages
**ISBN 0-9651042-7-3**                          **$15.95**

## ANGRY WOMEN IN ROCK
by A. Juno

"[Today], indie chicks proliferate, all tousled and tight-trousered and signed to major labels. ANGRY WOMEN IN ROCK gives us some portraits of women whose 'independence' is their substance and not just their style." —*Seattle Weekly*

"This book—stuffed with ideas, history, wise (and wise-ass) remarks, and most importantly, hope for the future—will be thumbed through often." —*Puncture*

"Creativity, sexuality, politics, fame, misogyny, strapping on rubber phalluses, all this is clearly dissected in question-and-answer format ." —*Q*

Includes interviews with: Chrissie Hynde (The Pretenders) Joan Jett, Kathleen Hanna (Bikini Kill), 7 Year Bitch, Jarboe (Swans), Tribe 8 (the all-dyke punk band), Kendra Smith, Naomi Yang (Galaxie 500), and much, much more!

**MUSIC/WOMEN'S STUDIES/CULTURAL STUDIES**
Paperback, 7 x 9 inches, 224 pages, lots of photos
**ISBN 0-9651042-0-6**                          **$19.95**

## INCREDIBLY STRANGE MUSIC
by A. Juno & V. Vale

"The bible of lounge music is INCREDIBLY STRANGE MUSIC." —*Newsweek*

"Fans of ambient music, acid jazz, ethno-techno, even industrial rock, will find the leap back to these genres an easy one to make." —*Rolling Stone*

INCREDIBLY STRANGE MUSIC is a comprehensive guide to little known yet amazing vinyl recordings—mostly from the 50s, 60s, and 70s—like *Muhammad Ali Fights Tooth Decay*, Jayne Mansfield reading *Shakespeare, Tchaikovsky and Me*, Sebastion Cabot (yes, Mr. French of *Family Affair*) "singing" songs by Bob Dylan, and tons more!

Impress your friends! Drive your roommates out! with • Brazilian Psychedelic • Outer Space • Exotica-Ploitation • Singing Truck Drivers • Yodeling • Abstract Female Vocals • Religious Ventriloquism • Sitar Rock • Theremin • Mallet Mischief • Phantom Surfers • Moog • Music for Bachelors • Hot Boppin' Girls • Eartha Kitt • "Where Did You Come From?" by Art Linketter • "Satan Is Real" by the Louvin Brothers • "U.S. Senator Robert Byrd, Mountain Fiddler" • etc.!

**MUSIC/LOUNGE CULTURE**
Paperback, 7 x 9 inches, 176 pages, lots of photos
**ISBN 0-940642-21-2**                          **$17.99**

**www.JunoBooks.com**

# Favorites!

## CONCRETE JUNGLE

**A Pop Media Investigation of Death and Survival in Urban Ecosystems**

Edited by Mark Dion & Alexis Rockman

"CONCRETE JUNGLE stands as one of the finest works in urban anthropology to appear in recent years. A plentitude of provocative essays, bizarre photographs, marginal quotes, and weird diagrams are to be found in this exploration of 'the intersection of urban living and Nature.'" —*Fringeware Review*

"This wry and often grotesque look at the food chain shows just how active nature is despite our unflagging attempts to pave it over." —*Utne Reader*

"CONCRETE JUNGLE looks oddly like a high school science text book, but…the content is oozily compelling." —*Artforum*

"The next time you throw a dinner party, bring this provocative, compelling, and amusing volume to the table." —*Time Out*

**ECOLOGY/CULTURAL STUDIES/ART**
Paperback 7 x 9 inches, 224 pages, over 260 line drawings and halftone photographs
**ISBN 0-9651042-2-2**                    **$24.95**

## BODIES OF SUBVERSION

**A Secret History of Women and Tattoo**

by Margot Mifflin

"In this provocative work full of intriguing female characters from tattoo history, Margot Mifflin makes a persuasive case for the tattooed woman as an emblem of female self-expression." —Susan Faludi, Pulitzer Prize-winning author of BACKLASH

"An indelible account of an indelible piece of cultural history." —Barbara Kruger, artist

"BODIES OF SUBVERSION is a comprehensive and clear-eyed account of tattooing and women in Western society over the past century. Margot Mifflin…furthers understanding of this complex art as it exists among women. It is essential reading for anyone interested in the subject." —Don E. Hardy, renowned tattooist and historian

"…An outstanding read, and long-overdue addition to the growing body of literature on tattooing…" —*International Tattooing*

**CULTURAL STUDIES/WOMEN'S STUDIES/BODY ART**
Paperback, 8.5 x 11 inches, 192 pages, over 200 halftone photographs
**ISBN 1-890451-00-2**                    **$23.95**

## Dangerous Drawings contains these slammin comix artists!

- Art Spiegelman
- Dan Clowes
- Julie Doucet
- Chris Ware
- G.B. Jones
- Diane Noomin
- Emiko Shimoda
- Chester Brown
- Ted Rall
- Eli Langer
- Aline Kominsky-Crumb
- Phoebe Glockner
- Keith Mayerson
- Matt Reid

## HORROR HOSPITAL UNPLUGGED

**A Graphic Novel**

by Dennis Cooper & Keith Mayerson

"Youthful angst is rarely portrayed as this terrifying." —*Library Journal*

"This book will definitely become a classic." —*International Drummer*

"Trippy and brilliant." —*Attitude*

"Bound to reign in cult stardom status, HORROR HOSPITAL UNPLUGGED is the ultimate generation whatever's coming of age tale of Trevor Machine, the 90s answer to Holden Caulfield…. Filled with stimulating art and cynically amusing text, HORROR HOSPITAL UNPLUGGED is a rare treat offering its readers intelligent entertainment on every page." —*Cover*

"Cooper's idiosyncratic morality meets cartoonist Keith Mayerson's manga-like style in this ruthless and totally rude book." —*Gay Times*

**GRAPHIC NOVELS/MUSIC/GAY LETTERS**
Paperback, 8.5 x 11 inches, 256 illustrated pages
**ISBN 0-9651042-1-4**                    **$24.95**

# The Juno Books Individual Order Form for Caring Persons Not Living by a Great Bookstore!

## BILLING INFORMATION

Your name

Today's date:

Your address

Want to get special e-mail notices on private sales offers?

Tel

Fax:

E-mail:

City

State

Zip

## PAYMENT INFORMATION

Please charge my: ☐ MC ☐ Visa ☐ Amex

Your credit card number:

Exp date:

Signature

☐ Check enclosed

## SHIPPING INFORMATION    ☐ CHECK IF SAME

Name

Address

City

State

Zip

Tel

Fax

| QUANTITY | TITLE | AMOUNT |
|----------|-------|--------|
|          |       |        |
|          |       |        |
|          |       |        |
|          |       |        |
|          |       |        |
|          |       |        |

SPECIAL SHIPPING INSTRUCTIONS:

SUBTOTAL

add 8.25% tax if you live in NY

DOMESTIC: SHIPPING & HANDLING ($4.50 1ST BOOK, $1.50 EACH ADDITIONAL)
FOREIGN: $10.00 SURFACE, $25.00 AIR MAIL 1ST BOOK; $5.00 SURFACE, $10.00 AIR FOR EACH ADDITIONAL

*Please note that books will be sent when available.*

TOTAL

**HELP US THROW EVER MORE ELABORATE BOOK LAUNCH PARTIES AND PROVOCATIVE, UNUSUAL PR CAMPAIGNS! ANSWER OUR QUESTIONNAIRE AND RECEIVE A 20% DISCOUNT!**

1) How did you first hear about us?

2) What do you love most about our books?

3) Which of our books are your favorites?

4) What's your sex?          Your age?

5) What do you do?

6) How much do you make?

7) What kind of liquor do you drink?

8) What catalogs do you buy from on a regular basis?

9) What web sites do you buy from?

**Don't worry! All this info will be kept confidential, and be used for statistical purposes only!**

## please now do one of these things:

1) Mail a copy of this form to: **Juno Books Sales Desk**, 180 Varick Street, Suite 1302, New York, NY 10014-4606
2) Fax a copy to: **212 366 5247**
3) e-mail a copy to: **orders@JunoBooks.com**
4) Call us toll-free at: **1-877-pH-is-joy**